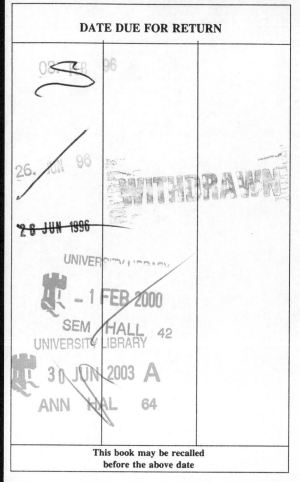

Jean Toomer
and the Prison-House
of Thought

Robert B. Jones

Jean Toomer
and the Prison-House
of Thought

A PHENOMENOLOGY
OF THE SPIRIT

The University
of Massachusetts Press

Amherst

Copyright © 1993 by
The University of Massachusetts Press
All rights reserved

Printed in the United States of America
LC 93–18609
ISBN 0–87023–860–4

Designed by Susan Bishop
Set in Galliard by Keystone Typesetting, Inc.
Printed and bound by Thomson-Shore, Inc.

Library of Congress Cataloging-in-Publication Data
Jones, Robert B.
Jean Toomer and the prison-house of thought : a phenomenology
of the spirit / Robert B. Jones.
p.   cm.
Includes bibliographical references and index.
ISBN 0–87023–860–4 (alk. paper)
1. Toomer, Jean, 1894–1967—Philosophy.   2. Phenomenology and literature.
3. Afro-Americans in literature.   4. Philosophy in literature.   I. Title.
PS3539.0478Z69   1993
813'.52—dc20   93–18609

British Library Cataloguing in Publication data are available.

10 0 0 3 5 7 8 6 9

With love and gratitude,
to my mother, Queen E. Jones,
who taught me to read and write
when I was three

A reincarnationist would derive me from the Orient, I'm sure.
—*Jean Toomer*

. . . to be lost in spiritlessness is the most terrible thing of all.
—*Søren Kierkegaard*

CONTENTS

CONTENTS

ACKNOWLEDGMENTS

There are several people I wish to thank for assisting me in completing this book. It was in the seminar "The Twenties in American Literature," conducted by Walter Rideout at the University of Wisconsin, Madison, that I was introduced to the writings of Jean Toomer; under Rideout's expert guidance I completed a dissertation on Toomer and Gertrude Stein. During our work together he was not only my mentor and major professor but also a trusted and cherished friend. For his fatherly advice and continuing support over the years, I owe him a great debt. Two other people also provided careful, considered, and sensitive readings of my work. My good friend and colleague Melvin Friedman took time away from his many ongoing projects to read and comment on the entire manuscript, as did Barbara Foley who, notwithstanding her heavy responsibilities as director of graduate studies in English at Rutgers University, Newark, offered numerous helpful suggestions. I am also pleased to thank both Marjorie Content Toomer and critic Kenneth Burke for answering my many queries about Jean Toomer. On several occasions Mrs. Toomer followed up our conversations with letters and materials she alone possessed, while Mr. Burke's unfaltering memories of his friendship with Toomer transported me into the 1920s and 1930s in ways I shall always fondly remember. I also wish to thank Margot Toomer Latimer, Toomer's daughter and my faithful coeditor of *The Collected Poems of Jean Toomer,* for not only granting me permissions to bring formerly unpublished manuscripts into the public domain, but also for her enduring support of my projects. Like her father, she is a courageous pioneer in the country of the spirit. Several librarians have also generously given of their time and expertise: Beth Howse and Ann Shockley in the Special Collections Library at Fisk University; Julie Campbell, David Schoonover, and Ralph Franklin in the Beinecke Rare Book and Manuscript Library at Yale University; Jerry Frost and Claire Shetter in the Friends Historical Library at Swarthmore College; Bar-

ACKNOWLEDGMENTS

bara Richards in the Little Magazines and Special Collections section of Memorial Library at the University of Wisconsin, Madison; and Michael Tyree of the Golda Meir Library at the University of Wisconsin, Milwaukee. Finally, I wish to thank the Beinecke Rare Book and Manuscript Library for permission to quote from the Jean Toomer Collection, as well as *Studies in American Fiction, Black American Literature Forum,* and the University of North Carolina Press for permission to reprint parts of the present study which first appeared in slightly different forms in their publications.

PREFACE

This book began as an attempt to find a comprehensive system for understanding one of America's most enigmatic writers, Jean Toomer. After several years of examining the vast network of published and unpublished texts, both in the Fisk University Library and in the Beinecke Rare Book and Manuscript Library at Yale, I was able to assign specific works to periods in Toomer's intellectual development. Soon a literary canon evolved, comprising almost four decades of writings; concomitant with this evolution there emerged a remarkably systematic devotion to the possibilities of idealist philosophy. The present study examines how this perennial devotion to idealism influenced his philosophy and art. While this study constitutes the first comprehensive critical survey of Toomer's literary canon, examining works written between 1918 and 1955, it is also a critique of the subjective idealism that is consistently at the center of these works. In this context, I discuss the problem of idealist reification in his life and works as the basis for perpetual alienation. In formulating a heuristic strategy for examining idealist reification, I employ a dialectical methodology. Thus my purpose is not only to lay bare specific manifestations of reified consciousness in the themes, character types, and formal strategies, but also to discuss Toomer's struggles *against* reification. This dialectic, between the synchrony of form and the diachrony of history, should then provide an appropriate metacommentary useful in analyzing these works.

While no writer's life can be facilely reduced to discrete stages, Jean Toomer's search for spiritual systems of thought consistent with his idealism produced inflections and oscillations that truly represent moments in a phenomenology of the spirit. The present study develops in three parts, paralleling Toomer's literary and philosophical development with Kierkegaard's stages of spiritual evolution. Part 1, "The Aesthetic Sphere," examines the works composed between 1918 and 1923 in the light of Orientalism, Symbolist idealism, and Imagism. In chapter 1 I discuss Toomer's early literary experimentation in poetry and consider the emergence of racial themes in the short stories "Bona and Paul" and "Withered Skin of Berries," in the plays *Balo* and *Natalie Mann,* and in *Cane.* Here I suggest that the emergence of these themes represents his struggles against the forces of reification. Chapter 2 comprises a comprehensive examination of Toomer's masterpiece, *Cane,* on two levels of interpretation. On the micronarrative level, I discuss the structure of language and the structure of plot in terms of Modernist-Formalist aesthetics. On the macronarrative level, I interpret the structure of plot as a dramatization of consciousness, in which racial identification is ultimately eclipsed by the reascendancy of reified idealism. I conclude this chapter with an assessment of form in *Cane.* Given Toomer's adaptation of Symbolist and Imagist aesthetics and his acceptance of Orientalism as both philosophy and religion, it is appropriate to designate this first stage in his literary development as the aesthetic sphere. In accordance with Kierkegaard's categories, the aestheticist lives in a world of poetry, apart from the world of realities, and takes pride in being an *observateur.* "The Aesthetic mode of life," writes Reidar Thomte, "leads to isolation from society. The individual has himself as the greatest good and the goal in life. Everything else becomes a tool to this end. The individual is magnified and society becomes insignificant. The aesthetic may be regarded as a-ethical and a-religious."[1] Only through an absolute choice can an individual progress from the aesthetic to the ethical stage; for Jean Toomer, this choice was universalist consciousness.

Part 2, "The Ethical Sphere," analyzes the literary works Toomer produced from 1924 to 1939, during his apprenticeship with the Russian mystic Georges Ivanovitch Gurdjieff. The two chapters which compose this unit explore the idealist and ethical dimensions of Toomer's art in light of Gurdjieffian philosophy. In chapter 3 I examine Gurdjieffian "objective consciousness" in the poems and "higher consciousness" in the novels *York Beach,* "The Gallonwerps," "Caromb," and "Eight-Day World." This chapter also examines for the first time Toomer's unpublished Gothic tale "The Eye," as well as a group of local color works imaging the landscape of the American Southwest. Chapter 4 turns away from the landscape of the self to the landscape of society in the decade after World War I. Here I discuss the unpublished short story collection "Lost and Dominant," Toomer's manifesto of the Lost Generation, as well as social themes in the plays and the uncollected short stories. In this context I argue that Toomer's vision of the modern world as a wasteland again represents his efforts against materializing abstractions. Given the shift in his thinking from racial to universalist consciousness during this period, I designate it as the ethical sphere. As Kierkegaard defines it, the ethical expresses both the universal and the individual, for only when the individual becomes the universal can the ethical be realized.[2] On this plane of thought, the individual attempts to interact with the social order to create a social and civic self, as evident in Toomer's "New American" social philosophy.

Part 3, "The Religious Sphere," considers the influence of Quaker religious philosophy on Toomer's art and thought in the works written between 1940 and 1955. Here I discuss the social and historical dimensions of "The Angel Begori" and "The Colombo-Madras Rail" as representing efforts against reification, while in the poems I examine the conflict between Toomer's earlier forms of idealism (human spirituality; the claims of man) and Quaker religious idealism (Christian spirituality; the claims of God). According to Kierkegaard, the self has its highest and most comprehensive unity in God, an assumption he shares with Hegel and German idealism.[3] Yet, as we shall see, the antinomies between Toomer's ethical and religious spheres of idealist consciousness, as well as the existential perspective that inheres in Quakerism, provide the basis for not only reified consciousness but also Christian existential themes in the religious lyrics of this period. Notwithstanding Toomer's efforts to counter reification, we witness the ascendancy of idealist consciousness throughout his canon, and with it the attendant mystification of thought.

Jean Toomer
and the Prison-House
of Thought

Idealism and Alienation

In his pioneering commentaries on Jean Toomer, Darwin Turner summarizes Toomer's life and career in metaphors of alienation.

> At the age of twelve, physically debilitated and humiliated because he no longer was respected as the leader of his gang, Eugene Pinchback withdrew from his friends, climbed a post, and contemptuously observed his former playmates from his isolated seat. In *Cane* he wrote of isolated individuals seeking not to belong but to be. After *Cane*, Toomer, self-exiled from all races and from the material and style which served him best, names the isolated protagonists Nathan or Hugh, or Hod, but they were all self-portraits of Jean Toomer, exile.[1]

To be sure, Toomer was an exile, alienated from both society and himself. Fully aware that society classified individuals of dubious racial heritage as quadroon, octoroon, and mulatto, and that he himself was of "mixed blood," he began looking at himself through the eyes of others, a phenomenon W. E. B. DuBois defined as "double-consciousness": "It is a peculiar sensation, this double-consciousness, this sense of always looking at one's self through the eyes of others, of measuring one's soul by the tape of a world that looks on in amused contempt and pity. One ever feels his twoness—an American, a Negro—two souls, two thoughts, two unreconciled strivings; two warring ideals in one dark body, whose dogged strength alone keeps it from being torn asunder."[2]

As DuBois defines it, double-consciousness describes a phenomenon experienced by black Americans who, despite their second-class status, continue to think of themselves as Americans, an idea eloquently expressed by writers of the Harlem Renaissance. The example of Jean

1

Toomer provides a curious variation on this syndrome, however. For throughout his adult life, except for a brief hiatus of ancestral consciousness from September 1921 to July 1922, he consistently and preeminently described himself as an American, ostensibly having transcended double-consciousness. Indeed, if one does not perceive oneself as an African-American, then this malady is avoided, at least as DuBois defined it. And even during the months of his "lapse" into ancestral consciousness, Toomer's identification with African-American people, life, and culture was quintessentially spiritual and intellectual rather than ethnic. "Double-consciousness," then, neither accurately nor precisely defines Toomer's alienation, for his "split in personality" derived from society's alternating impressions of him as white or as black and, ultimately, from his alienation from both races. Because he could not fathom the racial categories society idolized as laws unto themselves or locate himself within "the system," he capitulated to a much more insidious form of alienation, which Georg Lukács terms reification.

Reification refers to the process of regarding an idealized abstraction as if it were a concrete, objective thing with a material existence. On an economic level, Lukács's theory of reification describes the alienation of laborers from the product of their labor, whereby workers apprehend a "split in personality" between their status as human beings and their function as objects of commodity exchange.[3] Marx defined this phenomenon as commodity fetishism: "A commodity is therefore a mysterious thing, simply because in it the social character of men's labour appears to them as an objective character stamped upon the product of that labour; because the relation of the producers to the sum total of their labour is presented to them as a social relation, existing not between themselves, but between the products of their labour."[4] From this definition, Lukács deduces the concept of alienation of labor, which describes how one's labor becomes an objective, independent thing or commodity which the laborer can neither transform nor control. From the objective side, then, "commodification" ("reification") means the creation of a "second nature" of pseudo things, while from the subjective side it means the alienation of human activity for laborers forced to work within this second nature.

From the alienation of labor Lukács proceeds to the abstraction of labor. As commodity production takes place in increasingly larger proportions, workers begin perceiving themselves as mere cogs within a factory system, as they succumb to mechanical, repetitive, standardized, isolated activities which are quantifiable and calculable. This process culminates in the "progressive elimination of the qualitative human and individual attributes of the worker," the full rationalization of which is the fragmentation of labor production into mechanical elements, each a predictable result of specialized, partial operation.[5] More important, workers become even more fragmented as their labor becomes an abstraction to them. On the one hand, Lukács argues, the worker's activity becomes purely objective as labor power is transformed into a thing that can be sold on the market, like the various objects of the external world. On the other hand, the worker's subjectivity is reduced to contemplation of his or her own (and other workers') alienated activity. Moreover, this contemplative stance implies passivity toward a work process that conforms to fixed laws "enacted independently of man's consciousness and impervious to human intervention."[6]

Having established the economic foundations of capitalism as the basis for reification, Lukács now applies his theory to society, still using the factory model. The bureaucratic administration of the state, he argues, is analogous to the capitalist organization of a factory. This implies that all aspects of life within the culture of capitalism are standardized and reduced to easily calculable partial systems that obey what are, ostensibly, "natural laws." Not only work but gradually all human activity is alienated and made part of a "second nature" impervious to human control. The fate of the worker, then, becomes the fate of society as a whole when the internal organization of the factory becomes the microcosm of the whole structure of capitalist society. Even bureaucrats are not excepted; as Lukács argues, one-sided specialization is most clearly dehumanizing in the case of the bureaucrat, as a single aspect of the bureaucrat's mental faculty is detached (abstracted) and mechanized. The result on both economic and social levels is passivity (contemplation) and isolation in a world that is seen in fragments and as fundamentally unchangeable.

Idealism is a classic response to reification, with its promise that the alienated individual, socially fragmented and divided, can be made whole again in thought. Idealist philosophy seeks to discover the subject of action, the maker of reality, and to posit the world as conceived by thought. Yet as Marx states in his "First Thesis on Feuerbach," idealism does not comprehend praxis, as it is devoid of "sensuous human activity," or real, lived experiences: "The chief defect of all hitherto existing materialism . . . is that the thing, reality, sensuousness, is conceived only in the form of *the object or of contemplation,* but not as *sensuous human activity, practice,* not subjectively. Hence, in contradistinction to materialism, the *active* side was developed by idealism—which, of course, does not know real, sensuous activity as such."[7]

Lukács similarly regarded idealism in terms of contemplation, rather than praxis, devoted to the mystification of thought: "Classical philosophy is able to think the deepest and most fundamental problems of the development of bourgeois society through to the very end—on the plane of philosophy. It is able—in thought—to complete the evolution of the class. And—in thought—it is able to take all the paradoxes of its position to the point where the necessity of going beyond this historical stage in mankind's development can at least be seen as a problem."[8] Within the realm of pure philosophy, contemplation cannot be transcended; indeed, any contemplative stance on the part of the subject leads to a divided relation with the object of contemplation. "The 'purer' the cognitive character of thought becomes and the more 'critical' thought is," writes Lukács, "the more vast and impassable does the abyss appear that yawns between the 'subjective' mode of thought and the objectivity of the (existing) object."[9] Idealism, therefore, rather than transcending the subject-object dialectic to form "the identical subject-object," actually restores and restates the dialectic on a higher level. Only through the realization that thought and existence, theory and practice, are aspects of the same historical and dialectical process can the identical subject-object be achieved.

To comprehend the basis of Toomer's reified thinking, especially on the subject of race and society, and his subsequent adoption of philosophical idealism, we must first understand that for generations racial identification was a problematic issue within his family, originating with his famous grandfather, P. B. S. Pinchback (1837–1921), who was governor of Louisiana during Reconstruction.[10] The son of a white planter and a "mulatto" slave, Pinchback was labeled Negro in accordance with America's prevailing system of racial taxonomy, although he was white in appearance. Despite his ability to "pass," he publicly defined himself as an African-American. During the Civil War, in 1862, he was assigned to recruit a company of free blacks for the Union army, although a year later he and other black leaders of the company resigned because of unfair racial treatment. Soon afterward, however, he attempted to organize a company of black cavalry but later gave up the idea and settled into the army unit of the Second Louisiana Regiment without a commission. At the end of the war, he traveled to Alabama to protest the treatment of newly freed African-Americans. After acts of violence were committed against blacks during the reorganization of Louisiana's civil government in 1866, he formed a political action group in 1867, the Fourth Ward Republican Club, to protect their civil rights.

Not all of Pinchback's family supported his racial disclosure and activism, however. In April 1863, he received a letter from his sister Adeline, who lived in Sidney, Ohio, sternly warning him to dissociate himself from blacks and urging him to pass as white.

> If I were you Pink I would not let my ambition die. I would seek to rise and not in that class either but I would take my position in the world as a white man as you are and let the other go for be assured of this as the other you will *never* get your rights. Know this that *mobs* are constantly breaking out in different parts of the north and even in Canada against the oppressed colored race. Right in Cincinnati they can hardly walk the streets but they are attacked. . . . *I* have nothing to do with the negroes am *not* one of them. Take my advise *dear* brother and do the same.[11]

Although Pinchback disregarded his sister's pronouncements, he kept the letter for many years. When he died in 1921, the letter became the property of Jean Toomer, who preserved it as a family heirloom. It apparently had quite a different impact on Pinchback than it did on Toomer.

In March 1894 Pinchback's daughter Nina married Nathan Toomer, a man who, like Pinchback himself, was the son of a white planter and a woman of "mixed" races. "Living in Georgia between Augusta and Macon, he was known to have some colored blood . . . [but] lived with both white and colored people. The rigid division of white and Negro did not apply in his case."[12] Both of Toomer's parents could have passed as white, although they listed themselves as "colored" on their marriage license. In December 1894 Nathan Eugene (Jean) was born, and a year later the father deserted the family. For the next eighteen years the young boy oscillated between living as black in Washington, D.C. and living as white in New Rochelle, New York. Significantly, when he returned to live in Washington, following the death of his mother in 1909, he experienced total immersion in black culture, attending the all-black Dunbar High School in the fall of 1910. By now, he had developed a sense of himself as different from the other (black) students, and he began to withdraw and isolate himself. "After fourteen years in the white group, by his count, and four in the black, he was ready to be done with groups and find his way as an individual."[13] Whereas his grandfather had chosen life as an African-American, Toomer thought it best to employ, variably, one of three alternatives: to advance a transcendental conception of race, to appear to be white and pass, or to remain silent on the issue. To understand precisely why he would employ these alternatives, rather than proclaim his African-American heritage, we must first understand racism and its relationship to reification.

People have not always been classified into races. Historically, the idea of race is a relatively recent phenomenon, dating back to the seventeenth century. Between 1700 and 1900, Europe completed its worldwide colonization. During these two centuries the awareness of race was converted into an ideology of racism, serving the political imperatives of colonialism, nationalism, imperialism, and slavery. In the United States, slavery promoted the ideology of racism, resulting in such formal and legal classifications as "octoroon" (one whose ancestry is one-eighth African-American), "quadroon" (one-fourth African-American), "mulatto" (one-half African-American), and "griffe" (three-fourths African-American). Generally, Americans hold one of several views on racial classifications. The first is that racial taxonomies are necessary and should be maintained. This view proposes racial classification as a neutral, objective demographic instrument, despite the fact that such groupings are used by America's agencies and institutions as an instrument of social management. This view is also held by proponents of racial segregation, of all stripes and colors. The second is maintained by a growing number of Americans who are the progeny of a mixed racial heritage. They often resent having to choose one or another ethnic strain for purposes of identification and therefore propose the creation of some "other" category to define their status. Proponents of this view are quick to remind us of America's democratic pluralism, pointing out that "mixed Americans" represent a new, progressive social order. The third view proposes eradicating all racial taxonomies, maintaining that "the idea of race represents one of the most dangerous myths of our time . . . the belief that physical and mental traits are linked, that the physical differences [in the varieties of humankind] are associated with rather pronounced differences in mental capacities, and that these differences are measurable by IQ tests and the cultural achievements of these populations."[14]

There is yet a fourth view, however, which is that racial classifications constitute a legal fiction that has been reified to camouflage class consciousness, and that the "facts" or "natural laws" of racial classification are but the parts of a total process that have been artificially isolated and frozen (reified) into a fixed objectivity, a plantation system on a national scale. Jean Toomer's philosophy of race and race classification coincides with our second view, as a corollary of his democratic idealism. Thus, instead of campaigning to dismantle the system of racial injustice, as he campaigned for "New American" social thought, he attempted to transcend the polemics of race via idealist metaphysics.

The philosophy of idealism asserts that the essential nature of reality lies in consciousness, rather than in the phenomenal world. It is a philosophy of the spirit that locates autonomy in the experiences of the self. This is a Romantic notion, with origins in both Eastern and Western philosophy. In Eastern theosophy, for example, Taoism affirms the unity of self and world. As *tao* describes order and harmony in nature, *te* describes that same order and harmony within the self. A mystical state of enlightenment, *te* involves an inner transformation that allows the individual to achieve harmony with *tao*. As a consequence, self and world are collapsed to create a transcendental self. Taoism, then, is Being, the Universal One, the Harmony through which all opposites are reconciled. It is therefore a philosophy of oneness in duality. Similarly, Buddhist theosophy teaches that humankind's constructions, definitions, and philosophies represent mere human efforts to grasp, freeze, and contain reality; that our clinging to the illusion of individual identity is our greatest source of anxiety and pain. Salvation consists in relinquishing this illusion in order to achieve the transrational mystical state of nirvana, wherein all sense of ego ceases in surrender to the Buddha-Nature. Enlightenment then comes from one's complete realization that taxonomies cannot contain essence or identity, since the self is united with the perfect spiritual freedom of the Buddha-Nature, which is one with the phenomenal world.

In Western philosophy, David Hume was the first philosopher to structure a formal theory of epistemology around this idea, arguing that all knowledge is derived exclusively from the senses. Immanuel Kant similarly argued that substance, time, and space are notions that must be imposed on sense data by the individual in order to fabricate a coherent unit of knowledge. For Kant, time and space are a priori elements of knowledge, as both are assumed by the individual before perception occurs. This concept of the individual also forms an integral part of the philosophy of Henri Bergson, who maintained that numerical multiplicity is made possible only by the accompanying intuition of space, and that it is the task of the mind to synthesize a coherent whole from these two dimensions. That is, the individual's ability to synthesize a coherent whole from nonsimultaneous events requires that time have, in addition to the characteristics of space, the potential for duration. For Bergson, duration is a function of consciousness. These and other philosophers share in a radical conception of the self that is the very foundation of idealist philosophy.

"In Idealism," writes Evelyn Underhill, "we have perhaps the most sublime theory of Being which has ever been constructed by the human intellect: a theory so sublime, in fact, that it can hardly have been produced by the exercise of 'pure reason' alone, but must be looked upon as a manifestation of that natural mysticism, that instinct for the Absolute, which is latent in man."[15] An important corollary of idealism, then, is mysticism, with its theory of direct spiritual union with the Absolute. Mysticism may be defined in terms of the mind's quest for unmediated union with the highest state of consciousness. As A. Seth defines it, mysticism "appears in connexion with the endeavor of the human mind to grasp the Divine essence or the ultimate reality of things, and to enjoy the blessedness of actual communion with the highest. The first is the philosophical side of mysticism; the second, its religious side. The thought that is most intensely present with the mystic is that of the supreme, all-pervading, and indwelling Power, in whom all things are one."[16]

Symbolist idealism shares many similarities with the philosophy of mysticism. Both emphasize subjective experience, locating ultimate reality in a realm that transcends phenomena. According to Andrew Lehman, "the mystic's approach to literature differs in little but its terminology from that of the 'idealist'; each sees in poetry, and by extension in every other form of art, the communication not of 'information' but of some strong emotional experience."[17] As for time, Symbolism shares with mysticism a belief in the unity and continuity of time and space. Symbolist writers are noted for their representations of time in arresting the immediacy of the moment through synesthesia, simultaneity, epiphany, and spatial form. By comparison, the mystic's emphasis on absolute unity bridges the gulfs of human experience, including distinctions between time and space. Finally, in terms of language, Symbolism shares with mysticism a devotion to the possibilities of symbolic discourse. Symbolist writers often employ a private symbology, like the mystic who tries to translate the truth of visionary experience into symbol and image.

> The mystic, as a rule, cannot do without symbol and image, inadequate to this vision through they must always be: for his experience must be expressed if it is to be communicated, and its actuality is inexpressible except in some side-long way, some hint or parallel which will stimulate the dormant intuition of the reader, and convey, as all poetic language does, something beyond its surface sense. Hence the enormous part which is played in all mystical writings by symbolism and imagery; and also by that rhythmic and exalted language which induces in sensitive persons something of the languid ecstasy of dream.[18]

With mysticism as its animating spiritual force, idealism provided for Toomer not only the potential to reconcile self and world but also the spiritual conviction of intensely felt religious belief.

Jean Toomer was formally introduced to the philosophy of idealism at the age of twenty-six, in 1920. For more than eight months, he abandoned writing to study Oriental philosophy.

> I came in contact with an entirely new body of ideas. Buddhist philosophy, the Eastern teachings, occultism, theosophy. . . . These ideas challenged and stimulated me. Despite my literary purpose, I was compelled to know something more about them . . . and my religious nature, given a cruel blow by Clarence Darrow and naturalism and atheism, but not, as I found, destroyed by them—my religious nature which had been sleeping was vigorously aroused.[19]

9

On the basis of these studies, he formulated theories of being and consciousness, and when he returned to writing, he sought literary equivalents for his idealism. Symbolist and Imagist aesthetics provided those equivalents.

Toomer's Symbolist aesthetic derives from both French and American sources. Of the French Symbolists his mentor was Charles Baudelaire, whose *Petits poèmes en prose* provided models for the prose poems and lyrical narratives in *Cane*. A Romantic reaction against realism, the French Symbolist movement advocated unique, immediate, emotional responses as the proper province of art. Toward this end, Symbolist poets employed private symbolization—what Edmund Wilson calls a medley of metaphors—to communicate personal feelings. Their works are thus characterized by indirection, as ideas are presented obliquely through a variety of symbols and must be apprehended largely by intuition and feeling. In their efforts to capture the essence of the object and not the object itself, they often used words for their magical suggestiveness, what Baudelaire termed *une sorcellerie évocatoire*. In the words of Arthur Symons, Symbolism may be defined as an attempt to spiritualize literature, an attempt to evade the old trappings of rhetoric and exteriority. "Description is banished that beautiful things might be evoked, magically; the regular beat of verse is broken in order that words may fly, upon subtler wings. Mystery is no longer feared, as the great mystery in whose midst we are islanded was feared by those to whom that unknown sea was only a void."[20] There was an analogous Symbolist movement in American literature, as seen in the writings of Emerson, Thoreau, Hawthorne, Melville, and Whitman. Among the American Symbolists, Walt Whitman's democratic idealism and his mystical conception of the self appealed to Toomer's idealist imagination. "The 'I' of Whitman's poems," writes Charles Feidelson, "speaks the world that he sees, and sees the world that he speaks, and does this by *becoming* the reality of his vision and of his words." The American Symbolist imagination, according to Feidelson, tried to find "a point of departure outside the premises of dualism—not so much an attempt to resolve the old 'problem of knowledge' as an effort to redefine the process of knowing in such a manner that the problem never arises."[21] American Symbolist writers thus sought to view the subjective and objective worlds as functions of each other; the medium for recapturing unity in a world artificially divided was the self.

Like his French and American Symbolist forebears, Toomer was similarly concerned with the exigencies of inner and outer, self and world, both as a philosopher and as an artist. Indeed, his idealist imagination consistently ventured to transcend the rigorous imperatives of dualism. "A flash bridges the gap between inner and outer," he declares, "causing a momentary fusion and wholeness."[22] As a philosopher, he reiterated the power of the human mind to reconcile and transcend self and world. "In life nothing is only physical," he argues; "there is also the symbolical. White and Black. West and East. North and South. Light and Darkness. In general, the great contrasts. The pairs of opposites. And I, together with all other I's, am the reconciler." As an artist, he advocated the privacy of the literary symbol, declaring "a symbol is as useful to the spirit as a tool is to the hand."[23] And he insisted that the creative process demanded selfless absorption in the human mind. Toomer believed that human nature, which stimulates self-consciousness, interferes with the act of literary creation. The human mind, however, is able to engage in a loss of self-consciousness in order to induce a state of negative capability wherein the mind can reconcile and transcend both self and world in a higher or spiritual self. It is in this transcendental state of awareness that one is capable of engaging in what he calls "purification of the senses," which allows the writer to create works of art.[24] "The subject matter of art is inner experience," says Toomer; "the more exalted the inner experience, the greater and more significant the art content."[25]

Symbolist idealism also figures prominently in Toomer's early fascination with Imagism. In his attempts to fashion experience as a mystical moment of vision and to create the immediacy and presentness of portraiture in literature, he welcomed the Imagist movement as having aesthetics consistent with his own. "Their insistence on fresh vision and on the perfect clean economical line was just what I had been looking for. I began feeling that I had in my hands the tools for my own creation."[26] Imagist influences are evident not only in Toomer's poems but in his lyrical sketches and prose poems as well. But the aspect of Imagist aesthetics most clearly manifested in his writings is Pound's Doctrine of the Image. Indeed, Pound's insistence upon rendering the wholeness and immediacy of experience in "an emotional and intellectual complex" finds expression in Toomer's aesthetic.

> In writing I aim to do two things. One. To essentialize experi-
> ence . . . to strip a thing of its nonessentials and to experience
> the concentrated kernel of the thing. Two. To spiritualize
> experience . . . to have one's psyche or spirit engage in a process
> similar to that of the body when it digests and assimilates food.
> To spiritualize is to digest, assimilate, up-grade, and form the
> materials of experience—in fine, to form oneself.[27]

Imagist poetics thus provided for him the ideal medium to make the reader "see," almost in mystical fashion, the "fresh vision," the distilled essence of an insight or experience.

Shortly after the publication of *Cane* in October 1923, Toomer came into contact with the austere idealism of Georges Ivanovitch Gurdjieff, and in 1924 he attended the Gurdjieff Institute for the Harmonious Development of Man at the Château de Prieuré in Fontainebleau, France. "Ever since my arrival in France," he wrote to Alfred Steiglitz, "I have been working in the Gurdjieff Institute. My conjectures to you concerning its significance have been confirmed. It is by all odds the best *general* instrument that I have found and it is just possible that I shall return to America with the teacher . . . [to] help her instruct in the elementary exercises."[28] He sailed back to America after two months but returned to the institute again in 1926 and in 1927. While Gurdjieffian philosophy is arcane and obscure, we need not concern ourselves with its esoterica in order to formulate the major tenets as they relate to Toomer.

The "ordinary man," Gurdjieff tells us, "is a three-brained being," with his ontological status shared among three autonomous centers: physical (itself divided into instinctive, moving, and sex centers), emotional (feelings), and intellectual (the mind). In some people the center of gravity is located in the moving center; in others, in the intellectual or emotional center. Beyond these centers, however, there exist higher levels of "objective consciousness," which Gurdjieff calls the "higher emotional center" and the "higher thinking centre."[29] On these levels of mystical awareness, the self is the recipient of a miraculous energy from a nonmaterial source, in direct communion with the supernatural In religious philosophy, this state of consciousness is often called illumination, enlightenment, or epiphany. One is able to move from lower to higher planes of consciousness through the assiduous practice of austere self-observation. In this way, one comes to understand the Gurdjieffian distinction between "essence" and "personality": "It must be understood that man consists of two parts: *essence* and *personality*. Essence in man is *his own*. Personality in man is what is 'not his own.' . . . Essence is the truth in man; personality is the false."[30] According to Gurdjieff, the self identifies with its outer personality (appearance, education, culture) to the exclusion of its inner or spiritual self. The self, therefore, knows and understands little of its own essence, since it is overwhelmed and stifled by personality. One's true "I," one's individuality, can grow only from one's essence; thus the self must awaken from the trance of habituation and claim its right to "true consciousness," as a precondition for "objective consciousness."

On the level of objective consciousness, knowledge becomes the corollary of an idealist or transcendental epistemology. That is, truth is experienced by consciousness directly and immediately, and as an intense conviction. Rather than viewing an object from different perspectives and giving a general description of it, thereby affirming the separation between subject and object, objective consciousness creates a mystical union between the knower and the thing known. In the words of Richard Gregg, "There is not only a blending of subject and object, a mutual absorption, a forgetting of everything else; there is often delight, an exultation, an enthusiasm, a rapture, a deep and abiding joy. . . . It is not a knowing from without; it is a knowing from within. It is not knowing-about; it is unitive knowledge. Unitive knowledge is much more complete and deeper than knowing-about."[31] Within this realm of unitive knowledge, one is impressed not by the diversity of experience but by its unity. Thus the closer one gets to pure, objective consciousness, the more one is absorbed into a nameless entity immeasurably greater than the self. In this way, Gurdjieffian idealism posits the self as undifferentiated consciousness, energized by what Richard M. Bucke calls cosmic consciousness; that is, the mystical union of self and cosmos.[32] Gurdjieffian philosophy assiduously differentiates between the Absolute and the Judeo-Christian concept "God." Indeed, in the passage from self-consciousness to objective consciousness, a person is "transhumanized into a God" as he or she becomes one with the all. Gurdjieff's concept of the Absolute is therefore essentially cosmic and pantheistic, as illustrated in the accompanying diagram of his Ray of Creation theory of the universe.

13

Absolute
↕
All worlds
All suns
Our sun
All planets
↕
Earth
Moon
Nothing

In the series that ranges from the Absolute to the moon, there occurs an interval between the planets and the earth which can be bridged only by organic life on earth. In this way, "The whole of life on earth could be regarded as forming a kind of sensitive film which first absorbed and then liberated energies coming from the higher region of the ray."[33] Maintaining that all forms of matter, including human beings, possess psychic and cosmic as well as physical properties, Gurdjieff further argues that organic life on earth functions both as an organ of perception and as an organ of radiation, transforming energy before transmitting it back into the earth. Indeed, Gurdjieff's Ray of Creation theory holds that the "divine" sun, not God, is the genesis of life on earth.

Finally, it is important to understand Gurdjieff's conception of art, particularly in light of an affective aesthetic that generally animates the literature Toomer wrote during this period. Gurdjieff's art aesthetic is perhaps most clearly revealed in his theory of "objective art." "I measure the merit of art by its consciousness, you by its unconsciousness. A work of objective art is a book which transmits the artist's ideas not directly through words or signs or hieroglyphics but through feelings which he evokes in the beholder consciously and with full knowledge of what he is doing and why he is doing it."[34] In view of this aesthetic and its influence on Toomer, one would be correct in surmising that the literature of this period was written to inspire cosmic consciousness. Yet in reviewing the years between 1940 and 1955, we witness a conspicuous shift in Toomer's idealism, owing to his conversion to Quakerism. With its mystical quietism, its emphasis on the self's direct communion with

God, and its premise that God is both imminent and transcendent, Quaker religious philosophy appealed to his idealist thinking.[35]

When Jean Toomer moved to Doylestown, Pennsylvania, in 1936, he had not planned to associate with any religious sect. "I had felt that the church was more reactionary than forward-moving. The power radically to change lives seemed to have departed from it."[36] In 1935, he renounced his affiliation with Gurdjieff, and by 1938 his interest in Quaker religious philosophy led him to believe that the Religious Society of Friends provided a radical venture beyond objective consciousness to "Inner Light consciousness."

> Quakers assembled I had been told, for silent worship and waited for the spirit to move them. This appealed to me because I had practiced meditation. Years before I had read a brief account of George Fox that impressed me. I had heard of the Quaker reputation for practicing what they preached. . . . Prior to coming into contact with Friends I had been convinced that god is both imminent and transcendent, and that the purpose of life is to grow up to God; that within man there is a wonderful power that can transform him, lift him into new birth; that we have it in us to rise to a life wherein brotherhood is manifest and war impossible. . . . The more starkly I see the human situation the more urgent is my conviction that nothing less than a radically changed life, wrought by supra-personal love and light, will enable us to resolve the terrific problems we have brought on ourselves and to advance a decisive step toward our true destiny.[37]

During his apprenticeship with the Society of Friends, he immersed himself in Quaker religious philosophy, reading George Fox's *Journal*, Fox's epistles entitled *A Day Book of Counsel and Comfort*, Robert Barclay's *An Apology for the True Christian Divinity*, William Penn's *Rise and Progress of the People Called Quakers* and *No Cross, No Crown*, Issac Pennington's *Letters*, John Woolman's *Journal*, and Rufus Jones's multi-volume edition of the Quaker History Series. Toomer wrote numerous essays on George Fox and Quakerism, and in 1940 he joined the Society of Friends. Quaker religious philosophy is founded on the idea that the Inner Light of divine presence is the ethical and religious essence of being. The individual is capable of direct communion with God's presence, which resides deep within the self, and knows what is ethical through inward, subjective conviction. Within the Society of Friends there is no objective religion, for religion is not a doctrine but a mode of life; and there are no ethical systems, for ethical action derives from within the self. Quaker religious philosophy, however, observes sharp distinctions between the divine and the human, maintaining that truth lies *outside* of consciousness. Restoration of the union between God and the individual is not an achievement of identity, as in Oriental philosophy and in Gurdjieffian idealism, but is brought about by the descent and incarnation of God in the individual. Toomer himself defines the philosophy of Quakerism as follows:

> The message of Quakerism is that there is that of God in every man. Indeed the message is the immediacy of God. . . . Quakerism says here is a way to God. Here are practices that will lead you to discover God in yourself and your fellowman. Here are means and methods that enable you to recover the indwelling divinity and realize you are part of it. . . . Quakerism is not unique in proclaiming that something of God is in man. Hinduism proclaims the same . . . [and] Catholic mystics made the same discovery.[38]

At first, Toomer envisioned Quaker religious philosophy as a bridge between two levels of consciousness: the ethical or social concerns of being consciousness, and the religious or theistic concerns of Inner Light consciousness. After several years, however, he began realizing the futility of reconciling these philosophies. Indeed, in the last decade of his career as a writer, the shift away from monistic, pantheistic, cosmic consciousness to dualistic, Christian, religious consciousness achieved its apotheosis in the poetics of alienation and praise. Thus, for more than three decades Toomer's devotion to idealist metaphysics reveals that he sought to materialize (reify) ideas and abstractions. This fact is most clearly manifested throughout his canon in his conceptions of characters, in his philosophy of race and society, and in his conception of history.

In Toomer's works we are able to discern a pattern of idealized or reified versions of the self in his creation of character types. There is the Divided Self, which is sometimes dramatized as a divided protagonist and sometimes as a Socratic dialogue between a "real" and a "projected"

16

self; there is the Mystical Self, most often represented as a prophet of higher consciousness; and there is the Alienated Self, exiled from society and itself. Toomer's reification of thought is evident in the way he consistently proposed idealism as the solution to racism and social problems, yet without the praxis of social activism. Using an idealized version of himself as the foundation of a new, raceless social order reveals precisely how he sought to materialize an abstraction. Finally, his reification of future time via utopianism and millennialism suggests his general indifference to historical consciousness. Indeed, in many of his works history is transmuted into a timeless world of myth, as seen in his uses of literary portraiture and spatial form techniques. As we shall see, these dimensions of his reified thinking are manifested throughout his canon.

PART 1

The Aesthetic Sphere
1918–1923

1. Aesthetics of Orientalism and the Emergence of Racial Consciousness

IMAGIST AND SYMBOLIST POETRY

As literary corollaries of his idealism, the Imagist and Symbolist poetry Toomer wrote during this period reveals varying degrees of reified consciousness, both in its highly personal visions of reality and in its art-for-art's-sake aestheticism. The best examples of Imagist poetry are "And Pass," "Storm Ending," "Her Lips Are Copper Wire," and "Five Vignettes." A sustained impressionistic portrait of twilight fading into darkness, "And Pass" images a picturesque sea setting in two brief movements, each introduced by "When."

> When the sun leaves dusk
> On far horizons,
> And night envelops
> Empty seas
> And fading dream-ships;
> When the stars have eyes,
> And their light blends
> With darkness—
> > I stand alone,
> > Salute and pass
> > Proud shadows.

The poem concludes in a moment of visionary awareness, as the poet's imagination is suddenly arrested by the passing clouds, the fleeting and majestic "proud shadows." Concomitant with the poet's sense of exaltation comes a sense of his own loneliness and mortality, as "night envelops / empty seas / and fading dream-ships."[1]

21

Also richly impressionistic in design, "Storm Ending" unfolds as an implied comparison between two natural phenomena, thunder and flowers, although imagery remains the crucial vehicle of meaning.

> Thunder blossoms gorgeously above our heads,
> Great, hollow, bell-like flowers,
> Rumbling in the wind,
> Stretching clappers to strike our ears . . .
> Full-lipped flowers
> Bitten by the sun
> Bleeding rain
> Dripping rain like golden honey—
> And the sweet earth flying from the thunder.

This scene captures the momentous return of sunshine and tranquility following a tempest, as the sound of thunder fades into the distance.

In "Her Lips Are Copper Wire," desire generated by a kiss is compared to electrical energy conducted between copper wire, here imaged as lips. The evocative and sensuous opening lines, addressed to the imaginary lover, convincingly illustrate Pound's Doctrine of the Image.

> whisper of yellow globes
> gleaming on lamp-posts that sway
> like bootleg licker drinkers in the fog
>
> and let your breath be moist against me
> like bright beads on yellow globes

"Five Vignettes" is a series of imagistic sketches modeled after Japanese haiku poetry. The first is a seascape portrait of "red-tiled ships" shimmering iridescently upon the water. The ships are "nervous" under the threat of clouds eclipsing their watery reflections:

> The red-tiled ships you see reflected,
> Are nervous,
> And afraid of clouds.

The second captures a dynamic tension between stasis and motion.

> There, on the clothes-line
> Still as she pinned them,
> Pieces now the wind may wear.

The third vignette depicts an old man of ninety, still living courageously, "eating peaches" and unafraid of the "worms" that threaten his very existence. The fourth is reminiscent of an Oriental proverb, especially in its idea that suffering teaches wisdom, and the fifth portrays a Chinese infant, as well as our common humanity.

> In Y. Don's laundry
> A Chinese baby fell
> And cried as any other.

Vignettes four and five are as moral as they are imagistic, each in its own way commenting on the human condition.

Several of the poetic sketches recall the linguistic impressionism of Gertrude Stein's *Tender Buttons,* especially "Face" and the lyrical quartet "Air," "Earth," "Fire," and "Water." In *Tender Buttons,* Stein attempted to defamiliarize our automatic linguistic perceptions by creating noun headnotes without naming them, as in "A Carafe, That Is a Blind Glass":

> A kind in glass and a cousin, a spectacle and
>   nothing strange
> A single hurt color and an arrangement in a system
>   to pointing
> All this and not ordinary, but unordered in not
>   resembling.
> The difference is spreading.[2]

This lyrical sketch is reminiscent of a riddle: "What is made of glass (and its 'cousin') but is different from a drinking glass in the way it spreads (bulbously) at the bottom?" The answer would be a carafe. Like Stein, Toomer attempted to register precise nuances of perception and name them with a unique word or phrase. Here he renders a portrait of an old woman, using the noun headnote "Face."

> Hair—
> silver-gray,
> like streams of stars,
> Brows—
> recurved canoes
> quivered by the ripples blown by pain,
> Her eyes—
> mists of tears
> condensing on the flesh below.

Toomer's quartet ensemble demonstrates how linguistic impressionism serves as a poetic medium for communicating both the uniqueness and the universality of our common perceptions of the cosmic order, as in "Fire":

> Flickers, flames, burns.
> Burns into a thing—hence, depth, profundity.
> "Hot after something,"
> Sparking, flowing, "in a fever"
> Always stewing smoking panting
> Flashy.

Yet another form of linguistic impressionism is revealed in "Sound Poem" (I) and "Poem in C," both of which represent adaptations of French Symbolist aesthetics. The French Symbolists maintained that the purpose of language is to evoke a reality beyond the senses, rather than to state plainly or to inform. In their attempts to describe the essence of an object and not the object itself, they sought to produce the effects of music, thinking of images as having abstract values like musical notes and chords. Sounds and associations, then, perform the act of communication, while meaning is eclipsed, as in "Sound Poem" (I):

> Mon sa me el kirimoor,
> Ve dice kor, korrand ve deer,
> Leet vire or sand vite
> Re sive tas tor;
> Tu tas tire or re sim bire,
> Rozan dire ras to por tantor,
> Dorozire, soron,
> Bas ber vind can sor, gosham,
> Mon sa me el, a som on oor.

Here Toomer uses sounds and words from several languages, such as French ("mon se me" or "mon sommeil," "vite," "tas," "bas"), Latin ("kor" and "soron"), Spanish ("me," "el," "dice," "tu," and "por"), Japanese ("kirimoor"), and English to open poetic avenues to thought, in the tradition of Rimbaud, Baudelaire, and Laforgue. An exercise in formalism and a lesson in the mystical powers of language, this sound poem also employs -or end rhymes, -ire internal rhymes, repetition ("mon sa me el"), parallelism ("Leet vire or sand vite" and "Tu tas tire or re sim bire"), and linguistic cognates to create the illusion of meaning, while sounds guide us through the process of poetry. The Symbolist

24

lyric "Poem in C" produces the effect of music, as hard *C* sounds take on the abstract values of musical notation, as in this excerpt:

> There behind us lay the sombre catacombs
> Ready to catapult their dead
> Among us living catilines and caterans;
> "Needest thou catharsis?" I asked the first.
> "Nay," said he, "My place of birth was
> Ancient famed Cathay, whence go roads
> To the flaming cauldron, which has
> Long since cavorted me."

In addition to the specifically Imagist and Symbolist lyrics composed during this period, there are also conventional poems which treat the ecstasy of love, the idealist imagination, and the modern world as wasteland.

A love song in four stanzas, "I See Her Lovely There" expresses the agony and the ecstasy of love, the former resulting from a loss of masculine pride, the latter from an awareness of his lover's beauty.

> Lord bring her from that distant place,
> Inaccessible to my fate,
> That my heart may break and break
> Against her anviled loveliness.

"Evening Song," from *Cane,* comprises a portrait of a lady, Cloine. Following an evening of romance, the poet and his companion spend the night together. As she drifts toward sleep, he imagines her in stages of tiring, sleeping, and dreaming.

> Cloine, curled like the sleepy waters where the moon-waves start,
> Radiant, resplendently she gleams,
> Cloine dreams,
> Lips pressed against my heart.

"Delivered at the Knighting of Lord Durgling" develops as a dialogue between two personalities within the self: the elder Lord Davey Durgling, who symbolizes petulance and cynicism, and the young Davey, who represents good humor and idealism. Young Davey's idealist imagination prevails in the end, when he defiantly confronts his elder self:

25

Go kick yourself and be chased by cats,
The world is full of sweet-lipped interests,
Not to mention hot-lipped interests, and
Transcendental polygons are the forms of breasts.

In "Banking Coal" the poet uses metaphors of fire and air to evoke the élan of life as a divine spark or flame that animates the human spirit. As the poem describes it, the fiery coals of imagination and creativity should never be "banked" conservatively within the furnace of the mind. "Roaring fires never have been made that way." Rather, by "touching the air" the mind "takes a flame" from the phenomenal world:

. . . one grand flare
Transferred to memory tissues of the air
Is worth a life, or, for dull minds that turn in gold,
All money ever saved by banking coal.

"Skyline" and "Gum" portray the urban landscape of the modern wasteland in images of cultural and moral failure. A lament for modern humanity's loss of spiritual identification with nature and the primordial past, "Skyline" unfolds through contrasting images of past and present, as symbolized, respectively, by the fossilized remains of a cow sealed underneath asphalt, and the upper asphalt jungle itself. "Gum" declaims the ascendancy of materialism in the postwar decade, as two lighted billboards provide the central symbolism in the poem. One offers a religious exhortation:

STAR
J E S U S
The Light of the World.

The other carries a commercial advertisement:

WRIGLEYS
eat it
after
every meal
It Does You Good.

As the billboards flash intermittently upon the streets below, they illuminate a small park, the scene of a Salvation Army rally. They also shed light on the loss of asceticism in the modern world, as symbolized by the gum-chewing missionaries, preaching in a world that "jaws Jesus" while "jawing gum."

Jean Toomer participated on equal terms with Gertrude Stein, Ezra Pound, Amy Lowell, H.D., and Richard Aldington in the creation of a uniquely modern vision of art. These were American writers who, in accordance with Pound's famous dictum "make it new," were engaged in "threshing and winnowing, testing and experimenting with words, stretching them and refocusing them, until they became the pliant instruments of a new idiom."[3] Yet modernist innovation and experimentation is itself born of alienation. As Renato Poggioli reminds us, alienation from society manifests itself on the level of form as alienation from literary tradition.[4] In this way, Toomer's formalism reflects his alienation, which he sought to transcend via idealist aesthetics. Thus the circle is complete, and we witness the return and restoration of the original dialectic, the return of reified consciousness.

In "Skyline" and "Gum" Toomer holds the mirror up to nature. What we see is the modern, postwar world as a wasteland, ravaged by materialism and moral failure. The rest of the poetry of this period, however, reveals the poet's almost complete absorption in the art-for-art's-sake aesthetics of Symbolism and Imagism. "And Pass," "Storm Ending," "Her Lips Are Copper Wire," and "Five Vignettes" all present time as a spatial form, as a moment of vision, rendering history as static portraiture; "Sound Poem" (I) and "Poem in C" use arbitrary and abstract sounds to transcend language, sacrificing meaning to linguistic impressionism; and both "Delivered at the Knighting of Lord Durgling" and "Banking Coal" assert the predominance of idealist consciousness. The most striking illustration of reified consciousness is evident in Toomer's representation of the divided self in "The Knighting of Lord Durgling," the symbolic self torn between cynicism and idealism in which the latter prevails. As we shall see, however, the short stories and plays of this period reveal his struggles against idealist reification in their representations of social and racial consciousness.

"LIKE GREEN BLADES SPROUTING IN HIS CONSCIOUSNESS"

When Toomer arrived in Georgia in September of 1921, ready to assume his duties as headmaster of Sparta's all-black Agriculture and

Industry Institute, he seized upon the opportunity to explore his black heritage. Living as a black American in a small, segregated, Southern community liberated his latent identification with black folk culture. And knowing that his own father, Eugene, had lived in Sparta some twenty-five years earlier contributed to his Platonic conception of himself as a prodigal son returning home. It is precisely this spiritual identification with his African-American heritage that provided the creative impulse for *Cane* (1923). But *Cane* was not the first work in which he employed black characters and racial themes. As early as 1918 he had written of the awakening of racial consciousness in "Bona and Paul," a story he later revised for inclusion in *Cane*. This story will be discussed in chapter 2. Race is also a major theme in the short story "Withered Skin of Berries" (1920). In the months following his return from Georgia, while composing and revising works which would later compose *Cane,* he wrote two plays: *Balo,* which treats mysticism within three generations of an African-American family, and *Natalie Mann* (1922), which examines the issue of female self-actualization within the social constraints of the black bourgeois. In sum, between 1918 and 1923, African-American characters and racial themes occupy center stage in Toomer's writings.

In "Withered Skin of Berries" the author presents his "First American" or "New American" social philosophy as the solution to racism. This story allegorizes the relationship between two mulattoes as the model for racial amalgamation in America—Vera, a neurasthenic woman, and David Teyy, a poet, mystic, and philosopher portrayed as her spiritual guide. The first part of the story focuses on the failure of Vera's relationship with Carl, who is white, and Art, who is black, neither of whom represents a solution to her spiritual lethargy. In the second part of the story Teyy's idealist racial philosophy emerges. He first reveals his vision of transcendental unity in addressing Carl's bigotry.

> Dead leaves of Northern Europe, Carl, have decayed for roots tangles here in America. Roots thrusting up a stark fresh life. That's you. Multicolored leaves, tropic, temperate have decayed for me. We meet here where a race has died for both of us. . . . They have resolved their individualism to the common stream. . . . have you ever felt overpowered by the sum of something, of which plowed fields, blue sky, and sunset were a

part, overpowered till you sank choking with wonder and reverence?[5]

Symbolically described as "the man of the multicolored leaves," Teyy proclaims that a "new world soul" unifies all races in universal harmony. As the narrative ends, he reiterates his philosophy of transcendental unity.

> Know you, people, that you sit beside the boulder where Tiacomus made love. Made love, you understand me? Know you, people, that you are above a river spattered with blood. With blood, you understand me? John Brown's blood. Know you, people, that you are beneath the stars of wonder, of reverence, of mystery. Know you that you are boulders of love, rivers spattered with blood, white red blood, black red blood, that you are stars of wonder and mystery.[6]

Teyy's allusions to the Indian Tiacomus and to the abolitionist John Brown, as well as to the commonly spilled blood of blacks and whites in founding the nation, emphasize how all Americans have "resolved their individualism to the common stream." Indeed Teyy himself symbolizes both Native American and African-American strains. Earlier in the narrative, in his conversation with Carl, Teyy (who is described as dark and who sings a Negro folk song) refers to himself as a pale-faced Indian, signifying his Native American status.

A modern-day morality play, *Balo* allegorizes the spiritual values of three generations of African-American mystics, represented respectively by Uncle Ned, Will Dickerson, and his son, Balo. Uncle Ned allegorizes the prophetic dimension of mysticism. Gray-haired, bearded, and blind, Ned is the wise and intuitive patriarch. Like Father John in "Kabnis," he decries the presence of sin. "Boll Weevil come ter tell us that its time ter change our ways. Aint satisfied with sinnin, but getting wus. An th Lord looks down an is angry, an he says 'stop,' says He, 'Kin you stop now? If you kin you kin be saved. I'm awarning yer."[7] Ned's warning, specifically directed at the cardplayers in this scene, symbolizes the assertion of spiritual values over the encroachment of materialism.

A youthful mystic and a lightning rod for spiritualism, Balo allegorizes the charismatic aspects of mysticism, for he possesses an uncanny gift for seizing the moment and converting it into an exhilarating and unifying religious experience. Early in the play, he is mesmerized by the language of the Scriptures, as if spiritually transported outside of the scene. Toomer achieves this effect by having all sound cease on stage while the actors mime laughs and shouts in the background. This foregrounds Balo and his chanting, thereby allowing the audience to share in his moments of religious ecstasy. In a later scene, he is suddenly inspired to play a stirring Negro spiritual on the organ. This, in turn, inspires everyone on stage to join in singing a song of praise. When the music ends and all is still, Balo begins speaking as if in a somnambulistic trance. The closing scene uses the biblical account of Saul's transformation to Paul to emphasize Balo's own religious conversion. Like his father and Uncle Ned, he is now also a spiritual leader of his race. As the curtain descends, only Uncle Ned and Balo remain on stage. Their embrace symbolizes the union of past and present in a shared recognition of spiritual harmony.

Will Dickerson allegorizes the social dimension of mysticism. A backwoods preacher, he is extremely loving and generous; indeed, his home is a sanctuary for members of the community. Will's charity extends beyond his home, however, to include his poor-white neighbors, the Jennings. During hard times, Dickerson and Jennings share their produce. There is no dividing line between the two homes, except a solid stake of oak, which symbolizes the strong bond between the families. Indeed, the heavy oak bed and the oak dresser, gifts from the Jennings family, are considered heirlooms in the Dickerson household.

A drama in three acts, *Natalie Mann* satirizes the traditions of restraint and "right reason" within the Victorian black bourgeoisie. Reminiscent of Ibsen's *Doll's House* in its representations of female independence, the play revolves around the characters of Natalie Mann, a young middle-class woman who liberates herself from gender socialization, Etty Beal, a sensual cabaret dancer who becomes the model for self-actualization, and Nathan Merilh, Natalie's "instrument of achievement," mentor, and spiritual guide. A kindred spirit of D. H. Lawrence's Rupert Birkin in his conception of personal relationships, Nathan is an eccentric writer and philosopher absorbed in his own theories of individual and social development. Like Birkin, who desires a mystical "pure balance of two single beings," an impersonal union that leaves one "free," Nathan dissuades Natalie from thinking her life must revolve exclusively around him or any man. Indeed, he admonishes her to liberate herself from the authority of gender socialization before becoming a wife or mother.

> You have not found yourself. You cannot function. You can conceive of no joy transcending the bliss of surrender to partial love. You think that your love for me is the sum of your capabilities. But even a char-woman gets more from life than bed and home and babies. If only once in a life-time, she is conscious of her own being. At that time she knows that a man does not include the universe. Your possibilities are greater. You would curse me if you awoke too late to realize them.[8]

Much of the drama in *Natalie Mann* develops through character doubling. Described as "imperfect doubles," Natalie and Nathan not only share similar names and socioeconomic backgrounds; each also suffers from a deficiency in emotional development, a neurasthenia derivative of a sterile, Victorian upbringing. Society, here associated with hypermorality and "right reason," thwarts "the spontaneous union of souls," resulting in the failure of love. In this context, Natalie's promiscuity represents her attempts to compensate for a lack of parental love, while Nathan's neurasthenia defines his lack of emotional development. Toomer also counterpoints Nathan, who symbolizes the masculine, reflective self, and Etty Beal, who symbolizes the feminine, impulsive self. In search of an ideal complement to balance his pervasive inability to feel, one which will "prove sufficiently independent and vital" in overcoming the conventions of "right reason," Nathan dances with Etty to achieve a momentary stay against self-consciousness, to achieve harmony with his unconscious or impulsive self. Their dancing, "a spontaneous embodiment of the struggle of two souls, against external barriers, for freedom and integrity," symbolizes the unification of emotion and intellect. Thus, when Nathan collapses during the most intense moments of his dance with Etty (as he similarly falters during passionate moments with Natalie), his failure symbolizes the inability of reason to achieve a proper balance with emotion. The most dramatic use of doubling, however, occurs between Natalie and Etty in the closing scene of the play. Following Nathan's collapse, Natalie is curiously aloof and composed. As she exclaims defiantly, "You silly women, who see him only a man!" she is motivated not by jealousy but rather by "a truth of which she is at this moment fully conscious." When Natalie and Etty face each other "in the glow of an instant and mutual recognition," each experiences an epiphany, a mutual realization that women must develop independent of both men and social conventions if they are to transcend gender socialization and achieve true selfhood.

In contrast with the poems of this period, the short stories and plays show Toomer's struggles against idealist reification. Yet even in these realistic narratives, idealism mitigates against focused and unified critiques of racism and sexism. In "Withered Skin of Berries," for example, transcendental consciousness ultimately achieves ascendancy over racial consciousness. For although Teyy censures Carl's racial bigotry, he does so in order to advance a "New American" philosophy of race, a philosophy which signals the reemergence of reified idealism. To be sure, privileging individuals of mixed racial heritage as the "First Americans" represents, at best, a naive view of history and social evolution. Teyy's views on women similarly betray his idealism. That he presumes to guide women into the light of self-realization reveals not only his missionary zeal for idealist philosophy but his chauvinism as well. In *Balo* Toomer treats the theme of spiritualism in African-American culture, and how spiritual values contribute to positive race relations. Here, African-American history is defined in terms of religious mysticism, rather than the social struggles which constitute that history. As in "Withered Skin of Berries," he privileges the mystical seer as hero, implying the ascendancy of mysticism over historical and social reality. In *Natalie Mann* we again see the male hero and mystical seer (Nathan) as "an instrument" of self-realization for women, a role which undermines the play's apparent satire on sexism and gender-based restraints. Moreover, in this work, as in "Delivered at the Knighting of Lord Durgling," reified consciousness is evident in Toomer's allegorization of the divided protagonist (Nathan and Natalie), as two halves of an entity unable to reconcile itself.

Between the winter of 1921 and the fall of 1922, Toomer maintained his interest in African-American subjects, as he continued to write and revise the works which were to compose his masterwork, *Cane*. The book was completed in December 1922 and published in October 1923. Because *Cane* is the centerpiece of his canon, I accord it extended analysis in the next chapter, examining both its micronarrative and macronarrative structure, as well as its degrees of idealist reification.

2. *Cane:* Hermeneutics of Form and Consciousness

In his foreword to the 1923 edition of *Cane,* Waldo Frank properly locates the pulse of Toomer's Symbolist-Modernist aesthetic, heralding him as "a poet in prose." In describing his own writing, Toomer corroborates Frank's assessment: "As for writing—I am not a romanticist. I am not a classicist nor a realist, in the usual sense of those terms. I am an essentialist. Or, to put it in other words, I am a spiritualizer, a poetic realist. This means two things. I try to lift facts, things, happenings to the planes of rhythm, feeling, and significance. I try to clothe and give body to potentialities."[1] In words reminiscent of Ezra Pound's summons to "make it new," Toomer asserts that the modern writer "has a wish to produce by experimentation a new form. Certainly he will aim to make an individual use of the old forms."[2] Toomer's original use of literary forms intermediate between poetry and prose not only accentuates his own search for form, it foregrounds the structure of language in *Cane.* In this context, Roman Jakobson's research on the nature of poetic language and Victor Shklovsky's theory of *ostraneniye* provide useful heuristic strategies for examining the book's range of verbal art.

The character of verbal art, according to Jakobson, is twofold: it develops either by contiguity, as in prose, or by similarity, as in poetry. The former is described as *metonymic* discourse, the latter as *metaphoric.*

> In verbal art the interaction of [metonymy and metaphor] is especially pronounced. . . . [In poetry] The primacy of the

metaphoric process in the literary schools of romanticism and symbolism has been repeatedly acknowledged, but it is still insufficiently realized that it is the predominance of metonymy which underlies and actually predetermines the so-called "realistic" trend, which belongs to an intermediary stage between the decline of romanticism and the rise of symbolism and is opposed to both.[3]

The "contiguous," or metonymic, language of realistic narrative is essentially denotative and explicitly referential, as it advances by combination and contexture. The "similar," or metaphoric, language of poetry, however, is essentially connotative and explicitly reflexive, as it advances by selection and substitution.

Jakobson also isolates six functions of language, noting that every "message," though often fulfilling more than one role, is framed in a predominant context. He defines the domain which is specific to poetry by extension of his distinction between the metonymic and metaphoric poles of language: "The poetic function projects the principle of equivalence from the axis of selection onto the axis of combination."[4] That is, the principal way in which the poetic function manifests itself is by *projection* of metaphoric language onto the metonymic speech act. "By emphasizing resemblances of sound, rhythm, and image, poetry thickens language, drawing attention to its formal properties and away from its referential significance."[5] Jakobson further observes that "similarity superimposed on contiguity imparts to poetry its thoroughgoing symbolic, multiplex, poly-semantic essence."[6] It is in this context that Victor Shklovsky's theory of defamiliarization complements Jakobson's description of the linguistic function which is specific to poetry.

In "Art as Technique," Shklovsky argues that as perception becomes habitual, it becomes automatic. Thus the purpose of art is to impart artfulness or *literariness* to life—by de-automatizing it, by defamiliarizing it—in order to distinguish it for sensuous perception. "The purpose of art is to impart the sensation of things as they are perceived and not as they are known. The technique of art is to make objects 'unfamiliar,' to make forms difficult, to increase the difficulty and length of perception because the process of perception is an aesthetic end in itself and must be prolonged."[7] "Defamiliarization" effectively transfers the object of perception into a new sphere of heightened perception. Victor Erlich, who labels the transference "semantic shift," describes this sphere as the very raison d'être of poetry. "By tearing the object out of its habitual context, by bringing together disparate notions, the poet gives a *coup de grâce* to the verbal cliché and to the stock responses attendant upon it and focusses us into heightened awareness of things and their sensory texture. The act of creative deformation restores sharpness to our perceptions, giving 'density' to the world around us."[8]

In "The Subject Matter of Art," Toomer uses three examples to illustrate the Symbolist notion that art which derives from inner experience is the product of the self's artistic defamiliarization, a process which evokes, in Toomer's words, "a range of experiences" within the reader. The illustration is of five people riding in a car, including a man who is a musician. What type of music is he to create for the occasion? On the one hand, if he makes music of the sounds of the car (e.g., the whir of the motor and the rattle of the body), he merely translates an experience common to all, inspiring no one. On the other hand, if he makes music of the ordinary moods of himself and his companions (e.g., the excited mood of starting; the tedium; the restlessness), according to Toomer, there is nothing in this type of art to warrant one's having spent years mastering the techniques of music. However, as a third alternative, if the musician uses techniques to express his true inner life and utilizes his technical facility to evoke higher levels of consciousness in himself and in his companions, then he evokes a *range* of experiences which neither the car nor their moods could provide. "Imaginatively place yourself in that car. Ask yourself which type of music you'd most like to hear and participate in. There is no doubt that the third type would mean most, precisely because it would transport you into a creative state of being, a state of being inner active as never before, whereas types one and two but repeat that with which you are already familiar." In other words, the musician's creative imagination *defamiliarizes* our common, habitual perceptions, distinguishing them for sensuous perception.

In narrative discourse defamiliarization is problematic, as it is in *Cane.* For whenever linguistic defamiliarization occurs within narration, a distinctly "poetic" dimension is introduced; that is, self-reflexive language in narration "makes strange" the metonymic speech act. When the "principle of equivalence" is projected from the metaphoric onto the metonymic axis of language, metaphor widens the gap between signifier and signified. The result is poetic verbal art, an aspect of creative deformation not unlike Brooks's dictum on the language of paradox, or Empson's types of ambiguity. In like fashion, Jakobson maintains that "ambiguity is an intrinsic, inalienable character of any self-focused message, briefly a corollary feature of poetry. . . . The supremacy of poetic function over referential function does not obliterate the reference, but makes it ambiguous."[9] For Jakobson, as for Shklovsky, the language of poetry widens the gap between the sign and its referent.

> The function of poetry is to point out that the sign is not identical with its reference. Why do we need this reminder? . . . Because along with the awareness of the identity of the signs and the referent (A is A1), we need the consciousness of the inadequacy of this identity (A is not A1); this antinomy is essential, since without it the connection between the sign and the object becomes automatized and the perception of reality withers away.[10]

Shklovsky's defamiliarization theory illuminates Jakobson's theory of poetic discourse. For if the metaphoric language of poetry is more defamiliarized than the metonymic language of prose discourse, then metonymy may be equated with linguistic habituation ("the automatism of perception"), and metaphor with linguistic defamiliarization (heightened perception). That is, in prose we do not notice individual words as words, because perception in reading "smooth" or referential language presents little difficulty. But in poetry, language is "roughened" or sign oriented; the autonomy of the word is emphasized. It follows, then, that mimesis in Symbolist or "poetic" fiction is a complex process indeed, involving not only the way in which the "real" world is reflected (and distorted) but also how genre conventions are observed (and subverted). This is what Jonathan Culler implies in citing "linguistic deviation" as a major hallmark of "the true structure or state of poetry," and what Ralph Freedman and Karl Uitti mean in employing the terms "distortions" and "deformations" to describe the techniques used by Symbolist novelists in their subversions of conventional, realistic narrative.[11] But clearly, all three critics understand poetic language to be a "heightened" form of prose, which transcends its sheerly mimetic qualities to achieve a higher level of *ostraneniye* than the corresponding act of "creative deformation" in realistic narratives.

In the light of Jakobson's and Shklovsky's research, we are able to posit a continuum illustrating the range of verbal art in *Cane* in terms of degrees of literary defamiliarization—that is, in terms of the predominance of self-reflexive poetic tropes, such as ambiguity, simile, metaphor, imagery, rhythm, and repetition.

METAPHORIC LANGUAGE

Poems: "Reapers," "November Cotton Flower," "Face," "Cotton Song," "Song of the Son," "Georgia Dusk," "Nullo," "Evening Song," "Conversion," "Portrait in Georgia," "Beehive," "Storm Ending," "Her Lips Are Copper Wire," "Prayer," "Harvest Song"

Prose poems: "Seventh Street," "Robert," "Calling Jesus"

METONYMIC LANGUAGE

Lyrical narratives: "Karintha," "Becky," "Carma," "Fern"

Prose narratives: "Esther," "Blood-Burning Moon," "Avey," "Theater," "Box Seat," "Bona and Paul," "Kabnis"

In order to specify the degrees of distinctions among these forms, as well as explore the structure of language which inheres in each, let us examine "Song of the Son," "Calling Jesus," "Karintha," and "Avey" as representative of their respective forms.[12]

Manifesting such lyrical tropes as imagery, metaphor, alliteration, repetition, and rhyme, "Song of the Son" represents the patently metaphoric pole of *Cane*'s verbal art. Composed in iambic pentameter, the poem develops in two movements, the first composed of three five-line stanzas (*a b b a a*), the second of two four-line stanzas (*a b b a*). The first movement opens with an invocation to a late-evening singer, whose song evokes the essence of the "sawdust glow of night" and pierces the twilight silence and stillness. Here night symbolizes the oblivion into which the African-American folk spirit is passing. "Velvet pine-smoke" from the sawdust pile, like incense, transports the essence of the evening song, the essence of the Southern black experience, toward heaven. The song symbolizes the truth of artistic beauty, transcending the mutable world. The poet declares himself a prodigal son, returning home "just before an epoch's sun declines" to preserve in art the fleeting legacy of a "song-lit race of slaves." The second movement comprises an apostrophe to the "souls of slavery," described in terms of "dark purple ripened plums / Squeezed, and bursting in the pinewood air" (12). This image suggests the cloying state of fruit as it passes into the oblivion of the post-harvest. Yet the poet affirms the power of art to preserve and immortalize "one plum" and "one seed" of the passing African-American heritage in his

> everlasting song, a singing tree,
> Caroling softly would of slavery,
> What they were, and what they are to me. (12)

Further along the continuum of verbal art in *Cane* are the prose poem "Calling Jesus" and the lyrical narrative "Karintha," both of which affirm Toomer's modernist predilection to "produce by experimentation a new form." Few critics have attempted to define the prose poem, although it has existed as an autonomous literary genre for over three hundred years. The tradition of the prose poem dates from the publication of Fénelon's *Les Aventures de Télémaque* (1699), although it is more generally acknowledged that this hybrid form was created by Aloysius Bertrand in his *poème en prose*. The most popular practitioners of the prose poem were the French Symbolists, particularly Charles Baudelaire in *Petits poèmes en prose* (1869), Lautrémont in *Les Chants de Maldoror* (1867), and Arthur Rimbaud in *Les Illuminations* (1886). Although both poetic prose and the prose poem reveal a writer's predilection for metaphoric discourse, they represent distinctly different yet contiguous forms. Poetic prose remains essentially *prose* discourse, whereas the prose poem is precisely a *poem*. Susan Bernard proposed three criteria for the *poème en prose: unité, gratuité,* and *breveté.* For Bernard, the prose poem

> presupposes a conscious will or organization into a poem; it must be an organic, autonomous whole, which allows it to be distinguished from poetic prose (which is but a raw material, or a form of the first degree if you prefer, starting with which one may construct essays, novels, or poems as well); this will lead to the notion of organic unity: as complex as it may be, and as free in appearance as it may be, the poem must form a whole, a closed universe. . . . a poem does not propose for itself any end outside of itself, not more narrative than demonstrative; it does utilize narrative or descriptive elements, it is with the condition that they are transcended and are made to "work" in a whole and to uniquely poetic ends. . . . the poem does not progress towards a goal, does not play out a succes-

sion of actions or ideas, but proposes itself to the reader. . . . the modern prose poem is always brief.[13]

According to Bernard, the *poème en prose* endeavors to transcend the double principle which inheres in its hybrid form: it wills to go beyond language while utilizing language; it strives to destroy form while creating form; and it struggles to escape from literature even as it exists as an autonomous literary genre. It is this internal contradiction, this essential antinomy, Bernard argues, that gives the prose poem the character of an Icarian art, reaching toward an impossible self-transcendence, toward a negation of its own conditions of existence. Owing to degrees of artistic defamiliarization, we are able to contrast the language of the prose poem "Calling Jesus" with the language of the poetic narrative "Karintha" in order to specify the distinctions between these forms.

A poem in three movements, "Calling Jesus" unfolds as an extended metaphor of the relationship between existence and essence, here symbolized by Nora and her "little thrust-tailed dog," respectively, to comment upon the dissociation of body and soul and the need for self-integration. Here, as in his poetry, Toomer employs such tropes as simile, metaphor, imagery, and repetition (parallelism) to establish lyrical form. The first movement opens with a simile comparing Nora's soul to a small dog separated from its mistress. The poet uses the vestibule of a house to symbolize the threshold that separates inner from outer, spiritual from physical. To be sure, Nora demonstrates a callous disregard for her spiritual self-development, leaving her dog in the cold vestibule overnight. Yet the poet envisions the force of transcendental unity, "soft as a cotton ball brushed against the milk-pod cheek of Christ, stealing in to cover the little dog" and uniting it with Nora, who "sleeps upon clean hay cut in her dreams" (55). That is, though her self-integration is thwarted by the city and its "vestibules," she dreams of union with her spiritual self, here described in rural nature imagery drawn from part 1 of *Cane*.

In the second movement we learn that during the day Nora experiences mystical flashes of self-integration, "when she has forgotten the streets and alleys, and the large house where she goes to bed at night." It is precisely during these moments that "a soft thing like fur begins to rub your limbs, and you hear a low, scared voice, lonely, calling, and you know that a cool something nuzzles moisture in your palms." In a moment of mystical union with the inner self, Nora's breath comes "sweet as honeysuckle whose pistils bear the life of coming song. And her eyes carry to where builders find no need for vestibules."

The opening lines of the third movement repeat the opening lines of the poem, reiterating Nora's self-fragmentation. Here the little dog is imaged as lagging along behind her by day and, again, enclosed in the vestibule by night. In the closing lines the poet reintroduces the force of transcendental unity developed in the first movement, again affirming its power to reconcile both inner and outer selves. The simile of spiritual intervention, described as "soft as a cotton ball brushed against the milk-pod cheek of Christ" in the first movement, is here imaged as "soft as the hare feet of Christ moving across bales of southern cotton." Thus this spiritual-mystical force is imaged as light and fleeting. The closing lines reiterate the need for spiritual awakening and self-integration. Again, as in the first movement, Nora's dreams are associated with the landscape of rural nature, "cradle in dream-fluted cane." In sum, language in "Calling Jesus" is highly symbolic and self-reflexive, as in poetry.

Like the *poème en prose,* the lyrical narrative also derives from a time-honored tradition, including Johann Wolfgang von Goethe's *Wilhelm Meister* (which Toomer greatly admired), Novalis's *Heinrich von Ofterdingen,* André Gide's *La Symphonie Pastorale,* J. K. Huysmans's *A Rebours,* and Virginia Woolf's *The Waves.* Yet a lyrical narrative is not a prose poem; rather, it employs patterns of reflexive references and poetic tropes to advance a narrative design. According to Ralph Freedman, "The characteristic differentiating lyrical from non-lyrical fiction is portraiture, the halting of the flow of time within constellations of images or figures.")[14] Thus while the lyrical narrative "tells a story," in accordance with E. M. Forster's maxim on the art of fiction, it also renders the immediacy of portraiture through spatial form achieved by reflexive references. Lyrical narratives, then, unfold simultaneously on both metaphoric and metonymic levels of interpretation. Yet, ultimately, a constellation of images emerges to advance what is primarily a *narrative* design.

On the metaphoric or self-reflexive level, "Karintha" manifests extensive use of "roughened" or poetic language. There is the artful use of simile (Karintha's skin is "like dusk on the eastern horizon," her beauty is "perfect as dusk," she is "as innocently lovely as a November cotton flower," her darting was "like a blackbird that flashes in light"), of metaphor (Karintha was "a growing thing ripened too soon" and "a wild flash," her darting was "a bit of vivid color" and her running was "a whir"), of descriptive imagery ("dusk on the eastern horizon," "feet flopping in the two inch dust," "smooth and sweet" pine needles which are "elastic to the feet of rabbits," smoke from a "pyramidal sawdust pile" which "curls up and hangs in odd wraiths about the trees" and "spreads itself out over the valley"), and of present tense verbs to arrest the immediacy of portraiture ("Karintha *carrying* beauty, perfect as dusk"; "Karintha *is* a woman. She who *carries* beauty"; "Karintha *smiles* and *indulges* her male suitors" (1).

On the metonymic or referential level, however, "Karintha" is a realistic and moral tale, narrating the untimely maturation of a beautiful young girl whose inner essence is ignored, especially by men. In this way, we come to understand Karintha as a victim of her environment. Even as a child her "perfect beauty" attracts men's attention. They dandle her on their knees, wishing "to ripen a growing thing too soon." Over the years, the community indulges her mischief because of her physical beauty, and by age twelve she ripens under the rays of un-disciplined free play: "She stoned the cows, and beat her dog, and fought the other children. . . . Even the preacher, who caught her at mischief, told himself that she was as innocent as a November cotton flower" (1). By age twenty she has been married several times and developed con-tempt for the men around her. Yet they all still desire to possess her, believing "that all they had to do was to count time." Several weeks before giving birth to an infant, she inhabits a pine forest living near a sawmill until the baby is born—onto a bed of "smooth and sweet" pine needles. If indeed Karintha buries the infant under the smouldering pyramidal sawdust pile, as the text seems to suggest, then the smoke, which curls up in odd wraiths about the trees and is so dense that everyone tastes smoke in the water, is an ill omen and reminder for the community of shared guilt. The closing lines of this story reiterate the contrast between Karintha's inner essence and her outer beauty and tell how the members of her community, especially the men, regard only her physical development: "Men do not know that the soul of her was a growing thing ripened too soon. They will bring her money; they will die not having found it out."

Representing the metonymic pole of language is "Avey," the most conventional "realistic" narrative in *Cane.* While this short story employs such metaphoric tropes as simile ("trees that whinnied like colts impatient to be set free," "Avey was as silent as those great trees," "soil of my homeland falls like a fertile shower upon the lean streets," "Their playing was like a tin spoon in one's mouth," "The Capitol dome looked like a gray ghost ship drifting in from sea"), imagery ("the moon was brilliant. The air was sweet like clover. And every now and then, a stale tang, a stale drift of sea-weed," "light spread like a blush against the darkened sky. Against the soft dusk sky of Washington," "She did not have the gray crimson-splashed beauty of the dawn"), and repetition ("the moon was brilliant. The air was sweet like clover. And every now and then, a stale tang, a stale drift of sea-weed"), the language of the text remains primarily metonymic (42–47). Most important, however, there is a conspicuous absence of the reflexive reference patterns and constellations of repeated images used in the prose poems and lyrical narratives to arrest the immediacy of portraiture. To be sure, in "Avey" plot and not image is the measure of narrative design.

Reminiscent of James Joyce's "Araby," "Avey" is a story of disillusionment and self-awareness. Avey herself represents modern woman in the postwar decade. Like Eliot's London secretary in *The Waste Land,* she countenances men's sexual advances with indifference. The plot unfolds in three intervals, each chronicling the narrator's increased self-awareness in terms of his encounters with Avey. Thus the narrator's quest, like that of Eliot's Parsifal, is directed by a debased Sybyl.

The first interval recounts a boyhood incident in which the narrator is sexually awakened by romantic illusions of Avey. Later in this account, his illusions are partially realized during an amorous encounter with her on board the *Jane Moseley.* His masculine pride is bruised, however, when she meets his affection with maternalistic condescension. "I could feel by the touch of it that it wasn't a man-to-woman love. . . . I itched to break through her tenderness of passion. . . . I gave her one burning kiss. Then she laid me in her lap as if I were a child. Helpless. I got sore when she started to hum a lullaby" (43–44).

During the second interval, which begins a year later, the narrator continues harboring romantic illusions about Avey, although his ideals are diminished when her indolence begins to offend him. Upon reflection, he surmises that it is precisely her environment (the modern world itself and Washington, in particular) which induces her spiritual sterility. Toomer's Sybyl leads the narrator on a quest of self-discovery, from

Washington to Wisconsin to New York, as her metaphysical presence continues to haunt him.

The third interval describes the narrator's newfound self-awareness in terms of an epiphanic experience. After five years, he again meets Avey in Washington "strolling under the recently lit arc-lights of U Street" with a male companion. By now Avey is a courtesan, while the narrator has learned "to find the truth that people bury in their hearts." Thus he attempts to lecture her on carelessness and inner self-development. In spite of his eloquence, however, when he turns to look at her, she is asleep, and his passion dissipates. Several hours later, watching the sun rise, the narrator experiences an epiphany. He is rid of his illusions about Avey forever. "I saw the dawn steal over Washington. The Capitol dome looked like a gray ghost ship drifting in from sea. Avey's face was pale, and her eyes were heavy. She did not have the gray crimson-splashed beauty of the dawn. I hated to wake her. Orphan-woman" (47). The range of *Cane*'s verbal art reveals Toomer's search for form, particularly a form consistent with his idealism. Here we note his transcendental vision of modern art, a vision in which poetry and fiction, metaphor and metonymy, are reconciled as interactive entities, each blending into union with its antithesis. It is precisely in this manner that Toomer's literary experimentation locates him within the Symbolist-Modernist tradition. As we shall see, not only his experiments with language but also his experiments with spatial form define his modernist aesthetics.

THE ART OF LITERARY PORTRAITURE

The individual works which compose *Cane* illustrate Toomer's art of literary portraiture. His innovative experiments with time and plot progression demonstrate an ever-present attempt to collapse self and world, lyrical and narrative—in sum, to introduce *poetic* strategies into narrative. Moreover, portraiture, which employs imagery and description primarily, breaks up the consecutiveness of plot, thus thwarting the conventional narrative surge toward completion. "To call a narrative a 'portrait' is to warn the reader at once not to expect much action, to look for resolution in the completion of an artistic pattern rather than in status achieved in the lives of the characters. In his precocious first draft of *A Portrait* Joyce defined a literary portrait as an attempt to present the present not in 'its iron memorial aspect' but as a 'fluid succession of presents.'"[15] Joyce was not the only modern writer who attempted to arrest the wholeness and immediacy of experience in "a fluid succession of presents." Indeed, the American who pioneered the art of literary portraiture was Gertrude Stein; in the context of Stein's portrait writing we are perhaps best able to understand Toomer's art of literary portraiture.

Stein often employed patterns of repetition, what she calls *insistence*, to spatialize form and produce literary portraits. Realizing that the spatial form which inheres in the plastic arts does not inhere in the literary arts, she sought to eliminate the illusion of time in her narratives, much in the way that Picasso sought to eliminate the illusion of depth during his Cubistic period. By de-emphasizing the temporal dimension of her art, Stein, like Picasso, was able to achieve heightened sensory perception, as well as the illusion of spatial creation. But the specific importance of Stein's experiments was the spatialization of literary form, which resulted in the introduction of a distinctly *lyrical* dimension into her art.

In creating literary portraits, Stein sought to create a "continuous present" by "beginning again and again." In commenting on this method she used in creating the portraits of Picasso and Matisse, Stein tells us: "Every time I said what they were I said it so that they were this thing, and each time I said what they were as they were, as I was, naturally more or less but never the same each time that I said what they were, not that they were different nor that I was different but as it was not the same moment I said I said it with a difference. So finally I was emptied of saying this thing, and so no longer said what they were."[16] Accordingly, in her "Portrait of Picasso" she uses two patterns of insistence to depict this famous artist:

I.   One whom some were certainly following was one who was
       completely charming (line 1)
      One whom some were certainly following was one who was
       completely charming (lines 5–6)
      Some were certainly following and were certain that the one
       they were following was one bringing out of himself then
       something that was coming to be a heavy thing, a solid thing
       and a complete thing (lines 9–13)
      One whom some were following and some were certainly
       following him (lines 23–24)

This one had been one whom some were following (line 35)
This one was one whom some were following (lines 68–69)
He did have some following (line 84)

II. . . . the one they were then following was one working and was
     one bringing out of himself then something (lines 7–9)
     One whom some were certainly following was one certainly
     working (lines 24–25)
     One whom some were certainly following was one having
     something coming out of him something having meaning
     and this one was certainly working (lines 26–28)
     This one was one who was working (line 39)
     This one was one going on working (line 42)
     This one was one who was working (line 77)
     This one was not one working to have anything come out of
     him. He always did have something having meaning that
     did come out of him (lines 80–83)
     He was one who was working (lines 84–85).[17]

Here Stein relies upon present participles and nouns ending in *-ing* to
create a sense of presentness and immediacy in narrative, much in the
way Imagist poets relied upon the sustained image itself.

Like Stein, Toomer similarly sought to create a continuous present
through lyrical "insistence" and an artful use of present tense forms. In
many of the selections in *Cane* Toomer uses a tripartite formal design to
approximate the presentness of portraiture: (1) an introductory lyric,
(2) an exemplum, and (3) a concluding lyric. This formal strategy is
evident in "Becky," "Carma," and "Calling Jesus," but it is perhaps most
artfully realized in "Karintha" and in "Seventh Street."

"Karintha" unfolds as lyrical statement, lyrical narrative, and lyrical
restatement. The lyrical statement and restatement frame this portrait of
dusky beauty. Within the narrative itself, three patterns of reflexive
references thwart the consecutiveness of narrative in favor of imagistic
description and portraiture:

I. Her skin is like dusk on the eastern horizon,
   O cant you see it, O cant you see it,
   Her skin is like dusk on the eastern horizon. . . .
   When the sun goes down (lines 1–4)

> Her skin is like dusk,
> O cant you see it,
> Her skin is like dusk,
> When the sun goes down (lines 36–39)

> Her skin is like dusk on the eastern horizon
> O cant you see it, O cant you see it,
> Her skin is like dusk on the eastern hori-
> zon. . . .
> When the sun goes down (lines 64–67)

II. . . . this Karintha, even as a child, Karintha
carrying beauty, perfect as dusk when the sun goes
down (lines 5–6)

> She carries beauty, perfect as dusk when the sun
> goes down (lines 40–41)

> Karintha at twenty, carrying beauty, perfect as
> dusk when the sun goes down (lines 62–63)

III. Karintha is a woman (line 41)

> Karintha is a woman (lines 45–46)

> But Karintha is a woman, and she has a child
> (lines 48–49)

Here is as artful an illustration of spatial form achieved by reflexive references as we will find in modern literature. Particularly significant is Toomer's emphasis upon "making you see" ("O cant you see her"). Indeed these three patterns function to depict (I) her dark skin, (II) her perfect "dusky beauty," and (III) her femininity, all of which lead men to ignore her inner, spiritual essence. As in Stein's portrait, Toomer's reflexive references occur as present-tense verb forms ("carrying," "carries," "goes," "Karintha *is* a woman," "she *has* a child"). Finally, in both Stein's and Toomer's portraits, the reader is able to "see" the total portrait only retrospectively, after having moved beyond the parameters of the continuous present. Each of the individual (and repeated) references must be connected by the reader and viewed as a whole before the portrait fits together, like a mosaic, into a meaningful pattern; knowledge of the whole is essential to an understanding of its parts.

The lyrical statement in "Seventh Street" images materialism and activity:

> Money burns the pocket, pocket hurts,
> Bootleggers in silken shirts,
> Ballooned, zooming cadillacs,
> Whizzing, whizzing down the street-car tracks. (39)

Within the lyrical narrative itself, reflexive images of "a wedge," "white and whitewashed wood," and "black reddish blood" attempt to capture the élan of Washington's Seventh Street in the Roaring Twenties:

> Seventh Street is a crude-boned soft skinned wedge of nigger life
> [Seventh Street is] thrusting unconscious rhythm, black reddish blood into the white and whitewashed wood of Washington
>
> . . . .
>
> Wedges are beautiful in the sun
>
> . . . .
>
> Black reddish blood. Pouring for crude-boned soft skinned life, who set you flowing?
>
> . . . .
>
> Flowing down the smooth asphalt of Seventh Street, in shanties, brick office building, theaters, drug stores, restaurants, and cabarets? Eddying on the corners? (39)

"Wedge" is an appropriate metaphor for Washington's Seventh Street, since this thorough fare thrusts ("wedges") throngs of blacks through the channel of an otherwise all-white area of the city, the "white and whitewashed wood of Washington." "Wood," then, is a metaphor for the city itself, and "black reddish blood" is a metaphor for the urban blacks swirling and flowing through the office buildings, theaters, and cabarets. Moreover, Toomer's use of present tense and present participial verbs stimulates the presentness of portraiture: "money burns," "pocket hurts," bootleggers are "zooming cadillacs" and "whizzing down the street-car tracks," Seventh Street itself is "breathing its loafer air" and "pouring unconscious rhythms," black reddish blood is "pouring for crude-boned song unconscious rhythms," and black reddish blood is "pouring for crude-boned soft-skinned life," "flowing," "eddying," and "swirling." The lyrical restatement concludes this portrait of vigorous spirit and movement.

On the micronarrative level, then, the individual works which compose *Cane* reveal Toomer's search for form within the Modernist-Formalist tradition. In terms of language, there are attempts to transcend dualistic genre distinctions to create new forms, like the prose poem and the lyrical narrative. As for plot, there are efforts to transcend history, to arrest time within constellations of images to create literary portraits. In both cases, these innovations represent the author's attempts to find literary equivalents for his idealism. Moreover, these literary experiments may be traced to Toomer's reified consciousness, specifically his efforts to reconcile his divided self, as well as self and world, within a unified philosophical system.

Beyond Toomer's formal uses of Symbolism to collapse poetry and prose and Imagism to create literary portraits, idealist reification is also manifested in *Cane*'s character typology and themes. As for character typology, we note the alienated narrator and the exiled hero figure in "Fern," "Beehive," "Harvest Song," "Bona and Paul," and "Kabnis." There is, moreover, the figure of the divided protagonist (Kabnis and Lewis) in "Kabnis." Also, as in "Withered Skin of Berries" and in *Natalie Mann,* there is the male spiritual guide and idealist philosopher who serves as the instrument of female self-realization, as seen in "Avey." Regarding themes revealing reification, we note the mind-body problem reconciled in favor of the mind and "inner essence" in "Karintha," "Calling Jesus," and "Prayer." Also, the theme of mysticism is presented in "Becky," "Georgia Dusk," "Fern," "Esther," and "Kabnis." Yet, other works manifest the author's struggles against reification. In terms of character typology, there is the first-person narrator or protagonist who participates in the community, as in "Becky," "Carma," "Song of the Son," "Fern," and "Kabnis." There are themes of racism and social justice in "Becky," "Esther," "Blood-Burning Moon," "Conversion," "Portrait in Georgia," "Bona and Paul," and "Kabnis." And the theme of the African-American past is treated from socially realistic perspectives in "Cotton Song," "Song of the Son," "Georgia Dusk," and "Conversion." Finally, there are satirical attacks on capitalism in the postwar decade in "Seventh Street" and in "Rhobert." Toomer's struggles against alienation and self-fragmentation are further manifested on the macronarrative level. Yet it is Toomer's own commentary on the structure of plot in *Cane* that provides the most compelling evidence of the author's capitulation to idealist reification.

SPIRITUAL DESIGN AND THE STRUCTURE OF PLOT

Although Jean Toomer shared in the postwar temper of literary experimentation and was influenced by both Symbolist and Imagist aesthetics in the years before writing *Cane,* few critics have attempted to examine his masterwork from the perspective of Modernist-Formalist criticism. For more than six decades reviewers and critics have debated the issue of form in *Cane.*[18] The polemical discussions on unity have centered on repeated elements within the book, from which general thematic analyses have developed. On the issue of genre, scholars remain divided over *Cane*'s status as a novel, critics on both sides failing to consider the evolution of new literary forms within the modernist tradition and subscribing to the practice of judging all narrative literature by standards appropriate only to the novel. In formulating a theory of narrative, the critic must consider technique in its relationship to two major concepts: subject matter and overall structure. In *Cane,* both may be explained in terms of the author's metacommentary on spiritual design, and both elucidate the structure of plot. While there have been discussions of unifying themes, to date there has been no systematic analysis of the structure of plot in *Cane.* To my mind, it is the author himself who provides the most comprehensive commentary on form and narrative design.

> From three angles, *Cane*'s design is a circle. Aesthetically, from simple forms to complex forms, and back to simple forms. Regionally, from the South up to the North, and back into the South again. . . . From the point of view of the spiritual entity behind the work, the curve really starts with Bona and Paul (awakening), plunges into Kabnis, emerges in Karintha, etc., swings upward into Theater and Box Seat, and ends (pauses) in Harvest Song. . . . Between each of these sections, a curve. These to vaguely indicate the design.[19]

According to Toomer, design in *Cane* may be interpreted in three ways: aesthetically, regionally, and spiritually, and all in terms of a circle. While several critics have alluded to the aesthetic and regional "angles,"

V
Loss of Unity Motif
("Harvest Song")

IV
Return from Union
Motif ("Theater"
and "Box Seat")

I
Awakening Motif
("Bona and Paul")

III
Empathetic
Union Motif
("Karintha" through
"Blood-Burning Moon")

II
Initiation Motif
("Kabnis")

only Charles Scruggs and Rudolph Byrd have attempted to analyze spiritual design in *Cane*. Scruggs and Byrd define unity in terms of myth and theme, respectively, rather than the structure of plot, however; and neither defines the book as a specifically *narrative* account of a spiritual odyssey.[20] A narrative is distinguished by two requirements: a teller and a tale. In *Cane,* the teller is represented by the metaphor of the "spiritual entity behind the work." This teller, the author's self in art, may be assimilated to the role of an implied narrator. "Even the novel in which no narrator is dramatized creates an implicit picture of an author who stands behind the scenes, whether as stage manager, as puppeteer, or as an indifferent God, silently paring his fingernails. This implied author is always distinct from the 'real man'—whatever we may take him to be— who creates a superior version of himself, a 'second self,' as he creates his work."[21] The tale itself allegorizes the narrator's experiences as successive stages of consciousness. Indeed, the five arcs in Toomer's cyclical narrative design correspond to Evelyn Underhill's five stages in the development of spiritual consciousness.[22] The subject of the tale, then, is the self, and the structure of plot may be represented as a mandala, as in the accompanying diagram.

50

As an instrument of the self's awakening and a chart of its spiritual evolution, a mandala comprises a constellation of images. Usually a formalized circular design containing or contained by a figure of five points of emphasis, each representing the chief objects of psychic interest for the maker, the mandala points toward spiritual perception. Carl Jung defines the psychic function of mandalas in Eastern philosophy as follows:

> "Mandala" means a circle, more especially a magic circle. . . . quite in accord with the Eastern conception, the mandala symbol is not only a means of expression, but works an effect. It reacts upon its maker. Very ancient magic effects lie hidden in this symbol for it derives originally from the "enclosing circle," the "charmed circle," the magic of which has been preserved in countless folk customs. . . . by means of these concrete performances, the attention, or better said, the interest, is brought back to an inner, sacred domain, which is the source and goal of the soul and which contains the unity of life and consciousness. The unity once possessed has been lost, and must now be found again. . . . The unity of these two, life and consciousness, is the Tao.[23]

Considering technique in its relationship both to subject matter and structure, we are able to read *Cane* as a dramatization of consciousness. In terms of the nature of narrative, the five arcs or stages of consciousness in Toomer's spiritual design may be assimilated to a Formalist critical perspective.

In his often-cited essay "Thematics," Boris Tomashevsky makes an important distinction between story and plot. In the latter, events are "arranged and connected to the orderly sequence in which they were presented in the work," while the former represents a background against which the plot arrangement is examined. The five arcs in *Cane*'s narrative structure constitute an *arrangement* of the events of the story into an artful design. Consistent with Tomashevsky's poetics on narrative, these arcs may be defined as "bound motifs": "Usually there are different kinds of motifs within a work. By simply retelling the story we immediately discover what may be *omitted* without destroying the coherence of the narrative and what may not be omitted without disturbing the connections among events. The motifs which cannot be omitted are *bound motifs;* those which may be omitted without disturbing the whole causal-chronological course of events are *free motifs.*"[24] The remaining "free" motifs in *Cane* are not inconsequential, for they sometimes dominate and determine the construction of plot. Yet it is the predominant "bound" motifs that chart a journey from spiritual awakening in "Bona and Paul" to spiritual loss in "Harvest Song."

"Bona and Paul" allegorizes awakening to racial consciousness in *Cane's* spiritual design. Set in Chicago, the story recounts Paul Johnson's awakening perception of himself as dark and different. Paul's romance with Bona, who is white, provides the basis for the central conflict. Upon entering a cabaret with her, he becomes self-conscious when they are greeted by a multitude of stares. In an epiphanic moment, he suddenly experiences alienation:

> A strange thing happened to Paul. Suddenly he knew that he was apart from the people around him. Apart from the pain which they had unconsciously caused. Suddenly he knew that people saw not attractiveness in his dark skin, but difference. Their stares, giving him to himself, filled something long empty within him, and were like green blades sprouting in his consciousness. There was fullness, and strength and peace about it all. He saw himself cloudy, but real. (75)

According to Underhill, the awakening of the self "entails a vision of the Absolute: a sense of divine presence: but not true union with it."[25] In the story this awakening is realized as Paul's mystical vision of the South and of himself.

> Paul follows the sun, over the stockyards where a fresh stench is just arising, across wheat lands that are still waving above their stubble, into the sun. Paul follows the sun to a pine-matted hillock in Georgia. He sees the slanting roofs of gray unpainted cabins tinted lavender. A negress chants a lullaby beneath the mate-eyes of a southern planter. Her breasts are ample for the suckling of a song. She weans it, and sends it, curiously weaving, among lush melodies of cane and corn. Paul follows the sun into himself in Chicago. (71)

His newly awakened identity is represented by his sudden spiritual identification with the black doorman, whom he addresses as Brother.

Their handshake at the end of the story symbolizes Paul's acceptance of his *total* self.

"Kabnis" allegorizes the second cycle in Toomer's spiritual design, which is preparation for union with the spirit of African-American consciousness. In the character of Kabnis, the author embodies both the portrait of an alienated individual who attempts to become integrated into the community and the portrait of an artist who must surrender his pride and suffer humility before experiencing the illuminated vision requisite for literary creation. Kabnis's initiation proceeds in three stages.

The first stage is marked by alienation, which prevents him from transforming Sempter's black folk tradition into literary art: "If I . . . could become the face of the South. How my lips would sing for it, my songs being the lips of its soul" (81). He is tantalized by the spirit of intellectual beauty which surrounds him: "Dear Jesus, do not chain me to myself and set these hills and valleys, heaving with folk-songs, so close to me that I cannot reach them. There is a radiant beauty in the night that touches and . . . tortures me" (83). Kabnis stands outside of the Southern black tradition because his own participation in producing it is mystified. As a detached spectator, he exemplifies the split between observer and participant. The next stage describes his apprenticeship in Halsey's workshop, as he overcomes alienation through associations with members of the community. During this stage, as Underhill defines it, there is a struggle between the inharmonious elements of the self.[26] Toomer dramatizes this struggle in doubling Kabnis (the artist-observer) with Lewis (the reformer-participant). Using this technique, he represents the hero's encounter with his alter consciousness as a highly symbolic epiphany. Lewis's eyes "turn to Kabnis. In the instant of their shifting, a vision of the life they are to meet . . . Kabnis, a promise of the soil-soaked beauty; uprooted, thinning out. Suspended a few feet above the soil whose touch would resurrect him. There is a swift intuitive interchange of consciousness. Kabnis has a sudden need to rush into the arms of this man. His eyes call, 'Brother'" (96).

Kabnis represents the reified self; he stands outside of the African-American tradition, and his participation in producing it is mystified. Lewis, however, represents the "real" self; he participates in reforming Sempter's social and racial climate, and he confronts Kabnis with the facts of racial heritage. In the final stage of his initiation, Kabnis descends into a cellar for an all-night party. By now he is a candidate for membership into the community, as symbolized by the robe he dons throughout the night, and he is soon referred to as Brother Kabnis. His most significant encounter during this stage, however, is with Father John, who symbolizes the perennial spirit of African-American consciousness. Initially, Kabnis denies any identification with Father John, while Lewis respects the old man as a symbol of racial heritage. Again, character doubling functions to suggest the blend of qualities Kabnis must possess if he is to capture the passing essence of the African-American folk experience. After a night underground, during which time the depths of his racial consciousness are tested, Kabnis takes off his candidate's robe, symbolizing initiation into the community. As he prepares to greet the rising sun of a new day and ascend the stairs ready to commence his labor as a humble blacksmith, he undertakes nothing less than the fulfillment of his desire to forge in the smithy of his soul the uncreated conscience of his race. That conscience is artfully realized throughout the next motif, which celebrates a vision of union with the spirit of African-American consciousness.

The works from "Karintha" to "Blood-Burning Moon" convey the empathetic union motif, which I shall also term the Karintha cycle. Here the narrator perceives an extraordinary radiance and mystery in rural Georgia, its inhabitants, and its African-American heritage. Underhill notes that such illumination is accompanied by the perception of visions and that literary art produced during empathetic union with "the joy of illumination" is lyrical and mystical in nature.[27] Indeed, the illuminative process is incomplete unless it is coupled with the perception of visions. Whereas "bound motifs" dominate the first two stages in *Cane*, here four "free motifs" determine the construction of plot, each group representing a moment of vision.

  I. Portraits of Southern black women
   "Karintha"
   "Face"
   "Carma"
   "Fern"
   "Evening Song"
   "Esther"

  II. Local color portraits
   "November Cotton Flower"

"Cotton Song"
"Nullo"

III. Swansongs for the black folk tradition
"Reapers"
"Song of the Son"
"Georgia Dusk"
"Conversion"

IV. Indictments of racism
"Becky"
"Portrait in Georgia"
"Blood-Burning Moon"

The Karintha cycle thus comprises four distinct subplots. The work in this cycle most representative of the narrator's empathetic union with ancestral consciousness is "Song of the Son."

"Song of the Son" is a celebration of the narrator's illuminated vision of spiritual union with the African-American past. The first movement uses time, nature, and music imagery to represent the persona as a native son returning home "just before an epoch's sun declines," intent upon representing in art the fleeting legacy of a "song-lit race of slaves" (12). The second movement symbolizes the African-American folk tradition as a plum tree nearly stripped of its fruit. Yet the poet is able to preserve "one plum" and "one seed" to immortalize the essence of an era in art. It is precisely this single, preserved "plum" which engenders the "everlasting song," the "singing tree" that is *Cane.*

The fourth motif in *Cane*'s spiritual design manifests a shift away from the illuminated visions that characterize the Karintha cycle to a spiritually sterile urban landscape during the postwar decade. The "Theater"–"Box Seat" cycle signals the narrator's return from empathetic union with the spirit of African-American consciousness following a period of sustained mystical activity. Underhill defines this stage as the Dark Night of the Soul: "The self which thought itself so spiritual, so firmly established upon the supersensual plane, is forced to turn back, to leave the Light, and pick up those qualities which it had left behind."[28] This stage is also marked by spiritual ennui and the return of alienation, as the self once again becomes cognizant of its dissociation from the transcendental state of illumination. The works in this motif may be grouped into the following categories:

I. Portraits of urban materialism
"Seventh Street"
"Rhobert"

II. Narratives of emotional and spiritual sterility
"Theater"
"Box Seat"
"Avey"

III. Portraits of the alienated self
"Beehive"
"Calling Jesus"
"Prayer"

The only illuminated moments of vision in the "Theater"–"Box Seat" cycle are "Her Lips Are Copper Wire," which intimates the possibility of love in the urban landscape, and "Storm Ending," which images the return of sunshine and tranquility following a storm. The most representative work within this cycle is "Calling Jesus."

In "Calling Jesus" imagery borrowed from the Karintha cycle symbolizes the narrator's nostalgia for the return of spiritual transcendence and for the unity of existence and essence in the urban wasteland. The text develops as an extended metaphor, comparing Nora's soul to a small dog separated from its mistress. Despite their separation by an urban vestibule, which symbolizes the gap between inner and outer reality, the narrator envisions a force of transcendental unity, "soft as a cotton ball brushed against the milk-pod cheek of Christ," intervening to unite Nora, who "sleeps upon clean hay cut from her dreams," with her spiritual essence: "Someone . . . eoho Jesus . . . soft as the bare feet of Christ moving across bales of Southern cotton, will steal in and cover it that it need not shiver, and carry it to her where she sleeps: cradled in dream-fluted cane" (55). In this way, the narrator allegorizes the dissociation and alienation that characterize this dark stage in consciousness. In Underhill's study, the Dark Night stage functions to bring the self "to the threshold of that completed life which is to be lived in intimate union with Reality."[29] As we shall see, however, in *Cane* the Dark Night is no harbinger of the self's union with the spiritual world.

Completing the spiritual design, "Harvest Song" dramatizes the narrator's loss of empathetic union with the essence of African-American culture and consciousness. Ironically titled, the poem describes an artist's inability to transform the raw materials of his labor into art. Reminiscent of Robert Frost's "After Apple-Picking," "Harvest Song" develops as an extended portrait of the poet as reaper. Although the poet-reaper has successfully cradled the fruits of his labor, when he cracks a grain from the store of his cradled oats, he cannot taste its inner essence. In vain, he attempts to stare through time and space to understand the sources of his inspiration; he also tries to make up the physical distance by straining to hear the calls of other reapers and their songs. But his dust-caked senses preclude any meaningful or helpful intervention. The "knowledge of hunger" he fears is the failure of consciousness and of the creative impulse. Thus he is reluctant to call other reapers, for fear they will share their truly inspiring grains, grains he is unable to assimilate.

> It would be good to hear their songs . . . reapers of the sweet-stalk'd
> cane, cutters of the corn . . . even though their throats
> cracked and the strangeness of their voices deafened me.

Still, he beats his soft, sensitive palms against the stubble of the fields of labor, and his pain is sweeter and more rewarding than the harvest itself. He is then comforted by the pains of his struggles, although they will not bring him knowledge of his hunger.

Cane allegorizes a spiritual odyssey from awakening to racial identity in "Bona and Paul" to loss of racial identity in "Harvest Song," and ends on a note of alienation rather than of union, which implies the narrator's loss of empathetic union with African-American consciousness. In this context, the "spiritual entity behind the work" is a metaphor for the reified self, divided between the "real" conception of himself as an African-American and the reified conception of himself as the transcendental "First American." Thus, the loss of racial consciousness signals the ascendancy of reified consciousness. As early as July of 1922, Toomer conceded that "the impulse which sprang from Sparta, Georgia last fall has just about fulfilled and spent itself." Still, the text remains a triumph of Romantic idealism. In John Keats's "Ode to a Nightingale," the poet achieves empathetic union with the immortal spirit of nature in a truly transcendental moment of vision. After the passing of this moment in the final strophe, he remains alone, his dissociation from the nightingale complete. Yet he is enriched by the experience, having achieved, if only momentarily, the transcendental unity of inner and outer, self and world.

The narrator in *Cane* achieves a similar transcendental union in the Karintha cycle, if only momentarily, and is similarly enriched. Indeed, retrospectively, Toomer viewed the book through the lens of his perennial idealism as a spiritual fusion, not only of life and consciousness, but also of life and art.

> While my instinct to dreams and reading built up that inner life by means of which the outer is transformed into works of art, by means of which the outer gets its deeper meaning, it must not be thought, however, that these two loves existed, as it were, side by side in a mutual and sustaining contract. For a long while just the opposite was true. Whichever was for the time being dominant would try to deny and cut off the other. And from this conflict a most distressing friction arose. In fact, only a year or so ago did they creatively come together. *Cane* is the first evidence of this fusion.[30]

In analyzing precisely why Toomer turned away from African-American subjects to Gurdjieffian "higher consciousness," we need only return to the metacommentary that inheres in *Cane*'s spiritual design. As the text allegorizes it, racial consciousness is awakened as a result of the narrator's alienation from white society, resulting in his identification with his African-American heritage, as seen throughout the Karintha cycle. Yet, after a period of heightened racial consciousness, he similarly experiences alienation from black society, as seen in "Harvest Song." His alienation is thus complete, as he exiles himself from *both* races and adopts Gurdjieffian idealism, with its transcendental conception of humanity united.

CANE: TOWARD A DEFINITION OF FORM

If we are able to posit Toomer's spiritual design as the basis for formulating a theory of narrative in *Cane,* then we are also able to examine the issue of genre, as well. In *Cane,* the text telescopes the author and the narrator into a lyrical perspective that defines the book as a lyrical novel and as metafiction. Genre conventions (and a writer's abrogations of those conventions) affect our interpretation of a text. It follows, then, that valid interpretation begins with a valid inference about genre and that to misconstrue the emphases of a text is surely to misunderstand it.

Indeed, artistry attributed to a given work often results from the way we perceive it. Thus the necessity remains for finding a method by which *Cane* may be understood in terms of its own constitutive features. In defining *Cane* as a lyrical novel, three issues must be considered: the concept of the self, the structure of language, and the structure of plot.

In a lyrical novel, the narrator or "symbolic hero" represents an idealized version of the self, the author's self in art. According to Ralph Freedman, this self-reflexive narrator creates a point of view analogous to the lyrical "I" in poetry.

> He is the cause of the novel's world, its landscape and stylized textures of faces and events. In his point of view, perceptions, illusory or real, are transmuted into imagery. But he also plays the role of the protagonist: he unifies not only symbolic images but also the novel's scenes. The relationship between these two roles played by an identical figure constitutes an important dimension of lyrical fiction . . . reflected in an ambiguous world composed simultaneously of a texture of images and of the linear movement of narrative.[31]

Thus, the lyrical novel is ideologically conditioned, as it reflects an idealist epistemology of narrative. That is, the text seeks "to eliminate the disjunction of self and world in the very genre that seems most to require their separation."[32] In *Cane*, the "spiritual entity behind the work," the author's self in art, assumes the role of a "symbolic hero," a self-reflective narrator who proceeds to draw a self-portrait as he allegorizes his symbolic encounters in art.

Any discussion of the structure of language in the lyrical novel is inextricably related to the structure of plot. For the presence of both metaphoric and metonymic poles of language within the same text, as in *Cane*, thwarts any overall narrative surge toward completion. To include lyric within narrative, "roughened language" within the language of discontinuous plot, deprives narrative of the second-degree semiotic system by which it is constituted. In sum, roughened language inhibits the production of discontinuous plot when these two modes of literary defamiliarization are included within the same text.[33] A theory of narrative in *Cane* must therefore postulate a mechanism which reconciles lyric and narrative defamiliarization. That mechanism is reflexive reference. Reflexive reference is a technique for combining primary and secondary semiotic systems (poetic language and discontinuous plot) into a ternary system that forms a pattern of meaning, as in the lyrical novel. "Depicting experience and enacting it through a progression of images, the hero renders himself as a symbolic vision."[34] In a lyrical novel, as in *Cane,* there is "a vast number of references and cross references that relate to each other independently of the time sequence of the narrative. These references must be connected by the reader and viewed as a whole before the book fits together into any meaningful pattern."[35]

As for the structure of plot, time in a lyrical novel is represented as a spatial form, resulting in literary portraiture. In other words, a constellation of images is fused with an underlying plot of spiritual evolution, from which a design of motifs emerges. "A lyrical novel assumes a unique form which transcends the causal and temporal movement of narrative. . . . rather than finding its Gestalt in the imitation of an action, the lyrical novel absorbs action altogether and refashions it as a pattern of imagery. . . . Ordering all parts [of the narrative] retrospectively in a total image . . . [the reader] sees complex details in juxtaposition and experiences them as a whole."[36] In *Cane,* the constellation of images composing the five arcs of Toomer's spiritual design represent experience as a circle and as a spatial form. The underlying plot of spiritual evolution is represented by the successive stages in the narrator's self-reflexive dramatization of consciousness. In the tradition of the lyrical novel, *Cane* renders spiritual design as a symbolic vision and as a portrait of the artist.

Cane may also be defined as metafiction. In *Writing Degree Zero,* Roland Barthes employs the term *écriture* (mode of writing) to differentiate style (verbal obsessions) and language (the author's linguistic heritage) from the function a writer gives to language, the set of institutional conventions within which the activity of writing occurs.[37] Borrowing Barthes's concept of *écriture,* Culler develops a spectrum of modern modes of writing, ranging from realistic (the "socially given" text and the "general culture" text) to self-referential (the "conventionally natural," or metafictional, text and the "parody and irony" text).[38] That is, as a text moves along a continuum from the sheerly mimetic to the sheerly self-referential, at some point its technique becomes its subject. It is at this point that a text crosses the line from the emphatically mimetic to the emphatically metafictional. Under Culler's system of "Naturalization," the lyrical novel—in its formal synthesis of metaphor and metonymy and in its combination of both discontinuous plot and "roughened language" within a coherent narrative design—is "naturalized" at the level of metafiction. At this level, the lyrical novel

> finds its coherence by being interpreted as a narrator's exercise of language and production of meaning. To naturalize it at this level is to read it as a statement about the writing of novels, a critique of mimetic fiction, an illustration of the production of a world by language. . . . The best way to explain this level of naturalization may be to say that citing or opposing conventions of a genre brings about a change in the mode of reading.[39]

A metafictional text establishes an opposition between itself and its genre, so as "to make a statement about the imaginative ordering of the world that takes place in literature." Thus, "We read the poem or novel as a statement about poems or novels (since it has, by its opposition, adumbrated that theme)," and we learn to "read particular elements or images as instances of the literary process."[40] While *Cane* is essentially a mimetic text, holding a mirror up to nature throughout its lyrical narrative design, the text also manifests metafictional impulses. In order to extrapolate or "lay bare" those impulses, the critic must locate *within the text* an appropriate perspective that allows mimetic elements to be read as "instances of the literary process."

Toomer's description of the "spiritual entity behind the work" may be assimilated to the role of a self-conscious narrator who plays upon the opposition between fiction and truth. As Fredric Jameson notes, metafictional analysis, or what he terms metacommentary, is of particular importance in understanding novels in which the narrator plays a significant role in shaping our perception of the plot. "In the novel of point of view, where little by little the action of the book comes to coincide with the consciousness of the hero, interpretation is once more interiorized, immanent to the work itself, for it is now the point-of-view figure himself who from within the book, reflecting on the meaning of his experience, does the actual work of exegesis for us before our own eyes."[41]

The metaphor of the "spiritual entity" as interiorized critic implies that *Cane* may be read on a metafictional level as the story about the writing of a story—more specifically, a story chronicling the stages of consciousness during the writing of a story. *Cane* reveals other metafictional perspectives, as well. "Kabnis," for example, represents the central character as a writer intent upon capturing the African-American folk spirit in art. And if we are able to read "Bona and Paul," which immediately precedes "Kabnis," as a symbolic awakening of the artist, then Paul Johnson is the prototype for Kabnis. Moreover, both "Song of the Son" and "Harvest Song" are patently metapoetic. In "Song of the Son" the writer figure as poet is imaged as a prodigal son returning to write about his homeland. On a metapoetic level, then, the "one seed" and "one plum" he saves are metaphors for the raw materials of his art; thus, the "everlasting song" and the "singing tree" are the text that is *Cane* itself. A similar metafictional perspective inheres in "Harvest Song." In an extended metaphor of the poet as reaper, this poem describes the poet's inability to transform the fruits of his labor into art. The "fatigue" the reaper experiences, from a metapoetic perspective, symbolizes the failure of the poet's creative imagination. A similar metapoetic perspective inheres in "Prayer," where the failure of creative powers is reflected in the lines "I am weak with much giving. / I am weak with the desire to give more." Through these perspectives, *Cane* examines its own ontological status as art.

In a letter to Sherwood Anderson, *Double Dealer* editor John McClure praises Toomer as a "lyrical genius" and locates him within the modern Symbolist tradition.

> [Toomer] can be an unusually good short story writer or a supremely fine lyrical rhapsodist, as he pleases. He should mold his stories into lyrical rhapsodies rather than attempt to present them realistically. . . . The lyrical genius is not restricted to poetry. A novel can be lyrical. Realism can be lyrical. . . . Toomer's character seems to me to be lyrical—he is so intensely an individual that it is useless for him to attempt anything other than to express himself. . . . Anything he touches will be transmuted into a personal expression.[42]

As Toomer sought literary equivalents for his idealism, he not only fused his inner and outer selves to form a transcendental or symbolic self in art, he also attempted to reconcile lyric and narrative, metaphor and metonymy, metafiction and mimesis within the same text. *Cane* was not Jean Toomer's total life; yet it remains his most ambitious attempt to create an art reflective of his Symbolist idealism.

PART 2

The Ethical Sphere
1924–1939

3. Landscapes of the Self: Art and Gurdjieffian Idealism

THE POET AS IDEALIST PHILOSOPHER

It is generally argued that Toomer's literary artistry declined, owing to the rise of didacticism in his works, following his conversion to Gurdjieffian philosophy. To be sure, Gurdjieffian idealism is affective, and its theory of so-called objective art evaluates literature by its capacity to inspire higher consciousness. Yet Toomer's own conception of literature as a medium for promoting consciousness predates his association with Gurdjieff, as seen in "Withered Skin of Berries" (1922), *Natalie Mann* (1922), and his 1921 review of Richard Aldington's "Art of Poetry."[1] Gurdjieff's objective-art theory, then, did not shift Toomer's literary aesthetic; rather, it allowed him to embrace an aesthetic already compatible with his established idealist thinking on the function of art. Much of the literature of this period is perhaps best described as ethical (in the Kierkegaardian sense) rather than didactic. In other words, much like Shaw and Ibsen, Toomer used literature as a medium for dramatizing ideas. Gurdjieff does, however, introduce a social and an ethical dimension into Toomer's thinking and his writing. Using the language and symbology of Gurdjieff's system, he dramatizes the idea that universal truth is ethical truth, that the individual is the universal, and that the individual must be "awakened" to universalist thinking. Accordingly, Toomer's favorite character is the mystic and seer; his favorite strategy, the drama of life reconciled by transcendental thought; and his favorite themes, transcendentalism, pantheism, and millennial consciousness. There is a notable absence of African-American characters or themes in these works; yet absence itself constitutes a metaphor for Toomer's attempts to assimilate racial taxonomies and racial alienation into idealist philosophy. Having experienced alienation from both races, as allegorized in "Bona and Paul" and in "Harvest Song," he now seeks refuge within the prison-house of Gurdjieffian thought. There remains, nevertheless, an inner dialectic that struggles against the forces of idealist reification.

The works Toomer composed between 1924 and 1939 generally fall within two categories: those which treat idealist metaphysics and higher consciousness, which I term "landscapes of the self," and those which treat social themes in the context of the postwar decade, which I term "landscapes of society." In the former category we witness Toomer's almost total absorption in Gurdjieffian idealism, with its attendant reification, whereas in the latter we witness his efforts against reification, as he attacks the moral and spiritual bankruptcy of the 1920s.

Of the works on idealist metaphysics and higher consciousness, the poetry perhaps best reveals the highest degrees of reified consciousness. Toomer wrote scores of "objective consciousness" poems during this period, and they may be grouped as follows: poems on being consciousness and self-integration, such as "The Lost Dancer," "Unsuspecting," and "White Arrow"; poems depicting mystical experiences, such as "At Sea" and "The Gods Are Here"; poems of cosmic consciousness, as represented by "Peers" and "Living Earth"; and his Whitmanian hymn to democratic idealism, "The Blue Meridian."[2]

"The Lost Dancer" expresses the poet's quest for unity of being and self-integration in terms of the failure of idealism. The dancer-artist figure is "lost" because he is unable to discover a "source of magic" whereby he can transcend the rigorous imperatives of subject-object dualism—inner and outer, essence and personality, self and world, art and life—here symbolized, respectively, by the metaphysical "vibrations of the dance" and the physical "feet dancing on earth of sand."

> Spatial depths of being survive
> The birth to death recurrences
> Of feet dancing on earth of sand;
> Vibrations of the dance survive
> The sand; the sand, elect, survives
> The dancer. He can find no source
> Of magic adequate to bind

> The sand upon his feet, his feet
> Upon his dance, his dance upon
> The diamond body of his being.

Unity of being then follows when the dancer is able to synthesize "the birth to death recurrences / Of feet dancing on earth of sand" (object), with "the diamond body of his being," the prismatic brilliance of inner essence (subject), to form a unified complex, the transcendental self.

"Unsuspecting" utilizes imagery borrowed from horticulture ("culls," "trims," and "prunes"), as well as reflexive rhyme ("mind" and "rind") to suggest that refined, cultivated intellect without corresponding inner development is naive and superficial.

> There is a natty kind of mind
> That slicks its thoughts,
> Culls its oughts,
> Trims its views,
> Prunes its trues,
> And never suspects it is a rind.

Composed in iambic pentameter, "White Arrow" sketches the poet's Lawrentian notion of female self-actualization in contrasting images of sleeping or existing and waking or being, images drawn from the language of Gurdjieff's system. The poem unfolds as an affectionate admonition to an unnamed individual to liberate herself from the "sleep and fear" induced by the authority of gender socialization: "In faith and reason you were swift and free, / White arrow, as you were, awake and be!"

Both "At Sea" and "The Gods Are Here" are expressions of mystical experiences. "At Sea" dramatizes an ephemeral and fleeting moment during which the poet is transfixed by the awesome power and beauty of the sea. While in this mystical state of consciousness, he experiences a "pang of transience," when the spirit of the universe briefly reveals itself in the life and order of the cosmos.

> Once I saw large waves
> Crested with white-caps;
> A driving wind
> Transformed the caps
> Into scudding spray—

"Swift souls," I addressed them—
They turned towards me
Startled
Sea-descending faces;
But I, not they,
Felt the pang of transience.

"The Gods Are Here" develops as an extended contrast between two forms of asceticism, both of which release the soul from bondage and permit its union with the divine—that of the hermit on a mountain among the wilds of nature, and that of the poet within a domestic environment.

This is no mountain
But a house,
No rock of solitude
But a family chair,
No wilds
But life appearing
As life anywhere domesticated,
Yet I know the gods are here,
And that if I touch them
I will arise
And take majesty into the kitchen.

Of the cosmic consciousness poems, the most representative are "Peers" and "Living Earth." "Peers" opens with an apostrophe to nature, here symbolized by a rock. For the poet, however, the mutual existence of humanity and nature confirms their ontological status as peers.

Some day I will see again
Your substance in the sacred flame
And meet you undisguised
In the root of all that lives.

Similarly, Toomer compares the life and order of the universe with human life and order in this excerpt from "Living Earth":

Is not Earth, Being,
Is it not a core of life,
Has it not organisms with spine,

Glands, entrails, and a sage navel?
Is it not a field of Force,
Force and field living?

Rejecting the idea that the earth is ruled by fate, blind force, and accident, the poet avers that the only conceivable accident is for us to attribute to the universe the blindness that is fixed within ourselves. The poem ends by questioning consciousness in nature, as a first step in understanding human consciousness.

Certainly the most ambitious poem of this period is "The Blue Meridian." As this work represents a milestone in his racial and spiritual consciousness, revised over a period of fifteen years, some background is necessary. Between the summer of 1920 and the fall of 1921, Toomer wrote drafts for the poem "The First American," later revised as "Brown River, Smile" (1931) and finally as "The Blue Meridian" (1936). "The First American" began as a response to what Toomer describes as the personal preference and prejudice he had encountered on the subject of racial problems in America.

> It was evident to me who had seen both the white and colored worlds, and both from the inside, that the authors of these writings had little or no experience of the matters they were dealing with. . . . among other things, I again worked over my own position, and formulated it with more fullness and exactitude. I wrote a poem called "The First American," the idea of which was that here in America we are in the process of forming a new race, that I was one of the first conscious members of this race.[3]

He continues this account in "On Being an American."

> Underlying all of the divisions, I had observed what seemed to me to be authentic—namely, that a new type of man was arising in this country—not European, not African, not Asiatic—but American. And in this American I saw the divisions mended, the differences reconciled—saw that (1) we would in truth be a united people existing in the United States, saw that (2) we would in truth be once again members of a united human race. Now all of this, needless to say, did not get into the poem. Years were to pass before that could happen, before

the germ of "The First American" could grow and ripen and be embodied in "The Blue Meridian." But into "The First American" I did put something of my actuality, something of my vision of America—though it needed explaining.[4]

The most comprehensive accounts of Toomer's "New American" consciousness appear in several preliminary drafts of "A Fiction and Some Facts" (variously entitled "A First Ride," "Thus May It Be Said," and "The Inside Story") and in a polemical essay entitled "The American Race." In these tracts he argues that a new American race has evolved in the United States, one which is neither white nor black, red nor brown, but a synthesis which defies conventional racial taxonomies. He further maintains that although American consciousness lags far behind racial consciousness, the biological fact of ethnic intermingling is a fait accompli.

> From my early years I have felt and known I was a member of the American people and of the American race, the new race that is gradually forming in this country owing, not only to the various strains, but to the geography of the North American continent and to the effect of the social and psychological conditions which exist here. . . . I was aware of this long before I wrote *Cane*. . . . this realization is coming to more and more people of all groups; and when it finally becomes a dominant thing, something of great social value is going to happen in this country. . . . the important thing about any individual man or woman is not his color or features, not his external identities and affiliations—the important thing is his essence, his nature, his humanity, and the degree of essential development, are obscured because we have identified with and valued only comparatively unimportant and secondary features. . . . we have labeled the bottle and forgotten its contents.[5]

He further argues that a drop of Negro blood does not make one Negro, any more than a drop of English blood makes one English. He concedes that "full blood" does indeed make one entirely of, say, Indian or Caucasian descent; yet he consistently maintains that individual concerns with ancestry have eclipsed the experience and realization of what we are now. "For me then," writes Toomer, "to be true to my race means, and cannot mean anything else or less, that I must be true to all races, namely, that I must be true to the human race." Describing the several races as branches of a human-life tree, he admonishes all Americans to overcome what he calls branch consciousness and attain the "tree consciousness" of humankind united. "The only hope of mankind is to rise above egotism, extend beyond partisanship, overcome separations of all kinds and re-merge the now different and often antagonistic elements into a unified and harmonious whole. In my thought, in ideals, and in the very life I live from day to day I stand for Mankind United. This perhaps is the largest and most significant single fact of my life."[6]

Toomer believed that his own blend of ethnic strains, like the blend of strains within America itself, conferred upon him a mystical conception of the self and a transcendental vision of America. He also believed, like Walt Whitman, that there is a central identity of self which is the foundation of freedom, that each individual is unique and yet identical with the all, and that democracy is the surest guarantee of individual values. Also like Whitman he attempted to resolve the conflict between individual and society at the transpersonal level by positing his own self, "the First American," as the self of all human beings. In *Leaves of Grass*, Whitman writes:

> Singing the song of These, my ever-united lands—
> my body no more inevitably united, part to part,
> and made out of a thousand diverse contributions
> one identity, any more than my lands are
> inevitably united and made *One Identity.*[7]

Toomer echoes this idea in "The Blue Meridian."

> We are the new people,
> Born of elevated rock and lifted branches,
> Called Americans,
> Not to mouth the label but to live the reality,
> Not to stop anywhere, to respond to man,
> To outgrow each wider limitation,
> Growing towards the universal Human Being.

To be sure, Whitman's radically democratic Weltanschauung, creating unity out of diversity, excited Toomer's transcendental consciousness, for he too heard the "varied carols" and the "strong melodious songs" of American singing. For both Whitman and Toomer, then, democratic idealism is a corollary of a transcendental or mystical conception of the self. Toomer's Adamic conception of himself as one of the first conscious members of a united human race is the very cornerstone of his First American or New American consciousness. Such an exalted mind, carrying with it the conviction of absolute novelty, is reminiscent of what psychologist R. M. Bucke calls cosmic consciousness. "Along with the consciousness of the cosmos," writes Bucke, "there occurs an intellectual enlightenment which alone would place the individual on a new plane of existence—would make him almost a member of *a new species.*"[8] Having formulated an Adamic self, Toomer proceeds to become the maker of his own conditions by creating a model society. And this is precisely what he does in "The Blue Meridian." In the words of R. W. B. Lewis, the American Adam *"projects* a world of order and meaning and identity into either a chaos or a vacuum; he does not *discover* it. The poet may salute the chaos; but he creates the world."[9] Toomer expresses this same idea in *"The Blue Meridian."*

> When the spirit of mankind conceived
> A New World in America, and dreamed
> The human structure rising from this base,
> The land was a vacant house to new inhabitants,
> A vacuum compelled by Nature to be filled.
> Spirit could not wait to time-select,
> Weighing in wisdom each piece,
> Fitting each right thing into each right place,
> But had to act, trusting the vision of the possible.

A minor classic in American literature, "The Blue Meridian" is a Whitmanian affirmation of democratic idealism, a poetics for democracy. Composed in free verse, the poem displays such standard poetic tropes as assonance, alliteration, repetition, inverse word order, parallelism, metaphor, symbolism, and imagery. As in *The Waste Land,* form in "The Blue Meridian" is governed by constellations of reflexive references designed to render the poet's millennial vision for America. Toomer employs several constellations of images within the poem, some of which are drawn from the cosmology of Gurdjieffian mysticism. But the dominant patterns which emerge portray a new American selfhood and a new model for American democracy.

"The Blue Meridian" develops in four movements, each beginning with the pronouncement "It is a new America." In the opening lines of the first movement the poet associates the spiritualization of America with millennial consciousness, "It is a new America, / To be spiritualized by each new American." The images of sleeping and awakening are drawn from Gurdjieff's notion that individuals must awaken from the trance of habituation and claim their right to true, or cosmic, consciousness. Images of darkness and of hidden resources, the "black light" and the "inland lake," are contrasted with the "waking forces" and "energy" of cosmic spiritualization, here symbolized by the rays of "The Big Light." "The Big Light," Gurdjieff's Ray of Creation conception of the Absolute, inspires people to "crash the barrier to the next higher form." In an apostrophe to this radiant spirit of cosmic consciousness, "The I of earth and of mankind," the poet affirms the unity of humankind and the cosmos and calls for a new American selfhood which reconciles dualisms at the level of consciousness, thereby creating "Spirit-torsos of exquisite strength."

The poem shifts to describe "The Mississippi, sister of the Ganges, / Main artery of earth in the western world." The river symbolizes the poet's transcendental vision of America, uniting not only one person with another, as it links North and South, East and West, but all persons with the cosmos.

> Whoever lifts himself
> Makes that great brown river smile.
> The blood of earth and the blood of man
> Course swifter and rejoice when we spiritualize.

Emphasizing the unity of the American experience and the diversity upon which it is founded, the poet employs the metaphor of American as a granary, and each American a pod "perpetuating and perfecting / an essence identical in all."

Images of millennial consciousness dominate the next stanzas, as the poet contrasts past and present and envisions a new spiritual and social order. In lines reminiscent of Yeats, he decries the spiritual sterility of

> The old gods, led by an inverted Christ,
> A shaved Moses, a blanched Lemur,
> And a moulting Thunderbird.

He ends by declaring, "We are waiting for a new God." He similarly decries materialist consciousness for corrupting the spirit of America. The "old peoples" have been "Baptized in finance / Without benefit of saints." Thus he also declares, "We are waiting for a new people." In a review of the American past, the poet characterizes the pioneer spirit of the elder American Adam, who projected order and meaning into the chaos of the New World. America became the melting pot for "all the peoples of the earth," the homeland for newcomers and immigrants "Gathered by the snatch of accident, / Selected with the speed of fate." In a plea for cosmic unity, the poet petitions the Ray of Creation to "blend our bodies to one flesh, / And blend this body to mankind." Describing America's east coast as masculine and its west coast as feminine, he characterizes the middle region, the Mississippi River itself, as the child of that union. The river is then the "Reconciling force / And generator of symbols," the very symbol of meridian consciousness. In the closing lines of this movement, the transcendental self emerges, extending outward to fellow Americans and upward in higher consciousness.

> The prairie's sweep is flat infinity,
> The city's rise is perpendicular to farthest star,
> I stand where the two directions intersect,
> At Michigan Avenue and Walton Place,
> Level with my countrymen,
> Right-angled to the universe.

In the opening lines of the second movement the speaker envisions a new American consciousness, founded upon "Growth, Transformation, Love":

> Let new eyes see this statue in the bay,
> Let this be quarantine to unbend dreams,
> Let old eyes see it in Wall Street and the Loop,
> And through this clearing house
> Let all pass checks who may.

An eagle in the poem symbolizes America, encompassing within the span of its wings the polar extremes within society. But because American consciousness has developed so unilaterally toward materialism, the eagle has degenerated into a flying machine with a broken wing.

As the poem shifts to a cabaret scene during the depression years, the speaker meets a woman on the streets and invites her to a nightclub,

74

to "coax reluctant lust." His amorous advances are chided, however, by her devotion to higher love and spiritual consciousness. Indeed she is described in terms of

> the powers that heal,
> Sweeten, give new faith and make us remember
> That to live is to grow, to grow is to love.

The contrast between eros and agape here effectively illustrates the power of higher love to transform consciousness. The poem returns to the image of an airplane with a broken wing, now caught in a tailspin and descending with "terrifying speed," an image of the human race dissolving into materialism and war.

The poem now renders a vision of apocalypse in the thirties, with images of vermilion peaks, rosy-golden streets, clusters of squad cars, racketeers, and hijackers. Yet amid this chaos the poet opens his windows to greet his fellow citizens, affirming life over death, hope and affirmation over doubt and uncertainty.

> Yet in this crashing world
> Terrorized by bullet-athletes,
> I unbolt windows and ten-cents greet
> A happy simple thing—
> An organ grinder with jaunty hat,
> With wayward roaming feet,
> And his monkey,
> Sauntering along a spirit street.

The poet admonishes Americans to relinquish the materialism engendered by the modern machine age, here symbolized by a modern office "machined and ventilated / For everything but man," and awaken to the "terrible mistake / That we who have power are less than we should be." Toomer employs island symbolism to suggest the dangers of egoism and isolationism.

> Islanders, newly come upon the continents,
> If to live against annihilation,
> Must outgrow themselves and their old places,
> Disintegrate tribal integrators,
> And fix, as their center of gravity,
> As their compelling ideal
> The symbol of Universal Man.

Egoists and isolationists must then "find a larger truth in larger hearts, / Lest the continents shrink to islands" and society is destroyed.

The next section represents humanity as an imperfect crock, "shaped first by hand, now machined, / But not whole." The image of "radiant air," Gurdjieff's Ray of Creation, which symbolizes transcendental consciousness, is contrasted with "unholy rust," symbolic of self-regard. In the closing lines of this movement, the poet asks modern America to

> Uncase, unpod whatever blocks, until,
> Having realized pure consciousness of being,
> Knowing that we are beings
> Co-existing with others in an inhabited universe,
> We will be free to use rightly with reason
> Our own and other human functions—
> Free men, whole men, men connected
> With one another and with Deity.

A corollary of this New American consciousness, then, is a new cosmic theology, linking humanity and God in universal unity.

The third movement opens with light imagery, here representing a link between heaven and earth, or higher and "unawakened" consciousness. The speaker describes the "public and private scavengers" who seek to destroy higher consciousness, and the failure of love stemming from egoism and "split dominance." The scene then shifts to the landscape of the mystical or transcendental self. Here a mystical experience is described in terms of an implied comparison between a person and a millhouse, the former animated by music, the latter powered by a water-wheel. In lines reminiscent of Whitman, the poet dramatizes the emergence of the mystical self, inspired by both "sacred and profane extremes" of music, ranging from Gregorian chants to Duke Ellington and Eddy Duchin.

> And some rare times
> I hear myself, the unrecorded,
> Sing the flow of I,
> The notes and languages not of this experience,
> Sing I am,
> As the flow of I pauses,
> Then passes through my water-wheel—

> And those radiant others, the living real,
> The people identical in being.

The metaphor of the mill effectively portrays the self as a complex synthesizer, capable of essentializing and spiritualizing a diverse range of experiences. The unending stream of music, like the unending stream of water which powers the mill, animates the mystical self. In an image recalling Eliot's "still point in the turning world," the poet affirms the mystical powers of both music and nature to inspire higher consciousness: "May you be still within the flow / That always was and always is."

The final section of this movement describes yet another mystical experience, this one at sea. Inspired by the playful dance of sun upon the water, the poet experiences the presence of a female spirit.

> Her face was marvelously bright,
> My brain was fiery with internal stars,
> I felt certain I had brought
> The gods to earth and men to heaven;
> I blessed her, drawing with the fingers
> Of my spirit the figure of the cross;
> I said to her—
> "All my senses will remember you as sweet,
> Your essence is my wonder."

That she is inspired by the Ray of Creation, the sun, establishes her as a symbol of higher spiritual consciousness.

The final movement reiterates and summarizes the major themes of the poem—millennialism and New American consciousness, cosmic consciousness theology, and the tragedy of American materialism.[10] The poem ends on a note of hope and spiritual affirmation, with the appearance of the Blue Meridian god of New American consciousness.

> Blue Meridian, banded-light,
> Dynamic atom-aggregate,
> Awakes upon the earth;
> In his left hand he holds elevated rock,
> In his right hand he holds lifted branches,
> He dances the dance of the Blue Meridian
> And dervishes with the seven regions
>   of America, and all the world.

HIGHER CONSCIOUSNESS IN THE NOVELS

Of the fiction written during these years, *York Beach*, "The Gallon-werps," "Caromb," and "Eight-Day World" have received the least critical attention. These novels of mysticism and higher consciousness, like E. M. Forster's *Passage to India*, D. H. Lawrence's *Women in Love*, and Virginia Woolf's *Mrs. Dalloway*, compose an important subgenre in modern literature. A short novel comprising five chapters, *York Beach* is the story of a misanthropic writer, Nathan Antrum, who discovers his own dogmatic individualism as the source of his alienation from society. Throughout the narrative Toomer uses Bruce Rolams, Antrum's gregarious and well-liked counterpart, who is also a writer, to allegorize two halves of a divided self in need of harmonious balance. Indeed Antrum perceives his malady as the need for reconciliation of opposites, represented by two conflicting wishes within his psyche. "One was a wish for brilliant experience. . . . This wish belonged to that part of Antrum which made him a social human being, one who was strongly drawn towards people and who found joy and value in their company. The other was a wish for comparative solitude, difficult experience, friction, and much work. This wish arose from the part of Antrum that was Ishmael." His need to transcend the rigorous imperatives of dualism is represented by yet a third wish, which symbolizes his idealism. "There was a third wish: a force impatient with the opposites of human experience, an urge to reconcile these opposites and achieve one inclusive state of being. . . . Antrum affirmed this wish as a driving force. He was positive towards the possibility of its ultimate fulfillment. But he knew it was not yet able to achieve itself."

The major contrast between Antrum and Rolams is dramatized through their polemical Socratic dialogues on the difference between "the herd and the individual." Bruce interprets the difference in terms of "emotional intelligence," whereas Antrum understands it in terms of "mental intelligence." In accordance with Gurdjieff's levels of consciousness theory, each person is a three-level being, ranging at the top from the "mental center" to the middle "emotional center" to the lower "moving-instinctive center." Only when these centers are in harmonious balance can one achieve mystical union with the spirit of cosmic consciousness. As Gurdjieff defines it, the intellectual mind concerns itself with constructing theories and reasoned thought; the emotional, with feelings instead of ideas; and the moving-instinctive, with imitative behavior and reflexive movement. Thus Bruce symbolizes the sanguine self, while Nathan symbolizes the alienated self. In chapter 3, Antrum begins a process of assimilation into the small, New England community at York Beach, moving beyond the private realm of the self. By the end of the novel he implies that he has become one not only with York Beach but also with his alter ego, Bruce Rolams.

Complete with satire, burlesque, and humor, as well as characters with such names as Wimepime and Wistold Gallonwerp, Mrs. Plegeron Banty, Miss Marnee Waistboard, and Mr. Nockbut Prime, "The Gallonwerps" (1927) is a modern comedy of manners composed in the tradition of Restoration drama. Comprising 361 pages, the novel presents a grand array of characters, each representing a type of individual in need of awakening to higher consciousness. The narrative focuses primarily upon Wimepime Gallonwerp, however, who, like her counterpart, Prince Klondike, is adroit in the art of "diking"—that is, manipulating events so skillfully that people are compelled to act in accordance with the will of their manipulator. In the end she herself becomes the subject of an artful dike performed by Prince Klondike.

A middle-aged imperious aristocrat, married to a lecturer who desires to promulgate ideas on humanity's salvation to America's leaders, Wimepime Gallonwerp is a complex opportunist, a satirically drawn representative of the American upper class. She invites Chicago's foremost celebrities to her mansion, ostensibly to meet the mysterious and mythic Prince Klondike, reputed to be the wealthiest and wisest man in the world. In reality, she assembles this group to meet her husband and promote his views on "Ideal Concepts." Toward this end, she enlists the assistance of the prince himself. She herself, however, is described as "a remarkable woman of depth and beauty and understanding, with a rare ability to experience joy and sorrow and win significance from both." In sum, Wimepime is "a many-sided person, a woman of many different parts, any one of which was likely to dominate her consciousness and make her speak without reference to the others, as if it alone were her whole nature." Thus, she contains within her character the potential to change; at the end of the novel, we in fact witness such a transformation of her personality.

Throughout the novel, Wimepime is portrayed as cunning, manipulative, and neurasthenic. She is transformed, however, in the closing pages of the novel when Prince Klondike kidnaps Little Gasstar from Elginbora, the nurse. At first Wimepime wants revenge; yet, in an epiphanic moment, she begins feeling compassion.

> And then it was that Wimepime had a flash of lucid perception and saw her own state externalized and magnified by those others. So vividly did she see this, that it was almost a perceiving of the actual emotional forms. . . . With a start of despair she remembered that the Prince had warned her. "Our sins wait to visit us in heaven." She recognized its truth, and then she began to passionately deny it. It could not be so. Not if there were a God of love and justice in the world. Something in Wimepime that never before had lived took breath and prayed.

Suddenly, Prince Klondike appears in their midst, radiant and Christlike. He directs the most enlightened individuals present, Wimepime and Wistold, in one word, "Come," and they follow him into the bright morning sunlight, as if in a trance.[11]

Students of modern literature will note several striking parallels between "The Gallonwerps" and Virginia Woolf's *Mrs. Dalloway*. Both novels satirize the social customs, manners, and conventions of upper-class society, and in both novels the action focuses on one day in the life of the protagonist. Both Wimepime Gallonwerp and Clarissa Dalloway are middle-aged aristocrats, described as beautiful, yet cold, snobbish, and insensitive; both are superficial in personality and manner. Yet both undergo a spiritual transformation which leads to expanded consciousness. In both novels the heroine is portrayed as the perfect hostess, dedicated to the success of her evening dinner party, and in each case the party is interrupted by a tragic announcement which precipitates the heroine's epiphany. Moreover, in both novels the dinner party is the lens through which the reader perceives upper-class characters and their views on a diverse range of topics. Finally, both novels affirm the metaphysical power of epiphany to mediate union between self and other. In "The Gallonwerps," as in *Mrs. Dalloway,* expanded consciousness is dramatized by character doubling. In the former novel Wimepime realizes the paucity of spiritual values in her life through identification with her foil, Prince Klondike; similarly, in the latter novel Clarissa realizes the shallowness of her own life through spiritual identification with Septimus Warren Smith. In each novel, the heroine's spiritual identification with her foil derives from the author's sincere belief in the unity of experience.

Written in 1932, several months after his marriage to Margery Latimer, "Caromb" is Toomer's fictionalized account of the negative publicity and alienation the couple experienced following their move to Carmel, California. Society's reaction to their "mixed marriage" provides the basis for the novel, although the issue of race is never specifically mentioned. Instead the major theme is the triumph of love.

"Caromb" may be analyzed in four movements. The first, chapters 1–5, recounts the arrival of John and Marian Andrews amid the somber, gloomy landscape of Caromb. In these chapters images of darkness, evil, and fear, as well as the sinisterness of the ocean tides, symbolize threats to their existence at Gull House, an oceanside cottage. Chapter 4 introduces a malevolent, disembodied "force" which threatens to destroy their love and their marriage.

In the second movement, chapters 6–18, Toomer presents the major conflict of the novel, represented by the visit of a newspaper reporter, Cal Dunney. Ostensibly interested in John's philosophy of existence, in reality Dunney attempts to investigate the couple's recent marriage: " 'We hear that you and your wife are really in love!' The words came out under pressure. 'Are you?' He paused and twitched. 'Are you really? Will you verify that for me?' " Reluctantly, the couple consents to a photograph session, a decision they later come to regret, for several days later, the article and the pictures gain national notoriety. Marion, who is pregnant, is particularly disturbed by the adverse publicity. "Her glance was reproachful. Her face was pained, tortured, terribly hurt. He could see her state, in a flash he saw it and it shook him profoundly—shock, blame, distrust of him—her conflict, love and affirmation of him and their marriage, fear of what she would bring upon her parents, social ostracism, her blaming him for having gotten her into all of this, her wish to return to her old life. Would he lose her?"

The climax of the novel occurs in the third movement, chapter 18, when John drives into Caromb, leaving a feverish Marian alone. Throughout the novel Toomer uses the ocean waves, ominously pounding against the beach, to symbolize diabolical forces of public opinion threatening to drown John and Marian. In this context, the waves recall Forster's symbolism of the Malibar Caves in *A Passage to India*. As soon as John departs, Marian succumbs to the demonic lure of the waves and dashes from the house into the fog. "'I can't bear it,' she cried. 'I can't struggle no more. I'll go insane. I'll kill myself. I, you who would not pity me. O, you who would not help me. O, you who would not let me live as I must if I am to live. I hate you! I hate myself. I'll kill you and myself and life and love! Come kill me!'" Soon John returns and rescues her. Chapter 18 ends on a note of love and faith, as he praises God for her salvation.

Chapters 19–23 compose the final movement of the novel, marked by the restoration of calm serenity and the triumph of love. "They awoke in the morning, the cool bright-haze morning of clear and misty things, the forward-gleaming morning. Their mood was serene, tender, singing. . . . They sensed great land and something vast and spiriting. With consciousness blended and translucent, they experienced morning Caromb." To commemorate their triumph, they rename Gull House "Redwood," symbolizing their new perspective on Caromb and the world. Yet, having defeated the forces of hatred and evil, they decide to leave Caromb forever.

Reminiscent of D. H. Lawrence's *Women in Love,* particularly in its depictions of idealized male-male and male-female relationships and in its mystical bonding, "Eight-Day World" is an ambitious novel, comprising 436 pages and 53 chapters. The novel employs a voyage from New York to Paris as frame for a series of epiphanic or mystical experiences which advance a theme popularized by E. M. Forster—"Only Connect."

The first epiphany establishes Hugh Langley as a visionary and foreshadows his spiritual encounters with Hod Lorimer and Vera Arnold. Overlooking the Atlantic atop the bridge of the *Burgundy,* Langley succumbs to wind, spray, and sky in mystical harmony with the cosmos.

> In a flash of vision he saw the entire ship . . . its company disconnected yet enmeshed. . . . He had the tantalizing sense that something of great importance was about to break through to consciousness . . . all seemed right here, present, represented by the ship and its company—yet, try as he would, he could not bring it through. . . . What he did get was a glimpse of high in a light that both startled and amused him. He saw himself a tiny figure, sometimes dim, sometimes incandescent, standing on the bridge of a ship, broadcasting himself out into the sky.[12]

For the first eight chapters, Langley's relationship with the imperious Hod Lorimer is very stormy: "Relations with men were always twisted by rivalry, competition, a clash of egos" (38). Yet in the second epiphany Langley and Lorimer are reconciled in a moment of mystical connectedness, reminiscent of the *Blutbruderschaft* between Rupert Birkin and Gerald Crich in *Women in Love*.

> Just suddenly all the mixed feelings aroused in [Hugh] by Hod surged together in one single deep affection. With his blood he affirmed Hod. With his blood and his body he would fight for Hod against all and everything. . . .
>
> The world was in sunset, the sea-world, flushed with a soft radiant crimson glow. As if they had removed their shoes to enter the universe, they walked forward and felt they were being lifted up into a region of pure light and form, where the colors were their feelings, where the clouds were their thoughts, where the drama was their life enacted in a temple of the old mysteries.[13]

The third epiphany focuses on Vera and the problem of possessiveness in male-female relationships. "Relations with women were almost always blocked by nonessentials, indirectness, fear, and, most of all, possessiveness. Not yet had either sex learned to love without possessing and without being possessed" (38). For most of the voyage Vera is shy and retiring around Langley, although she is very attracted to him. When she confronts him with the sincerity of her emotions, they experience pure connectedness of being. "As they moved along their bodies fell into the same rhythm, the same cadence, flowing; and both knew that an experience was with them, they within it, gathering and lifting, dipping and rising with the ship. How complete! That man and woman have the nature to give each other such completeness! So unexpectedly it had come about . . . delayed for half the days of the ocean . . . but now claiming them."[14] After several romantic interludes, however, Vera begins exhibiting dependency and possessiveness. Yet Hugh remains independent and impersonal, gently lecturing her on the paradox of being purely alone and purely connected. "Here are the two directions, one, out into the world, the other, into oneself. Usually, however, neither of them is pure. Because both are impure they are in conflict and block each other. . . . The swing between an unsatisfactory participation and an unfruitful loneliness. We must learn to participate purely. We must learn to be purely alone. This means that we must recapture our full *being*. *Being* is the basis of everything."[15] Hugh's comments echo Rupert Birkin's remarks to Ursula in *Women in Love:* "At the last, one is alone, beyond the influence of love. There is a real impersonal me, that is beyond love, beyond any emotional relationship. So it is with you. But we want to delude ourselves that love is the root. It isn't. It is only the branches. The root is beyond love, a naked kind of isolation, an isolated me, that does not meet and mingle, and never can."[16]

Like Birkin, Langley desires a mystical bond or connectedness which transcends emotional and sexual bonding. Indeed, Langley's philosophy of human relationships implies the origins of a new social order: "We're going to stay together and return to America together, and begin building the country and a new people and a new world!" (416). Yet at the end of the eight days aboard the *Burgundy,* Langley remains faithful to his idealism; realizing his connectedness, he chooses to remain independent and alone.[17]

In addition to the poems and novels of higher consciousness Toomer wrote during his years as a disciple of Gurdjieff, he also wrote a lengthy Gothic tale of mystery and intrigue, "The Eye," as well as a series of works depicting the local color of the American Southwest. "The Eye" dramatizes the notion that evil and insanity inhere within the self in degrees of consciousness, each blending into union with its antithesis, while the works on the Southwest landscape reveal pantheistic worship of nature and mystical identification with the cosmos. In the Gothic tale, as in the local color works, we witness the ascendancy of Romantic and idealist philosophy.

"THE EYE": A STUDY IN TERROR AND INSANITY

Among the scores of unpublished short stories written by Jean Toomer, a newly discovered one is unique in its evocation of terror in the Gothic tradition. A disturbing tale of violence, guilt, and insanity, "The Eye" unfolds as a psychological drama of two Victorian spinster sisters, Edith and Eula Ogden.[18] While the action focuses on Edith's steady descent into paranoia and madness, it also highlights Eula's character as the evil, Gothic villain. In this way, Toomer explores the roles of evil and madness in terms of their links between personal identity and family relationships. Notwithstanding the vast amount of scholarship on Gothic fiction, critics generally agree on the basic conventions of the genre. In terms of character, there is the Faustian hero, the sentimental heroine, the grotesque villain; and the technique of character doubling is frequently employed. As for literary ambience, the mood is brooding and melancholic, the atmosphere charged with menace, fear, and terror; there is use of suspense and the supernatural; and the setting is often a castle or an old house, usually in a remote and exotic locale. The most frequently recurring themes are evil, guilt, insanity, transformation and metamorphosis, incest, and the family.[19]

In accordance with Northrop Frye's structure of romance theory, there are four primary narrative movements in literature: the descent from a higher world, the descent to a lower world, the ascent from a lower world, and the ascent to a higher world. "All stories in literature," he declares, "are complications of, or metaphorical derivations from, these four narrative radicals."[20] The descent themes, then, fall into two categories: those that suggest descent from one of the two higher worlds, Heaven and Eden, and those that suggest descent to a subterranean nether universe beneath the Edenic or natural world. As Frye defines it, Gothic fiction derives from the romance, although it represents a unique variation within its parent genre. In romance fiction the hero or heroine descends from the Edenic or natural world to the underworld in search of lost identity. In this underworld the protagonist undergoes ritual sufferings, culminating in a reclamation of identity. Following this achievement, the protagonist returns to the higher world and establishes a new Eden. In Gothic fiction there is a similar descent from the natural world to the underworld, in a quest for identity. Despite perpetual ritual sufferings, however, there is no achievement of identity, nor is there a return to the higher, natural world. Instead, the protagonist remains hopelessly fragmented in a demonic netherworld of cruelty, evil, and terror. In sum, romance fiction represents a fable of identity, whereas Gothic fiction represents a fable of the impossibility of identity. In "The Eye" the narrative pattern conforms to Frye's Gothic fantasy paradigm, as the structure of plot dramatizes Edith's loss of identity and descent into madness.

The first stage in Edith's descent occurs when the sisters were children, long before the action of the story begins. In an intentional act, born of "sullen hatred," Edith blinds Eula in one eye. As a result, Eula is disfigured and begins wearing an artificial eye. Recognizing her sister's guilt, Eula soon learns to use her handicap as a weapon. Indeed, she becomes an artful dissembler, skillful in projecting guilt and fear by means of her false eye. This stage continues into the present. For in the opening scene of the story, Edith absentmindedly sketches an eye, revealing her enduring, deep-seated guilt. "She let her eyes look straight at the pupil of the eye she had drawn on the margin of the letter, the lashes shaded and curled, the eye itself intense and vivid, like the great eye of some sin burning through one's flesh and fat, through the bone itself and the blood, into the soul" (2).

Periodically, Eula visits Edith to remind her of the crime, and on this day Edith ominously awaits her sister's terrible arrival. Upon arriving, Eula begins taunting her sister with memories of the past. Unable to endure the agony, Edith cries out and begs her sister to leave the house. This is precisely the behavior Eula had hoped to evoke. Slowly, she moves closer and closer toward Edith's face, allowing the full force of her bleary, false eye to wreak its terrorizing havoc.

> As she held herself solid and blank, Eula moved her head so that the strong light came down on her false eye that looked always ahead so that Edith could remember and see again that moment when it happened, her rage, her unthinking, stupid blow that was done for some sullen hatred and foolishness. She held her head so that Edith might take her fill of the deadly work, so that she might even hear the screams that were so terrible that people ran from their houses. She stopped breathing as she remembered her mutilation, her loss of faith, her loss of beauty through this senseless Edith. And as she remembered tears filled her other eye and rolled down her cheek and she pressed her lips tightly together but she did not speak out or cry aloud. Finally she said, "But even when you did it I forgave you, Edith. Even then I knew it would be worse for you than for me."(7)

Throughout the story, Eula's incessant (albeit feigned) forgiving is emblematic of her character, revealing the sinister nature of her perverse and maniacal mind.

The second stage in Edith's descent provides an ironic counterpoint in the structure of the plot. Here Edith attempts to liberate herself from

Eula's terrorizing influence and create a new guiltless, fearless identity. Set at night in Edith's locked, claustrophobic bedroom, this scene dramatizes Edith's anxieties as she sleeplessly endures the stillness, the quietness, the darkness. Yet during these bleak moments, as she stares blankly from her window, she comes to understand the universality of suffering, and how suffering must surely expiate guilt. With this realization comes the confidence to create a new life for herself, a life free of anxiety; by morning, she develops the resolve to confront her past.

Following her "dark night of the soul," Edith greets a new day, which is symbolically sunny and serene. She leaves her room and ascends the stairs to the attic. With its creaky, rusty-hinged door and its walls covered with crawling mice and rats, the room is terrifying to enter; yet, initially she feels no trace of fear.

> Her eyes suddenly visioned the walls covered with grey mice, working their claws into the rough wood as they lifted their loathsome bodies higher and higher, their stiff tails poking out behind, their round fat bellies pressing soft against the wood. And this vision that once would have made her cover her face and give a low terrible scream, did not produce even a flicker in her eyes or in her breast. She went on. Her body looked as if it were prepared, after this night, to meet any wild animal, any prowling beast that might have lurked since childhood behind the trunks, waiting for human flesh to rend with its white, firm teeth. (12–13)

Toomer's animal imagery—"soft long paws," "any animal claw," "any terrifying jaws," "the ravenous face of a tiger," "the death blow of an elephant hoof," "the snarling teeth of a leopard"—symbolizes Edith's fears and provides the link between her guilt and Eula, who is also described in animal imagery.[21] The final stage chronicles Edith's loss of identity, her descent into utter madness. Following her visit to the attic, she escapes from the old house and flees to the train station, en route to Seattle. At the ticket window, she impulsively wishes her sister were dead. In another moment, her impulse shifts toward suicide. Fearing her sister's arrival at the station, she locks herself in the dressing room until the train, the Pioneer, arrives. And when it does, she boards quickly, hurries to her compartment, and breathes a sigh of relief as the train leaves the station. "She closed her eyes, soothed by the swiftness of the flying train. She decided, half in her sleep, to will the house to Eula, to give everything to her. Something in her felt eased. She would pay in money and property to right her crime" (17–18). Having settled this matter in her mind, she calls a female attendant for a manicure. When the attendant arrives, Edith suffers a complete mental breakdown when she discovers, much to her horror, that it is Eula.

Throughout the narrative, Edith is described as if she were a mad woman, depicted as distracted, dazed, and bewildered. In her room alone, she exhibits signs of insanity, as she continually weeps and buries her face deeply into her bed. Yet it is on the second day of Eula's occupation that Edith's paranoia turns to madness, as symbolized by her wild hair and unkempt appearance. As she stands before the attic door, wearing the wrinkled suit and blouse she slept in the night before, she is a portrait of insanity. "She stood motionless, one hand lifted, her mouth opened idiotically, her hair slipped to the side with all the shining coils ruffled and distorted and one side of her face bearing the creases of the spread where she had pressed her face farther and deeper" (12). After she leaves the attic, she cannot remember where she is going or what she is doing. Before leaving the house, she places a white Panama hat lightly on top of her wildly styled hair. "The mushroom crown with its striped scarf gave her face an appalled, almost insane look . . . and her hair stuck out under the quaint Panama in long spears, in puffed ends and knots and loops, sliding crazily toward her shoulder" (14–15). In the final scene of the story, she entertains thoughts of suicide. And it is here that her madness becomes most acute.

Edith never regains the lost Eden she associates with the time before her crime. Her descent into the underworld of her dark and tortured past is symbolized by her visit to the attic, where her ritual sufferings could have led to a reclamation of her prelapsarian childhood. Yet in Edith's Gothic universe no such reclamation is possible. As William Day defines it, "The descent into the Gothic underworld becomes a descent into the self in which the protagonists confront their own fears and desires and are transformed, metamorphosed, doubled, fragmented, and destroyed by this encounter."[22] Edith is destroyed by her encounter with the past, as symbolized by the artifacts she discovers in the attic, each of which is an emblem of her fragmented self. The school dresses, "clean but unironed," symbolize the wrinkles in her sentimental character, the paranoia and guilt that remain after many years. The forget-menots on the leghorn hat represent her inability to forget the crime. The decaying dolls, exposed to mice, spiders, and dust, symbolize her vulnerable, innocent self, exposed to the villainous, perverse pleasures of her sister. The trunks and schoolbooks she used in college represent her attempts to escape Eula's terrorizing influence. To be sure, Edith remains a victim of the past, as she descends deeper and deeper into the black hole of psychic decay.

Eula is portrayed as Edith's powerful, imperious nemesis, the grotesque Gothic villain. According to Elizabeth McAndrews, there are three principal types of villains in Gothic fiction: characters whose madness and evil derive from the conflict within them, have a close affinity with the sentimental hero or heroine, and give rise to doubles figures; characters who have little or no relationship to the hero or heroine because it is their function to be the evil that opposes goodness; and characters who are figures of the grotesque and demonic, confronting the reader with unrelenting evil.[23] Eula demonstrates qualities of both the first and third types. For she is Edith's mad, evil double, and she is grotesque and demonic. Like Edith, she evidences signs of madness, although her insanity takes a different form. That is, her insanity derives from repressed feelings of hatred for Edith and alienation resulting from her defiled beauty. These repressed emotions are manifested as perverse acts of revenge, as she uses her "evil eye" to project guilt and terror.

The central symbol of the story is Eula's false, evil eye. The idea that one can project agony or torment through willful glances is a belief studied by many cultural anthropologists, for the belief is shared by many different cultures. Yet all of the studies share in their finding that the evil eye symbolizes aggressive feelings and the desire to destroy. In this way, the perpetrator reveals a deep-seated desire for power and mastery over another individual, usually a rival or enemy.[24] According to Joost Meerlo, "Being caught in the enemy's visual field is, as it were, the beginning of being attacked and destroyed. The victim is terrorized—stricken and immobilized. Indeed the eye of the predator often has a paralyzing and trapping influence on his prey."[25] Following the blinding incident and Eula's subsequent acquisition of the false eye, she becomes transformed into a masterful being, intent upon directing events with a glance. As Edith's guilt overwhelms her, powerfully assisted by her sister's calculated behavior and evil stares, Edith unwittingly endows Eula with supernatural power.

The relationship between the two sisters, then, may be described in terms of domination and submission. As Day defines it, the instability which derives from such relationships results in the creation of doubled identities.

> The figure of the double transforms the self-other relationship into a self-self relationship. Rather than finding the Gothic protagonist isolated in a hostile world, we see that the Other resolves itself into a version of the self, a fragmentation and externalization of identity that destroys the self as fully and as surely as the overt attacks of its nemesis. . . . Because the self embodies within it both sides of the dynamic of all relationships in the Gothic world, and because the self manifests this duality through the creation of doubles, we can see that the encounter of the self with the Gothic world leads to the transformation and metamorphosis of the self into its opposite, either into the Other or its own hidden double. . . . Doubling, then, is not simply a convention, but is the essential reality of the self in the Gothic world.[26]

It is precisely in this context that we are able to understand the transformation and metamorphosis of Edith's and Eula's identity. For each of them possesses a dual nature that is reflected in the other. Edith is the protagonist and sentimental heroine, consistently portrayed throughout the story as fearful and submissive. Yet she has been transformed into this personality as a result of guilt. Indeed, she is the same individual who, as a child, coldly and intentionally blinded her sister. Eula is Edith's foil and nemesis, the Gothic villain who willfully torments her sister into insanity. Yet she also enlists our sympathy because she is the victim of a senseless and brutal act of violence. Both characters are therefore passive and aggressive. In this way, Toomer's doubling technique evidences moral relativism, as neither character is totally good or totally evil.

One of the most famous of all Gothic conventions is the doubling of the castle or house with its owner, as in Horace Walpole's *Castle of Otranto* or Edgar Allan Poe's "Fall of the House of Usher." In "The Eye," the Ogden manse, and specifically the attic, similarly functions as Edith's double, an externalization of her decaying self. The house, like Edith's mind, is haunted by the past and by Eula's ubiquitous presence. As Edith lives imprisoned within the closed world of the house, she also lives within the closed world of her dark and tortured mind.

The omnipresent old house or castle is one of the most stable characteristics of the Gothic. A dire and threatening place, it remains more than a dwelling. It starts out as a stone representation of the dark, tortured windings in the mind . . . it bears the whole weight of the ages of man's drift away from an ideal state; and it becomes a lasting representation of the torments of the subconscious pressing upon the conscious mind and making a prison of the self.[27]

Despite her efforts to maintain the house as it was when she and Eula were children, she can not regain the prelapsarian innocence she possessed before her crime. Eula herself is the force that works against her, as seen in the dynamics of their relationship. When Eula arrives at the Ogden manse, she comments on her sister's attempts to retain the old house as it used to be. "Well, the house looks just the same, the furniture is just as it was when we were children" (6). In the next scene, however, Eula changes the setting to reflect the present-day scene. "Now everything was like a party, just as if Miss Edith had never lived there" (9), exclaims Emma, the maid.

Given their roles as doubles, Edith's and Eula's comments on the past reveal an ambiguous attitude toward history, a mixture of longing and repulsion that is a hallmark of Gothic fiction. For Edith, the past represents nostalgia for a time before the accursed crime began to destroy them. By contrast, Eula is repulsed by the past, as she associates it with the very origin of the violence against her. Diabolically, and paradoxically, she wishes to retain the horror of Edith's crime. Thus, parallel to a vision of a prelapsarian past is the concomitant vision of a perverse and paradoxical present. "The failure of the past on the one hand 'liberates' the protagonist from bondage to a dying tradition; on the other, it presents a challenge to which no one can rise: to create something out of nothing, to make an identity out of one's own power and nothing more."[28]

Throughout his career as a writer and philosopher, Jean Toomer reveals a perennial interest in the metaphysics of the self, as a corollary of his philosophical idealism. Drawing upon his studies in Oriental and Gurdjieffian theosophy, he consistently asserted a monistic vision of reality in which opposites are reconciled as interactive entities, each blending into union with its antithesis. Toomer uses this philosophy in formulating a poetics of terror, in which he dramatizes the idea that good and evil, as well as sanity and insanity, inhere within the self in degrees of consciousness. This is a Romantic notion, as seen in Toomer's forebears of the American Renaissance, especially Hawthorne, Melville, and Poe. "The Eye" well illustrates this conception of the self, as symbolized by Edith and Eula, both of whom contain within themselves the possibilities for evil and madness. It is this Romantic conception of the self, presented within a specifically Gothic literary tradition, that establishes "The Eye" as a significant contribution to modern American fiction.

"COSMIC CONSCIOUSNESS" AND THE AMERICAN SOUTHWEST

Among the newly discovered works of this period there exists a group of poems and a closet drama glorifying the landscape of the American Southwest.[29] In these works, as in *Cane,* Toomer is captivated by the beauty of nature, which inspires his mystical identification with the cosmos.

"I Sit in My Room" expresses the poet's experience of mystical union with the picturesque Southwest landscape. The first stanza describes his movement into a heightened state of union with nature, as the adobe walls of his room become transparent, suddenly revealing the mountainous scene around him. The second stanza recounts the union of self and world in a trance of cosmic consciousness.

> I, who am no more,
> Having lost myself to let the world in,
> This world of black and bronze mesas
> Canyoned by rivers from the higher hills.
> I am the hills,
> I am the mountains and the dark trees thereon;
> I am the storm,
> I am this day and all revealed,
> Blue without boundary,
> Bright without limit,
> Selfless at this entrance to the universe.

In "Imprint for Rio Grande" Toomer poses the problem of exile and being (i.e., alienation and integration) in terms of the relationship between natural landscape and consciousness. The first movement evokes the singing, dancing, and drumbeating of American Indians, in their "vast universe that comes to earth in New Mexico." Owing to their "quiet rituals which swing the body-mind to acquiescence," the Indians achieve union with the spirit of higher consciousness. Within this south-western landscape, the poet similarly experiences transcendental oneness with this spirit. "I beat thoughts against the drum of mind, sing music that never leaves my instruments, and dance without gestures." The second movement recounts the poet's life as an exile, a "cosmic outlaw" amid the mountains and mesas of New Mexico, before awakening to the mystical call of the landscape. "You there who have seen me but did not realize the Exile, who have seen this body of a man and a human mask walking plazas in Taos and Santa Fe and the main street of Española, how could you know my feeling that the earth and all her Nature, that heaven and all its gods were gunning for cosmic outlaws, you and I being of the driven band?" In the third movement, however, the focus shifts from exile to being, as the poet describes the ecstasy of being consciousness. "There is such marvel in the Rio Grande, such ecstasy of inner sun to outer sun, or inner breath to the blazing winds, that I and everyone seem re-born upon that ark which still rides high, straight above the mesas of all sunken lands." The poem concludes with the idea that the struggle between exile and being can be resolved only at the transpersonal level, when a person "gives utter allegiance to the radi-ant"—that is, the sun, which is the basis for Gurdjieff's Ray of Creation theory of the universe.

In "Rolling, Rolling" a train ride with a loved one "over the golden rails" to Santa Fe inspires panoramic evocations of natural beauty. As in "I Sit in My Room," the poet associates nature with religion.

> From the prairies to the mesas,
> From the blue lake to red plains,
> To the sacred mountain where the eagle sails,
> Over the golden rails,
> Rolling away to Santa Fe,
> My darling Emily.

Southwestern landscape imagery, with evocations of Native Ameri-can culture, also represents major movements in Toomer's Whitmanian celebrations of democratic idealism, "The Blue Meridian" and "It Is Everywhere." In the following passage from "The Blue Meridian," the

93

poet describes how the "seven regions of America" became spiritualized when the gods came down and dwelt among the American Indians.

> The great red race was here.
> In a land of flaming earth and torrent-rains,
> Of red sea-plains and majestic mesas,
> At sunset from a purple hill
> The Gods came down;
> They serpentined into pueblo,
> And a white-robed priest
> Danced with them five days and nights;
> But pueblo, priest, and Shalakos
> Sank into the sacred earth
> To fertilize the seven regions of America.

A newly discovered poem, "It Is Everywhere" is a celebration of America's geographic and cultural diversity. Here the poet describes the "life awaiting" in "the seven regions of America," stanzas in turn depicting New England, the eastern seaboard, the Blue Ridge Mountains, the South, the Northwest, the Midwest, and the California seaboard. The stanza imaging the American Southwest is particularly evocative.

> There's a life awaiting in the land
> Of flaming earth, canyons,
> Stark mesas and red valleys,
> Brown birth
> The grandeur of this planet;
> A giant hand holds pueblos
> And adobes,
> Swift limbs dance the marriage
> Of the eagle and the thunderbird;
> And as I dream—
> I must be going,
> There's a life awaiting in the Southwest.

Set in 1935 near Taos, the unpublished play "A Drama of the Southwest" opens with lyrical evocations of the southwestern landscape in scene 1; with allegorical characterizations of the realist, Buck Fact, and the visionary, Ubeam Riseling, in scene 2; and with an interpreter figure who introduces Lewis and Grace Bourne as pilgrims to Taos in scene 3. Yet when the action proper begins in scene 4, the play gradually devolves into a series of discursive commentaries by Bourne and his alter ego. Clifford Genth, on a range of topics, such as domination of males by females, practical versus ideal necessity, and life in the modern world. "A Drama of the Southwest" does succeed, however, in reiterating Toomer's thoughts on the mysticism of the Taos landscape, which he terms "the soul of Taos." In lines reminiscent of passages from *Cane,* Bourne tells Genth:

> I could easily become superstitious in Taos. The minute I get here I feel—something opens up. Night opens the wide gap. Night in Taos. . . . That of me which has always lived, the eternal dark "me" submerged, begins stirring. It brings to me the fears a man might have should he be walking a dark road alone and suddenly the rock crept from their places and the trees spoke in undertones and the air was thick with sinister animation.

In all of these writings reified consciousness is evident in the themes, character types, and formal strategies Toomer employs. In the objective-consciousness poems, themes of idealism, mysticism, inner or spiritual awareness, and pantheism reveal the poet's efforts to overcome alienation, both within himself and in his relationship with society. His efforts to establish unity between himself and society are most dramatically illustrated in "The Blue Meridian," although here themes of democratic idealism, racial transcendence, millennialism, and "meridian," or higher consciousness, propose thought rather than action as the foundation of a new American society. In the higher-consciousness novels, reification is similarly manifested in the themes that structure and unify each narrative. *York Beach* proposes the reconciliation of opposites through idealist thinking as the solution to Antrum's alienation from the community. In "The Gallonwerps," mysticism, as practiced by the messiah Prince Klondike, is presented as the salvation for society. In "Caromb" spiritual values ostensibly thwart the sinister forces of racial bigotry and alienation, and in "Eight-Day World" the theme of being "purely alone and purely connected" betrays the alienation that is a corollary of mysticism and idealist metaphysics.

Toomer's character typology similarly reveals his reified psyche. Within the poems, there is a recurring alienated persona who employs idealist metaphysics (e.g., "The Lost Dancer"), mysticism (e.g., "The Gods Are Here" and "I Sit in My Room"), and pantheism (e.g., "Peers" and "Imprint for Rio Grande") to heal his fragmented self. The novels also contain alienated narrators and isolated protagonists. There is the divided protagonist in *York Beach,* alienated from himself and from society; there is the visionary whose mystical vision locates him on a higher plane than his contemporaries, like Prince Klondike or Hugh Langley; and there is the racially alienated protagonist in "Caromb."

Toomer's formal strategies also manifest reified thinking. He dramatizes his fragmented self through the technique of character doubling, as in *York Beach,* or through the strategy of the dialogue between two versions of the self, as allegorized by the realist, Buck Fact, and the visionary, Ubeam Riseling, in "A Drama of the Southwest." He also uses techniques designed to arrest the mystical moment, as in the poems "At Sea" and "The Gods Are Here," as well as in the novel "Eight-Day World," where a series of epiphanic experiences attempt to capture the immediacy of mystical bonding. Finally, in "The Eye" Toomer draws upon idealist philosophy in formulating a theory of terror and insanity. In sum, Toomer's consciousness is manifested as form in his writings, revealing his reified thinking.

4. Landscapes of Society: The Postwar Decade

"LOST AND DOMINANT": LANDSCAPE OF THE MODERN WASTELAND

Beyond the mysticism and higher consciousness in the novels and in the poems of this period, in the short stories Toomer laments the moral and spiritual bankruptcy of the 1920s from social and political perspectives. In the decade following the First World War, a generation of artists, thinkers, and writers sought to dissociate themselves from the values of postwar America. "In much of the literature of the twenties," writes Frederick Hoffman, "there was a continuous statement of rejection; this was in part a naive awakening to the existence of new forms of evil in the world, but it also served as an indignant protest against a civilization that had played a bad joke on itself."[1] The postwar temper of rejection is evident in such novels of war consciousness as Dos Passos's *One Man's Initiation* (1920) and *Three Soldiers* (1921), as well as E. E. Cummings's *The Enormous Room* (1922) and Hemingway's *A Farewell to Arms* (1929). Yet it is also reflected in the expatriate movement and in the titles of little magazines, such as *Broom* (sweeping aside old ideas) and *Secession* (disaffiliation with the postwar world). It is reflected in writers' critiques of materialism and capitalism, as in Fitzgerald's *The Great Gatsby* (1925), and in satirical portraits of the modern business-man, as in Sinclair Lewis's *Babbitt* (1922). It is also reflected in the images and themes modern writers created to represent cultural and moral failure, such as Eliot's *The Waste Land* (1922) or Hemingway's *The Sun Also Rises* (1926), and in writers' formal improvisation and literary experimentation, as in the Imagist poetry of Ezra Pound and H.D., and in Faulkner's *The Sound and the Fury* (1929). Jean Toomer shared in the postwar temper of rejection, as Warren French demonstrates in his impressive comparative analysis of *Cane* and *The Waste Land*.[2] Toomer's most efficacious literary representation of the modern world as wasteland, however, occurs in "Lost and Dominant," an unpublished volume of short stories manifesting his dissociation from the cultural and moral failure of the twenties.[3] Begun in 1925 and completed in 1930, this volume presents symbolic portraits of modern man in the postwar decade.

"Lost and Dominant" opens with individual dramatizations of private life in the "unreal" city, then shifts to a panorama of the spiritually desolate landscape of the modern world.[4] The first two stories, "Drackman" and "Mr. Costyve Duditch," present parallel portraits of man as victim of his urban environment. The first portrait is of a New York businessman destroyed by materialism and egocentrism. Rich and powerful, with one of the city's finest skyscrapers bearing his name, Daniel C. Drackman is characterized as hard, cold, and dominant. The story represents the air and atmosphere of New York's business district as contaminated by germs of egomania. When Drackman succumbs to these germs, he suffers a series of nervous breakdowns. During one of his fits of insanity, he reveals tragic dimensions while railing at his wife: "Do you remember the old legend telling how the gods, jealous of man's power, fearful that man would dominate them, deliberately cut down and took away his force? My job is to assert myself! I've got to conquer the skies. I've got to rule earth and heaven!" As a "dominant" yet "lost" willful protagonist, Drackman is truly a tragic figure. Though he manages to recoup his sanity by the end of the narrative, the cycle of egomania and insanity is set to repeat itself for as long as he remains in the commercial atmosphere of the wasteland.

Set in Chicago, "Mr. Costyve Duditch" also portrays a modern businessman. Like Eliot's J. Alfred Prufrock in personality and temperament, Duditch is invited to tea parties hosted by society's elite, and like Prufrock he is plagued by feelings of insecurity when his pathetic side emerges and causes the world to come crashing down around him. As a result, he is a wanderer, aimlessly traveling throughout the world: "A product of the skyscraper age, Costyve was uprooted and had to be blown about, restlessly changing places." Like Drackman, Duditch finds solace in his daily worship of business, reverently attending the offices of his stockbroker and real estate agent, solemnly visiting his bank, and piously browsing in Marshall Field department store, described as "a cathedral of commerce." Yet Duditch's vulnerability to his mercantile environment becomes apparent when he accidentally breaks an expensive cut-glass bowl, symbolic of his own fragile ego. Embarrassed, he retreats to his skyscraper suite to regain his emotional security. Later that evening, as the center of attention at a tea party, Duditch experiences social acceptance and personal fulfillment. His house of cards begins to tumble again, however, when his untimely discussion of death casts a pall over the gathering, and the guests begin leaving.[5] "Poor Duditch knew he had broken something, but could not tell what." Suddenly realizing that he is perceived as pitiable, he again retreats to the skyscraper. There he experiences an intensive desire "to see no human beings on earth, of no need save to leave Chicago as fast as a train could carry him . . . for, rushing and active with fuss and to-do, surrounded by things and people though he was, his spirit hugged itself in loneliness and felt goaded by a thousand shattered hopes."

"Love on a Train" also recounts the tale of a Prufrock-like character, a neurasthenic neurologist named Dr. Meron Coville, whose timidity defines his tragedy. Early in the story, the narrator poses the primary oppositional symbolism, the dialectic of reason and love. Described as "a very clumsy young man," Coville himself symbolizes this unreconciled opposition: "He had given much thought to the apparent opposition between science and art, reason and love. . . . phrasing the problem in somewhat philosophic terms, he saw it to consist of an acute juxtaposition of the two dimensionally different worlds: the world of time, of becoming, and the world of space, of being. His career placed him in the world of time. . . . Love and art placed him in the world of space."

The narrator's ideas on time and space recall Yeats's interpenetrating cones theory of history: "These two worlds, so different, existed side by side, doubtless interpenetrating. Probably they were but aspects of a single higher reality. However this might be, their relationship and man's mode of functioning were such that no one could escape having part of a dual experience, sometimes experiencing becoming to the exclusion of being, sometimes, though less frequently, experiencing being to the exclusion of becoming." Having established Dr. Coville as a product of the time world, with tendencies toward the space world of art, love, and feeling, Toomer presents an exemplum of the failure of love. En route from Chicago to New York, Coville meets an attractive woman on a train. Like John in "Theater," however, he is too fearfully repressed to meet her.[6] She, in contrast, is spontaneous, displaying superior wit and intellect; moreover, she accurately diagnoses his malaise: "You are seven-tenths rationalistic, three-tenths emotional, and experience conflict between the two because you cannot blend them." Over the course of an evening, she invites him to bring his feelings in harmonious balance with his intellect. After challenging him to live fully, she bestows a kiss and leaves the train compartment. At this point, he realizes that he is an emotional cripple; yet he also realizes that the unnamed woman represents his hope for love and self-actualization. The next day he panics upon discovering that she has disembarked from the train and taken a ferry into New York's urban wasteland. As he waves to her in passing, she disappears in the distance, "lost forever in the world's people."

"Break" and "Easter" are illustrative of *le paysage moralisé,* that is, a symbolic landscape which assumes moral and spiritual significance. "Break" uses two contrasting settings to symbolize the disjunction between unity in nature and alienation in the city. The opening pages describe the pastoral beauty of grass-carpeted valleys around the Catskill Mountains: "Peace, an active repose rests on this valley, wells up from it as dawn and twilight rise upward from horizons. When bands of clouds hang over it or drift slowly like great airships, the scene is magical. Particularly it is so if looked down upon from a mountain top when the sun rises and strikes these clouds, causing them to lift, turning them to mist and iridescence." Throughout the day, the solitary narrator ponders his relationship with nature; as the sun gathers toward twilight, he gazes at the mountains, valleys, and purple sand dunes in uplifted awe. In this heightened state of awareness, he composes "The Lost Dancer," a poem expressing his quest for unity of being.[7] After a night in the Catskills, the narrator achieves transcendence when, in an epiphanic moment, he experiences complete union with nature: "Then I saw the swift-banded light of transformation." The remainder of the narrative describes alienation in the wasteland of the "unreal" city: "New York is unreal. A simple tree is more real than it. It is the fantasy of a mechanical God. . . . We just happened to drift to this place. We ourselves are strange and alien. We have no name. There is no one to identify us. We have no being. . . . I am alone. I have heard the echo of my voice around the world. I am strange and alien. . . . to ourselves we are lost."

The Symbolist sketch "Easter" introduces the theme of debased religion, representing the demise of God and the possibility for resurrection in terms of three waves of retreat from spiritual values. The opening scene uses animal imagery to depict a world devoid of courage ("no lions roared"; "no eagles screamed") and faith ("only a slim chance of a dove's descending"). Promises for hope and rebirth, however, are symbolized by sparrows that "had nests to build for sparrows eggs," and a peacock "that spread the colors of man across the landscape."

In the beginning of the story Toomer symbolizes a community of earth-beings living in Edenic innocence, harmony, and love. The initial retreat represents a shift from the prelapsarian values of the Garden, a time when "flies, monkeys, lions, eagles, buzzards, sparrows, peacocks and three men found the single lyric of all binding." For after a time, some of them leave the community. "Then something happened. Four hundred and sixty-six hastily got up and left the place. Their going was a single wind that hit the leaves with open pipes for whistling ten miles off. There remained two hundred."

The second wave represents a retreat from the values of agape. Amid a crowd of fellow earth-beings, an illiterate bootlegger stands up to advocate that wealth be redistributed to educate the masses. His exhortation is met by indifference, however: "Then something happened. One hundred and ninety-four persons jumped up and beat it, leaving a mere handful. Leaving, in fact, six." One of the persons who leaves is a provincial, narrow-minded minister, who symbolizes the failure of religion. He goes to Bethlehem and posts the following proclamation:

> We are coming toward Holy Week, and unless we can come together at the Cross, unless we are one in Christ we are not Christians; and this step toward the unification of the Church North and the Church South, and all the churches in the great Ecumenical Movement which includes all followers of Christ and excludes only the Hebrews, the Mohammedans, the Hindus, the Buddhists, and other such heathen cults, is a step toward making all one in Christ, the Lord of All.

The six remaining earth-beings represent a retreat from religious faith. Huddled in a sanctuary during April ("the cruelest month"), they anxiously await the arrival of Easter, with its promise of resurrection. Their waiting is tentatively rewarded when "at the climax of their torture the earth split open and He arose and shook himself like a dog from water." Toomer's simile of the Christ-figure as dog, however, suggests a degeneration of religious ritual, as in *The Waste Land*, where the anticipated resurrection of the dead god is jeopardized by a dog that threatens to dig up the corpse.[8] Similarly, for the six huddled refugees the effects of the risen god are ultimately inconsequential, as they soon abandon the sanctuary and return to the wasteland. Thus, when the Christ-figure arrives, the building is empty. The arrival of the risen god parallels the questing knight's journey to the Perilous Chapel in *The Waste Land:*

> In this decayed hole among the mountains
> In the faint moonlight, the grass is singing
> Over the tumbled graves, about the chapel
> There is the empty chapel, only the wind's home.
> It has no windows, and the door swings.[9]

Upon arrival at the deserted shrine, the quester discovers only emptiness and decay. Emptiness is perhaps the most significant feature of the chapel, for it is precisely the absence of belief that modern man must confront. Alone in the deserted house, the Christ-figure attempts to pray but is thwarted by the forces of 666, the trinity of evil. As his mind returns to the reality of his aloneness in the wasteland, he solemnly contemplates the hypocritical preacher who posted the Easter proclamation in Bethlehem.

Whereas "Love on a Train" dramatizes the failure of love in the wasteland on a personal level, "Two Professors" examines the problem on a social level. In the latter story, the setting aboard a transatlantic ocean liner symbolizes a model society spiritualized by cosmic unity and love.[10] Within this society, however, two cerebral professors reveal their unilateral development, as well as their social apathy, when they become hypnotically absorbed in reading during the eight-day voyage, completely oblivious to the spirit of community that pervades the ship's society. To be sure, they are lost in spiritlessness; throughout the narrative, metaphors of sleeping and awakening represent their spiritual dispassion.[11]

The next three stories are portraits of crass materialism. "Mr. Limp Krok's Famous 'L' Ride" recounts the events of an evening leading up to

Professor Krok's arrival at the Gallonwerp estate for a reception honoring the world-renowned Prince Klondike.[12] Krok's 'L'-ride-journey through the city takes on mythical dimensions, however, as he engages in cultural interpretations and criticisms of Chicago as symbol and symptom of the modern world: "Chicago had given rise to a class of modern barons, those associated with industry, public utilities, big business, and finance. . . . The trouble was that as yet [it] had failed to give rise to a class of modern priests." The central symbolism occurs near the end of the story, when he arrives at the estate. Here, much in the way that Fitzgerald represents Gatsby's mansion, Toomer uses the Gallonwerp mansion to symbolize the materialism of the twenties:

> Night shadows somewhat softened its hulking forms and crude angles; but, even so, it looked as though it had been fashioned by an unimaginative architect to house, perhaps, a breed of expensive mastiffs. It was somber and ungainly. . . .
>
> The house was near enough the loop to have the loop's lights and colors play on it. Reflections from huge electrical displays and lighted towers danced upon and around it, touching it with gleams of many colors. Now and again its dull dark stones seemed iridescent, alive with vibrations, seemed to be sending off strange colors and even stranger sounds. There was something fabulous about this mansion of the Gallonwerps. It pulsed with an elemental other-world life.

In "Fronts" a schizophrenic psychologist, Nathan Antrum, ponders the relationship between consciousness and society, specifically how the postwar landscape corresponds to the contours of modern consciousness. The narrative unfolds as an interior monologue between Antrum and his second-self, Bruce, on the idea that one can extrapolate both an understanding and a critique of society by analyzing the structures that humanity creates. According to the primary narrator, Antrum, the wasteland is a reflection of modern values, glorifying outer appearances over inner essences. Having established reality as a function of consciousness, Toomer implies that a shift toward inner reality is one solution to the wasteland condition.

A brief satirical attack on the climate of egoistic hedonism in the postwar decade, "Pure Pleasure" projects a vision of absolute self-gratification as tantamount to achieved perfection. Here an ironic narrator maintains that being pleased with oneself should be the highest goal in life: "To be pleased with himself. Each man wants it. He wants nothing else. The whole world seeks this pleasure, and the perfection of it. This is the perfect life. This is perfection. This is God."

A masterwork of modern American fiction, and the centerpiece of "Lost and Dominant," "Winter on Earth" is a carefully crafted narrative equivalent of *The Waste Land*. The story opens with a brief philosophical exposition on time and existence, followed by five panoramic frames, each depicting a moralized landscape, each commenting on life in the modern world. In this way, "Winter on Earth" employs spatial form to create multiple, parallel perspectives of life in the wasteland, thereby allowing the reader to contemplate diverse yet contemporaneous events in time.[13]

The first frame, set in mid-America, describes a cruelly cold winter: "Nature looked as if she had been turned into a rusty trash-heap and frozen stiff. Fields were colored a dark purplish brown. Foot-paths worn across them were so hard and lumpy that the men who stumbled along them had their spines jolted with each step." When two nondescript characters enter upon the scene, they curse their sterile world. As this frame ends, snow begins falling over the land.

The second narrative, entitled "The Young Man Tripped On," recalls the "young man carbuncular" episode in *The Waste Land*. This frame projects a world in which lust and betrayal have ascendancy over any redeeming or humanizing conceptions of love. As the story unfolds, a young reveler emerges from a raucous, all-night party, recollecting with pride his clever seduction of a friend's wife. The reveler's desire is uncomplicated by personal concern for the object of his gratification. His action is, in fact, an assault, although the victim of his desire, modern woman, is indifferent to his advances.[14] As the reveler continues jauntily down the street, he experiences an abrupt loss of memory and identity. "And then all of a sudden he forgot who he was. . . . He was suddenly blank, aware of nothing—but his body kept moving on." Toomer symbolizes the young man's lostness in the closing lines of the frame, describing him as having "stepped clear off the Earth." For now his jauntiness is hollow, as he clicks his heels "in the cold space."

The third frame represents a cross-section of life during winter on earth, with falling snow as the unifying image in each vignette. In these scenes, snow symbolizes the unity of humanity, as well as spiritual relief from the intense, sterile cold which grips the land: "But while it snowed, some force of nature thawed men out and allowed them to feel they were all in the world together." At least here, snow seems to counter the neurasthenia plaguing the land, creating feelings of hope and love: a man reading near his window in a modern apartment hotel senses "a swift jet of emotion" and recalls the first time he kissed his sweetheart; an old woman with insomnia arises to greet the snow and decides to read the biblical account of the birth of Jesus; and a young couple sitting near a parlor window suddenly realize true love when moments of intense honesty pass between them. Only a businessman perceives the snow negatively, cursing it because "no one wished to see or buy land in a blizzard."

The fourth frame shifts away from the wasteland to White Island, a romantic land of heart's desire. In a style of magical realism, Toomer projects a model society founded on spiritual values: "White Island, the legends ran, was so called because the angels, long ago, had descended and dwelt there. They had been sent down to earth by God, commissioned to teach and aid the men of earth to improve their way of living. Everywhere over the broad lands men had departed from universal harmony and as a result of this their bodies grew sick, and their souls became diseased." High on the summit of the island, there stands a house of God, "a symbol to those people of devotion and of the long chain of their ancestors." Indeed, their system of government is based on the spiritual philosophy of religious quietism: "Whoever felt compelled by some deep urge within his past to assume this office [governor of the island], which was at once a privilege and a sacrifice, stepped forth of his own accord and gave his life to guide them." And yet, transgressors against their ancient traditions of love and hospitality are sternly exiled. In this society Toomer represents the ecstasy of love in terms of sacred and enduring fidelity between Jend, "a marvelous flower of earthmanhood," and Naril, a beautiful young angel. After twenty years of separation, Jend returns by ship to the island and to his true love: "Even now she had climbed high to the summit of White Island and stood there, lithe and beautiful in the free winds and bright sun, near the house of God, alternately praying and dancing with joy for the first sight of the great Jend, her Jend, as he came sailing home." The image of Naril awaiting Jend's return recalls a similar vignette of Tristan and Isolde in *The Waste Land*.[15] This highly symbolic fourth frame is most important, however, in that it poses a supreme solution to the spiritual desolation which plagues the land. As the thunder echoes its admonition to give, sympathize, and control in *The Waste Land,* the values of White Island—love and temperance—harbinger salvation for the modern world.

The final frame signals a return to the cold wasteland, as it describes a couple driving across a prairie in a blinding snowstorm: "The glassy road lay across an endless flat-land, a cold white wilderness in which nothing grew or could grow." Like Eliot, Toomer describes "the dead land" in images of winter and snow. Also, like James Joyce in "The Dead," he poses the problem of interpreting the ending of the story. In "The Dead," the snow that is general all over Ireland is seen either as an agent of expanding consciousness and awareness for Gabriel Conroy, or as a symbol of total paralysis affecting both him and Ireland.[16] Similarly, in "Winter on Earth" the snow either signals death or anticipates rebirth in spring and the possibility of salvation, as seen in the third frame. Toomer's perennial optimism notwithstanding, "Winter on Earth" ends on a negative note. In this cold and sterile landscape, where "nothing could grow," the redeeming "falling snow" becomes, in the end, "blinding snow," threatening the couple's very existence. Thus, the snow only tentatively inspires spiritual awareness in a "closed cold world."

Like Eliot, Toomer lamented the idea that modern man no longer hears "the mighty voices of the past," and like Eliot, he created original and compelling metaphors for the spiritlessness and sterility of the twenties. In "Lost and Dominant" Jean Toomer joins his contemporaries of the Lost Generation in imaging the character and landscape of the era, providing an additional and special amplification of the wasteland theme. Toomer's originality lies in his creation of artful correlatives for moral and spiritual bankruptcy: satirically drawn representatives of business and commerce; symbolic, moralized landscapes; and situations depicting the failure of religion and love. A clarion call for love, asceticism, and spiritualism to awaken a lost generation, "Lost and Dominant" is a minor masterpiece of American literature, deeply rooted in the postwar temperament of dissociation from the modern world.

FURTHER SOCIAL PERSPECTIVES

Aside from the stories in "Lost and Dominant," Toomer wrote several other short stories which similarly address social issues of the postwar decade. Set in Chicago, "Hugh Lorimer Dreamed" develops on two levels: a dream sequence depicting the human condition, and Lorimer's epiphanic awakening to love and universal consciousness.[17] In the dream sequence Lorimer pictures himself dying, with his wife, Barbara, at his bedside, "in a private room smelly of hospital where the glint of bright steel instruments, to odor of antiseptic displaced human atmosphere." He regains consciousness after experiencing "a source of transforming moral energy" which wills his spirit to reenter his body. When he opens his eyes, he sees Barbara, who represents the energy of love. The sequence ends when surgeons, "like formidable ghosts," brush her aside and wheel him back into the operating room.

Lorimer awakens from this dream in his room at the Drake Hotel. As the narrator implies, the dream symbolizes human helplessness and paralysis in the modern world: "The dream was vivid in his mind. He recognized that it pictured one of his views of himself on earth in the midst of modern civilization—the steel, the scientifically administered pain, his own ultimate helplessness." Yet as he thinks of his wife's devotion and love, he realizes that he must "transform his dream-energy into the energy of imagination." As he looks out over Lake Michigan, Lorimer has an epiphany of universal love and cosmic consciousness: "He bent his head, as if before an unfinished portrait of himself, and went slowly to the window where he stood looking out over the strange grey-green waters of Lake Michigan. He did not see them. He was concerned with a new feeling sweeping up trying to find words. His countenance lifted." His pantheistic prayer, lines from "The Blue Meridian," expresses the majesty of America and the unity of humankind: "And thou, great fields, waving thy growths across the world, couldest thou find the seed which started thee? Can you remember the first great hand to sow? Have you memory of his intention? Great fields, and thou forests, and thou, stately trees, and thou the lands, all continents and seas, and thou, rain, snow, all gifts of the atmosphere."

"Lump," also entitled "Clinic," is an exemplum on the loss of egotism as a first step toward social awareness.[18] It is the story of Jonathan Curtis, who undergoes a spiritual and intellectual transformation during a visit to a clinic for removal of a lump in his mouth. Accustomed to position, influence, and special attention, he is routinely and unceremoniously routed throughout the clinic before the lump, symbolic of his egotism, pride and vanity, is finally removed. "He'd probably had a lump in his psyche far larger and far more harmful than the lump in his mouth. This time the idea struck him with such force that he sat bolt upright in amazement. So this was it! Here, by God, was the clue to what had been happening to him! Perceptions flooded him; and he saw, or thought he saw, it all." While no specific social or moral message follows from his epiphany, the story represents excessive self-regard as a potential cancer in the modern world.

"Elise" dramatizes the failure of love in the urban wasteland.[19] Set in Chicago, the story focuses on an illicit affair between Elise and her friend's husband. Initially, Elise is torn between passion and guilt; however, as the relationship develops, she succumbs to emotional paralysis. Like the neurasthenic women in *The Waste Land,* she engages in sex devoid of love or even desire: "The deciding factor that night was not any great desire, but simply that she was tired and wished to go to bed. If going to bed meant going with him—well—it was too bad—she wished it hadn't happened that way." As in *The Waste Land,* lust controls right reason: "There isn't even a yes-no pull. When the time for action comes, her mind seems to become completely paralyzed and she is as helpless, nay far more helpless, than any child. Not until it is over does her mind come to life again."

"Of a Certain November," also entitled "November Tenth," is an absurdist farce in the tradition of "The Gallonwerps."[20] Containing allusions from "Calling Jesus" (Nora), "Seventh Street" (bloodsuckers), and "Winter on Earth" (snow imagery symbolizing the cold wasteland), the farce focuses on Mr. Doofle Tack, a Prufrock-like character who relies upon "Tropic Glow" to protect him from the cold modern world. Whereas in "Seventh Street" Toomer attacked the war and Prohibition in the 1920s, here he attacks the depression, Roosevelt's election, and the "Booze, Beer, and Bullsoup" in the early 1930s as bloodsuckers which drain the very life of the American people. The central image in the story is an enormous glittering neon sign, which, like the eyes of T. J. Eckleburg in *The Great Gatsby,* oversees the cold wasteland. The glittering words themselves, like the newsreels in Dos Passos's *U.S.A.,* serve to contrast American ideals against wasteland realities: "American Standards . . . Progress . . . The Greatest Nation the World Has Ever Seen . . . Back to Prosperity . . . Forward to Abundance . . . This Means You and You and You . . . This Means All of Us . . . Three Cheers . . . Let Them Rise . . . Let God Hear . . . B E E R."

"Man's Home Companion" comprises one brief scene on the failure of love within the American family, resulting from modern technology and mechanization.[21] The scene dramatizes a husband's estrangement from his business-career-minded wife, and his subsequent reliance upon a bisexual maid-robot, Argive, and a television programmed to mimic human identities and provide companionship. Toomer aptly subtitles it "an a-drama," for it truly lacks dramatic action.

The Sacred Factory, on the other hand, is a fully developed Symbolist drama. Comprising four acts, the play develops on two levels of interpretation, the literary and the philosophical. The literary level highlights character and symbolism. The central characters, John and Mary, are patterned after Torvald and Nora in *A Doll's House.* Like Torvald, John is pretentious and egotistic, perceiving his wife as an extension of himself, rather than as a complement. He is also neurasthenic, atheistic, and intellectual; indeed, the central conflict of the play develops when he begins chastising Mary for having fallen "head over heels in love with God." To be sure, their marriage is reaching a breaking point, for she seeks a divorce. Like Torvald, who suggests that he and Nora continue to live together as brother and sister following Korgstad's disclosure of the forgery, John similarly suggests that he and Mary continue to maintain the appearance of harmony, despite their irreconcilable differences. And as Torvald sinks into a chair at the end of the play to lament Nora's departure, John also sinks into a chair following Mary's departure and engages in an imaginary conversation with his illusion of her.

Whereas John, like Torvald, remains a static and egotistic character throughout the play, Mary, like Nora, grows in stature and resolve. In *A Doll's House,* Nora's climactic decision to leave her family is founded upon her need for greater self-realization. Similarly, Mary's resolve to leave John and their young daughter is based on her need for self-development:

> You have wanted me to have your knowledge. I have wanted you to have my faith. We have succeeded only in opposing them. It has been knowledge opposed to faith; faith opposed to knowledge. You and I opposed—until now; the struggle is ended. I have gained in understanding, and for this I thank you. John, I bless you because you have helped me to be as I am. But you are still faithless. I cannot help you. So I, sepa-

rately, must act according to my faith, and now according to my need. So you, separately, must act according to your lack of it. Good-by John.[22]

Like Nora, Mary considers her role as mother in the final moments before she leaves, yet soon realizes that she must undertake the journey to higher consciousness alone.

Toomer employs symbolism throughout the play, much of which reflects the symbology of Gurdjieffian philosophy. According to Gurdjieff, an individual is a "three-storied factory," composed of three autonomous centers—intellectual, emotional, and physical. Each center is to complement the other, if harmonious development is to result. Thus the sacred factory itself symbolizes the processes of one's harmonious development. Divided into three distinct chambers, with distinct groups of people within each, the sacred-factory setting represents "life in the modern world." In the right chamber the Worker Group engages in a protracted pantomine allegorizing the routine of existence, while the central actions occur in the left chamber, which is the setting for the Family Group, representing middle-class life, and the Mass Group, representing the diverse range of humanity. The central chamber is a holy sanctuary, reserved only for saints, martyrs, and converts to higher spiritual consciousness.

Characters also function symbolically. John represents unilaterally developed intellect, knowledge, and agnosticism; Mary represents emotion, intuition, and faith; and their daughter, Helen, represents the consummation of their physical union. Thus these characters symbolize Gurdjieff's three autonomous centers: intellectual, emotional, and physical. Additionally, the Madonna, dressed in white, symbolizes pure spiritual consciousness, while the Being, robed in white, represents the godhead. There are also other symbols in the play. The brilliant white star which radiates through a triangular opening in the central chamber represents Gurdjieff's Ray of Creation and harmonious development, while the triangle itself symbolizes understanding in Gurdjieff's system. Thus the embroidered gold triangle surrounded by a circle the Being wears on his robe is an emblem of perfect understanding.

In these works, in which Toomer treats the landscape of society rather than the self, his struggles against reification are clearly evident in his critiques of the cultural and moral failure of the postwar wasteland society. It is these efforts that constitute the ethical dimension of his thinking during this period. Yet even in some of these works there is evidence of reified thinking. As for character typology, we note the recurrence of the divided protagonist in "Fronts," as Toomer employs an interior monologue to reflect Nathan Antrum's self-fragmentation. By creating two opposing versions of the self, engaged in a Socratic dialogue on the relationship between society and consciousness, Toomer reveals his reified thinking on the subject. As for themes, "Love on a Train" treats the failure of love in the wasteland, but from a personal rather than a social perspective; this failure is posed from the Gurdjieffian perspective of an unreconciled opposition between reason and love. "Break" uses mysticism and pantheism to dramatize the disharmony between pastoral nature and the urban wasteland. And "Hugh Lorimer Dreamed" proposes cosmic consciousness as one solution to the problems of the modern world. As for techniques, Toomer employs spatial form and "magical realism" in "Winter on Earth" in proposing a model, utopian society, resulting in a static, unrealistic solution for social change. "Of a Certain November" attacks social problems in the 1930s, but Toomer's uses of farce and fantasy confer an unrealistic atmosphere on the period and its historical events, in this way undermining the social realism that is the subject of the narrative. Similarly, in *The Sacred Factory* his use of an arcane symbology, adopted from the language of Gurdjieff's system, detracts from the critiques on the socialization and subjugation of women, investing the play with esoteric meaning known only to students of this philosophy. As we shall see, Toomer's devotion to Gurdjieffian rituals, ceremonies, and meditations, as well as his philosophy of inwardness, ultimately led him to a dimension of spiritual life that is the domain of religion.

PART 3

The Religious Sphere
1940–1955

5. Quiet Rebel: Quaker Religious Idealism

THE ETHICAL VERSUS THE RELIGIOUS

Although Toomer disaffiliated himself from Gurdjieff in 1935 and a year later moved to the Quaker community of Doylestown, Pennsylvania, he never repudiated Gurdjieffian philosophy. In 1937 he initiated a Gurdjieff group in Doylestown, and in 1942 he established a Gurdjieff commune in his home at Mill House. For the next decade, however, he attempted to exclude Gurdjieff from consciousness. Yet after hearing a lecture on his former guru in New York in 1952, Toomer recommitted himself and began attending group meetings in New York. In 1954 he attended Gurdjieff meetings in Princeton, New Jersey, and continued attending and leading these groups until plagued by ill health in 1957. It is significant to note, however, that during these decades Toomer was serving two masters, torn between conflicting idealist philosophies. For while he continued practicing the secular religion of Gurdjieffian idealism, he was also a devotee of Quaker religious philosophy. In 1938 he began attending Friends meetings in Doylestown. During his apprenticeship he immersed himself in Quaker philosophy and wrote numerous essays on George Fox and Quakerism. In 1940 he joined the Religious Society of Friends and immediately became actively involved. In 1941 he was appointed to four Friends committees, and in 1943 became clerk of the Ministry and Counsel committee for Bucks County. He was later appointed to this committee's executive council in Philadelphia. In 1945 he was appointed to the Religious Life committee, and in 1948 he gave the annual William Penn Lecture in Philadelphia. In

1951 he continued working within the society, giving a six-week lecture series on Quakerism at the Doylestown Friends meeting.

To be sure, these were turbulent times for him, as he tried to reconcile the claims of Gurdjieffian philosophy (the claims of man) and Quaker religious philosophy (the claims of God). At first, Toomer envisioned Quaker religious philosophy as a bridge between two levels of consciousness, the ethical or social concerns of cosmic consciousness and the religious or theistic concerns of Inner Light consciousness. In 1942 he sought to reconcile Gurdjieffian idealism with Quakerism by organizing a cooperative, composed of lay individuals interested in spiritual self-development and Quakers. He called this group Friends of Being.[1] Based in an old water-powered gristmill Toomer called Mill House, where they all worked and lived, the members of this cooperative dedicated themselves to "overcoming separation of all kinds" and to a philosophy of "co-opposition," that is, cooperating with creative and balanced self-development and opposing the forces which thwart higher consciousness. One Mill House resident recalls the experience as follows:

> There was plenty to be done. A good house to make into a place of peace, rest, beauty, and a place of energy, work, creation; an old wrecked stone shell, once a water-powered grist mill, to be re-created; a semi-abandoned farm to be brought back to life. Wood and stone and metal, weather and earth, animals and people. We worked with our hands, our bodies, our minds, and our hearts. . . . At the center was Jean Toomer, a gentle man with force. He was the prime mover; from him came the ideas, principles, purposes, insights, understandings. He saw the connections, he put it all together. More than anyone I have ever known Jean knew what and where man was, what he could become. As Jean moved we were ready to move. He opened doors we were ready to walk through, he rang bells we were ready to harmonize with. And as we moved so too did he. . . . The goal was development, the development of man, specifically the development of each man and woman. The dynamics were affirmation and denial, the basic yea and nay of human life.[2]

Yet despite his lofty goals, Toomer experienced only frustration in attempting to bridge gaps between these two idealist philosophies. To

116

understand the basis of Toomer's frustration in reconciling the ethical and the religious, let us examine the contrasts between Quakerism and his earlier forms of idealism, keeping in mind that both Oriental theosophy and Gurdjieffian idealism are Eastern in origin.

Both Orientalism and Gurdjieffian idealism posit the monistic assumption that reality is one organic whole and that God is an abstract force manifested in all life-forms. This pantheistic principle of mediation discloses the unity of opposites and the universal nature of all individuals; it holds that human and divine are one and that truth is a universal and inherent characteristic of humanity. Gurdjieffian philosophy, for example, discriminates assiduously between its concept of the Absolute and the Christian concept "God." By contrast, Quaker religious philosophy posits the paradoxical, dualistic assumption that there is an absolute discontinuity between humanity and God, although there is that of God within the self. That is, while the subject possesses the infinite within itself, the individual is nevertheless temporal (in the process of becoming), and truth lies beyond the self. While Quaker religious philosophy shares with idealism the assumption that the self realizes its highest and most comprehensive unity in the Absolute, Quakerism nevertheless rejects the notion that opposites can be harmonized and mediated in a higher unit, the idea being that mediation removes the absolute contradiction between good and evil, as well as the qualitative difference between God and human beings. Moreover, within the sphere of Toomer's earlier idealism, the self exists as undifferentiated consciousness energized by cosmic influences. One achieves authentic selfhood through identification with the spirit of universal consciousness, in a realm where individuality and universality are thoroughly integrated and corelated. By contrast, Quakerism affirms that overcoming the spiritlessness of existence necessitates differentiation between subject and object, self and world, and that everyone is an individual before God, and society is a lower category than that of the individual's personal relationship with God. Finally, in the years following Toomer's conversion from Gurdjieffian idealism to Quaker Christian mysticism, we note a shift in emphasis from meditative and discursive thought toward "pure faith" and passive contemplation. That is, in accordance with his new religious beliefs, the goal of which was union with God, he attempted to relegate self-will to God's will. To be sure, this was no mean attempt for one who had advocated the primacy of consciousness for over two decades.

Beyond the conflict between Toomer's Gurdjieffian claims of the universal and his Quaker claims of the religious, even beyond the conflicts between Quaker religious idealism and his earlier forms of idealism, Quaker religious philosophy is itself Christian existential in perspective. "It is an odd fact," writes Jessamyn West, "that a generation which has demonstrated so much interest in Zen Buddhism, Existentialism, and the writings of Martin Buber should not have noticed the many areas of likeness between these and Quakerism. . . . no quotations are necessary to show that there are likenesses between Quaker and Existential thought. Quakers are Existential Christians, and [George] Fox, though he had not the philosophical equipment of Søren Kierkegaard, attacked in his life the illusion against which Kierkegaard preached. . . . both saw so clearly that Christianity could not be an objective something—a system of teachings, a church, a code of ethics."[3] To be sure, there are many similarities between Quakerism and Christian existentialism. Indeed, they represent fundamentally the same religious philosophy, both in contrast with Gurdjieffian idealism. Although Kierkegaard shares with Hegel and German idealism the assumption that the self realizes its highest and most comprehensive unity in the Absolute, he nevertheless consistently attacked the Hegelian notion that opposites could be harmonized and mediated in a higher unity.

As in Quaker religious philosophy, Kierkegaardian existentialism reflects a philosophical dualism between the human and the divine:

> It is Kierkegaard's contribution to have drawn a distinct line between all human religiosity of imminence and the Christian religiosity of transcendence. The human individual does not possess the Truth nor the power to understand it. If he is to possess the Truth, God himself must reveal it to him. There is in Kierkegaard's philosophy an absolute dualism or discontinuity between God and human nature. This dualism is due to the fact that man is regarded as a created and derived self, but more essentially it is due to sin which is held to be a qualitative difference between God and man.[4]

Moreover, like Quakerism, Kierkegaardian existentialism focuses upon the category of "the individual." Indeed, Kierkegaard's famous thesis "truth is subjectivity" maintains that the self is the only reality for an individual and that ethico-religious truth derives from what he terms inwardness, or the self's consciousness with God. For Kierkegaard, then, as for Quakers, there is no objective religion or any codified ethical systems, for ethical action derives from existential inwardness. Neither the universal nor society provides the link between the individual and the Absolute; only in one's own personality can one study the ethical with any assurance of certainty. Finally, Kierkegaardian inwardness is quite similar to what Friends call quietism, a meditative state in which the mind is repressed or quieted to allow Divine Light to enter uncontaminated by any human element.

In contrast with both Quakerism and Christian existentialism, Gurdjieffian idealism (as well as Toomer's earlier transcendental Orientalism) makes the monistic assumption that reality is one unitary organic whole and that God is an abstract force manifested in all life-forms. This pantheistic principle of mediation discloses the unity of opposites and the universal nature of all individuals and holds that the human and divine are one and that truth is a universal and inherent characteristic of humanity. In contrast, the religious sphere of Toomer's consciousness is founded on religious dualism and paradox—that is, in the notion that there is an absolute discontinuity between God and human nature, transcendence and imminence, yet that there is something of God within the self. For Quakers as for Christian existentialists, truth is a corollary of the self's solitary consciousness with God.

Moreover, within the sphere of Toomer's earlier idealism, the self exists as undifferentiated consciousness, energized by cosmic influences. One achieves authentic selfhood through identification with the spirit of universal consciousness, in a realm where individuality and universality are thoroughly integrated and corelated. By contrast, Toomer's Quaker existentialism affirms that overcoming the spiritlessness of existence necessitates differentiation between subject and object, self and world; that everyone is an individual before God; and that society is a lower category than that of the individual's personal relationship with God. This is what Kierkegaard meant when he declared that the individual is higher than the universal. According to Kierkegaard, "The man of faith is not ignorant of the universal, he knows it as his home and abiding place. But he also knows that solitary path which winds outside the universal where there are no fellow-travelers, where because of his absolute relationship with God the man of faith cannot make himself intelligible to others."[5]

Thus in terms of Kierkegaard's model, Toomer's earlier idealism represented a "human spirituality," maintaining that truth inheres in human subjectivity and that God is imminent in the human personality, whereas his Quaker existentialism, a "Christian spirituality," maintained that truth is transcendent in God and that the self becomes actualized only when God becomes the measure of its ontology.[6] In terms of our Lukácsian model, the works written during this period may be divided into two categories: the "Passage to India" texts composed in 1939–40, in which Toomer treats social themes, and the poems he wrote reflecting the poetics of alienation and praise. In the former category, we note the author's efforts against idealist reification, while in the latter we see him struggling to supplant one form of idealist reification with yet another.

PASSAGE TO INDIA

In the four years following his disaffiliation with Gurdjieff, from 1935 to 1939, Toomer attended meetings of the Society of Friends, as he continued searching for a spiritual philosophy consistent with his idealism. While he was certainly attracted to Quakerism during this period, his larger plan was to return to the source of his earlier Orientalism by studying Eastern, specifically Indian, philosophy. In the months between August and December of 1939, during a tour of India in search of spiritual enlightenment beyond Gurdjieffian cosmic consciousness, Toomer began writing "The Angel Begori," a novel he never completed, and a one-act play entitled "The Colombo-Madras Rail." Both of these works employ a passage-to-India background, and in both the author appears with his wife and daughter. More important, these works chronicle Toomer's transition away from Gurdjieff, and they manifest social and political themes.

Comprising more than 200 pages of typed manuscript, "The Angel Begori" allegorizes a voyage of self-discovery and a quest for spiritual enlightenment. Begun in the first year of World War II and completed in 1940, this novel presents religion and war consciousness as major themes. "The central theme," writes Nellie McKay, "is the value of religion as a unifying force between man and God. Using the life-threatening uncertainties that WWII had created for most people, Toomer argued that in times of universal crisis there was a greater-than-ever need for a strong religious faith to restore stability to the world at large."[7] To advance these themes, Toomer employs several variations of the symbolic self, each a portrait of the author in fictional guise; he also uses the divided self, engaged in a Socratic dialogue. As we shall see, each version of the self has a specific function in advancing the themes and the narrative design. There is also the Angel Begori, the title character who bears an unmistakable likeness to Toomer's former guru, Georges Gurdjieff.

The book opens with a description of the incarnation of the Angel Begori: "'Good Lord!' said Begori; and the Lord, not having been praised for some time, bent down and elevated Begori to the status of an angel. This in brief is how Begori became an angel. 'Begori!' said I; and Begori himself, in a male human body, stood beside me. This is how Begori and I became acquainted."[8] In the next six pages, the narrator, Phillip Gosh, reflects on his sixteen-year association with Begori, Gosh now having reached middle-age, with "stiff legs and medicine bottles" (6). At their first meeting, the narrator was totally mystified by Begori's charismatic personality, as he succumbed to the angel's powers of spiritual seduction. Following a series of what Gosh calls "egotistical protests against egotism," he finally learns from Begori the path to cosmic consciousness: "I heard silence. I listened through the silence and heard music, grand music, moving and so beautiful, that awoke in my heart the memory of a forgotten world and started me longing for my home in the universe" (3). At this point in the narrative, Gosh introduces Robert Gee, who is twenty years his junior and singularly devoted to the angel. Gee is Gosh's youthful double, through which the narrator reveals an earlier and more idealistic version of himself. Having renounced "worldly career, fame, and fortune" to follow Begori, Gee is haunted by voices which accuse him of retreating from social responsibility: "Bob Gee, in following the way indicated by Begori, you are escaping from reality, neglecting your duties, evading the vital issues of the day, falling down on the job of saving civilization and making the world safe for democracy" (4).

The narrative now shifts from flashback to time present, as the three men—Begori, Gosh, and Gee—plan a journey in search of higher consciousness. The choices of destination are Russia, which the narrator describes in terms of "social engineering," and India, described in terms of "psycho-religious techniques." Begori asks Gosh to choose between the two, and ultimately the choice is India. "A phase had come to an end," says the narrator, "a new phase was about to begin" (6). The choice of India over Russia as well as the name symbolism represent a renunciation of Begori (i.e., Gurdjieff). Begori's prototype, Gurdjieff, is from Russia; instead, the narrator travels to India. Moreover, the names "Begori," "Gosh," and "Gee" well illustrate the demystification of Begori's role as saint. That is, all of their names are secular expletives: "gosh" and "gee" are obvious, while "Begori," a pun on "begorra" (a mild swearword for "by God") is an oath of irreverence and profanation. In this way, the "angel" is reduced to the human level of his disciples, Gosh and Gee, after sixteen years of deification.

The rest of the novel, which takes place in one day, is set aboard an ocean liner en route to India. Early in the voyage, we are introduced to yet another idealized version of the author in the character of Lincoln Ahwell, who appears with his wife and daughter. While there is much discussion of philosophy, goals, and methods, the central scenes depict a Socratic dialogue between the narrator and his alter ego, Lincoln Ahwell, two versions of the divided self. In this way, we are introduced to the political and social dimensions of war consciousness, as the text contains discourses on Hitler's perverted idealism, Germany's defeat of Austria and Czechoslovakia, and the evil nature of Nazism. On the one hand, Gosh symbolizes abstract and reified thinking on the subject of Hitler. As Gosh defines morality, right and wrong are relative to purpose, and purpose is relative to one's personal stage of self-development and consciousness. In his own words, "Except as the world impinges on me, I believe in letting the world alone." As Gosh explains it, "I'm a bit chary of speaking about Hitler and the Nazis because I have no personal experience of them. I like to speak from first hand experience, and if I lack the experience I am reluctant" (180).

Ahwell, on the other hand, who symbolizes political and historical consciousness, differs in his perceptions of Hitler. Almost unable to restrain himself, he exclaims:

> I don't believe in going on heresay either, and I've never met the gentleman nor seen a single brown shirt nor been in Germany since the plague broke out, but, after all, there's *Mein Kampf,* and there are scores of reports from perfectly reliable people who are there on the spot, and I have talked with people who have been there and come back, and there are refugees

whose very body, let alone their words, show the unmistakable marks of a most brutal persecution. I've met some of them and I've gone away feeling an indescribable mixture of pity, outrage and horror. What more evidence does a man need? (181)

Toomer's perennial idealism notwithstanding, Ahwell's considered and cogent critiques of the social and political contexts of Gosh's idealism are accorded the proverbial last word:

Purpose is surely something more than a private matter. Right and wrong are more than private matters. . . . suppose the world does not believe in letting you alone. . . . suppose the state, in order to become all powerful, would lay hold of you and all individuals, making them slaves of us all. . . . There is no stage of *human* development for which the purpose of becoming all powerful is a right purpose. . . . I recognize the need of each one contending with himself. But, trying as I do to keep my eye on the *total* situation, in which a person is related not only to himself but also to others, I also recognize the need of contending with others; and when I meet a man like yourself who is so firmly centered in the individual practice, I suppose I am moved to stress the importance of social measures. (184–90)

Ahwell's rhetorical triumph over Gosh constitutes a powerful reversal of Toomer's representation of idealism in Socratic dialogues. In most of them, as in "The Knighting of Lord Durgling," "Fronts," *York Beach,* or "A Drama of the Southwest," the voice of idealism clearly prevails. In this context, "The Angel Begori" dramatizes the triumph of the historical or real self over the idealized or reified self. The strategy of using a divided protagonist, nevertheless, reveals the author's intrinsic reification.

As for the theme of religion, a tone of religious skepticism recurs throughout the narrative. This is most evident in Toomer's portrait of the bishop as listless and unstimulating and in Ahwell's incisive critique of orthodox religion: "Religion is but a mistaken and impossible attempt to make man *other* than he is. It is artifice, a fantastic invention which no sane red-blooded man believes, a fiction which has nothing to do with reality, a refuge of the weak, a defense used by the weak as a protection against the strong, a dream indulged in by people incompetent to make their way in the real world (177–78)." In the character of Lincoln Ahwell, then, we witness Toomer's struggles against reification.

Set in South India during a train stop in Trichinopoly, en route from Colombo to Madras, "The Colombo-Madras Rail" (1940) is a one-act closet drama that is more a travelogue than a play. Indeed, this work fails as dramatic literature and as literary art. The characters are thinly veiled representations of the author and his family: John (Master) is Toomer; Mary (Lady) is his wife, Marjorie; and Missie (Grettie) is his young daughter, Margery. The most dramatically realized character, however, is the Sinhalese bearer from Colombo, Munasingha. Much of the play recounts (in a dull and prosaic manner) the travel experiences of this American family, living cramped in a small train compartment. The play's interest, rather, lies in its representations of poverty in India and its critique of the caste system. Surrounding the train compartment are hundreds of black Tamil vendors and beggars. In the midst of this scene, John sees "an old woman holding up a child, legless, starved, looking as though it had slept in ashes."[9] John is deeply moved by the scene and immediately empathizes with the Tamils. In contrast to the Tamils is the dutiful Munasingha, who is of a higher caste. Wearing a semicircular tortoise-shell comb in his hair to symbolize his caste (he does not carry objects on his head), he refuses to treat the Tamil coolies with respect. This seems to anger John, who sees the black coolies as a symbol of "the unconquerable vitality of the human race." While Munasingha does not contradict John, he clearly does not understand his master's source of identification with the lower caste.

In sum, "The Colombo-Madras Rail" attempts to dramatize the idea that dire poverty breeds conflicts between castes and contributes to a heightened desire for material acquisitiveness, thereby undermining the authority of spiritual values. Toomer's passage to India thus ended in disappointment and disillusionment, as he concluded that it would be impossible to pursue spiritual enlightenment in the midst of abject poverty. Near the end of his tour of India, he admitted that his search for spiritual enlightenment was unsuccessful. "A life of withdrawal from the world as I have seen it lived in India is not the life for me," he declares.[10] Rather, it is Quakerism which now gains ascendancy in his thinking: "If Quakerism had the catalytic action that it did in the days of George Fox and Robert Barclay, there would be nothing that we have seen and heard in the East thus far that could be as useful for the right process of American life. Even as Quakerism now is I think it better for Americans than any religion or way of life that we have seen here thus far."[11] Yet, although he had rejected Gurdjieff, he never repudiated Gurdjieffian philosophy. And the tension between this philosophy and Quaker religious philosophy is apparent in Toomer's Christian existential poetry of alienation and praise.

THE POET AS KNIGHT OF FAITH

While "The Angel Begori" and "The Colombo-Madras Rail" show the author's efforts to resist idealist reification, the poems of this period show alienation and estrangement from God. To overcome this reification, Toomer adopted the philosophy of Quaker religious idealism. Yet, ironically, Quakerism makes him more rather than less conscious of his alienation. The problem is that his human idealism or human spirituality (as evident in his earlier forms of idealism) allowed for specifically social and worldly dimensions, as well as the autonomy and supremacy of the self. His religious idealism or Christian spirituality (as evident in Quaker religious philosophy), however, allowed for only the paradox of religious faith—that God is both imminent and transcendent and that people must humble themselves before God. For Toomer, who had come to believe that the self was God, Quakerism meant alienation from God. Moreover, his thinking became increasingly reified as he experienced a split in personality between himself as a transcendental or mystical being and himself as a mere mortal before God. The former thinking is, by comparison, more reified, although both idealisms culminate in alienation and reification. The poetry of this period is thus defined by both alienation and praise.

The meditation verses and confessional lyrics which compose the Quaker period present a vision of the individual as alone, estranged from society, the universe, and God. Reflecting an evolution in the poet's spiritual consciousness, these poems fall into several categories: confessional lyrics manifesting tensions between being consciousness and Quaker consciousness, meditations for mediation between the self and God, confessional lyrics on asceticism, and lyrical verses of orthodox Quakerism.

The poems which perhaps best dramatize concomitant claims of both the ethical and the absolute are "Desire," "Prayer for Mending," and "Two Parts."[12] In "Desire," conflicting claims of consciousness are imaged as two types and levels of love. The poem opens with allusions to "suffering" and "the opened heart," reminiscent of the sacred heart. The imagery then shifts to reflect the poet's being consciousness.

> I seek the universal love of beings;
> May I be made one with that love
> And extend to everything
> I turn towards that love.

The line "In this new season of a forgotten life," however, suggests a change in perspective, and the images which compose the closing lines of the poem reflect a shifted emphasis away from agape, or brotherly love, toward Logos, or God's love:

> In this new season of a forgotten life
> I move towards the heart of love
> Of all that breathes;
> I would enter that radiant center
> and from that center live.

The image of the self merging with "that radiant center" which is the heart of love also recalls the Inner Light of Quaker religious faith.

In "Prayer for Mending" and its earlier version "Not for Me," image patterns again reveal a shifting emphasis toward religious consciousness. "Not for Me" is a lyrical petition for the success of the Mill House Circle and for self-renunciation. On the one hand, the poem exhibits ethical consciousness in its call for

> the transport
> Of consciousness from exile
> To the pure essence of life,
> To the deep center of being,
>
> . . . .
> . . . and the awakening of kinsmen.

Yet on the other hand, it manifests religious consciousness in its petitions for self-abnegation:

> That as broken instrument
> I may be mended, as an agent
> To do Thy will towards man,
>
> . . . .
>
> Not for me, except for my surrender
> To the One Self, do I ask Thy sanction.

In "Prayer for Mending" there is a change in the poet's perspective from "I" to "We," the tone is more homiletic and penetential, and being consciousness is eclipsed by religious consciousness. Unlike its earlier version, this poem concludes with the petition: "Take us into thy reality, / Blend us with thy Being." "Two Parts" also manifests this subtle tension between the claims of being consciousness and the claims of religious consciousness, here symbolized in terms of "control of self," on the one hand, and "oblation," on the other. These claims are reconciled, however, in one's "growing and perfecting on and on," and in one's greatest task before others and God,

> To life the wayward and the seeking,
> To plow these bounded fields
> Into the tractless universe.

The meditations for mediation poems, such as "Cloud," employ a variation of the five-line Japanese tanka to speculate on the "livid cloud" separating people from the "salient light" of Quaker religious faith:

> I lay on the great shadow
> Wondering
> Who cast this livid cloud
> Between
> Living beings and the salient light.

The confessional lyric "Here" similarly reveals the poet's sense of estrangement from the divine presence of God's Inner Light.

> Here I am
> And there you are, God.
> It does not make sense
> That I am as I am,
> A burdened speck,

A Clot of darkness,
With you within,
Without, everywhere
All light, all love.
(Box 50, Folder 33, JTC)

The confessional lyrics on asceticism and self-abnegation similarly reveal alienation from God. "Foundling" (Box 50, Folder 33, JTC) reveals a commingling of faith and doubt. Perceiving himself as a "child blindfolded in hide and seek," and God as "the inventor of the game, who sees / Those born of sight and children of the blind," the speaker is made to realize that it is easier for God to find us than for us to find God. His cynicism and sense of estrangement from God is reflected in the image of the God-man relationship as a game, of which God is the master. As a prerequisite for the game, one must repress the self and its consciousness, what the poet described as "the self that seeks in vain, / and the mind that follows its tracks." As the poem ends, doubt and cynicism are resolved into the quiet resignation that precedes faith, as the speaker declares himself "ready to be found."

"Motion and Rest" images white birds coming to rest in rendering a tranquil portrait of asceticism:

I have watched white birds alight on
    a barn roof
And come to rest, instantly still,
    effortlessly relaxed and poised,
In them no trace of former motion.
So would I come to rest, so should we
Come to rest at quiet time.

Within the Society of Friends, "quietism" refers to a mystical state of consciousness wherein one experiences annihilation of the will and passive absorption in God's Inner Light. The metaphor of motion and rest thus effectively dramatizes two contrasting states of consciousness— the realm of the world, with its emphasis upon social engagement, and that of the spirit, with its emphasis upon quietistic contemplation.

In "Prayer" (IV) the poet petitions God to enable him to suppress the transcendentalist self of his former idealism:

Heal me so I can forget me
Renew me so I can forget me
Regenerate me so I can forget me
And feel me
Lift me in new birth so I can forget me
And realize thee.
(Box 50, Folder 33, JTC)

A faithful acceptance of God characterizes the lyrical verses of orthodox Quakerism. In these poems Toomer accepts the paradox of religious faith—that there is an absolute discontinuity between human beings and God, yet that there is God within the self. "The Promise" reveals the poet's acceptance of the paradox of religious faith in contrasting images of spring in nature and human "new birth." Whereas Toomer had earlier sought to spread the gospel of pantheism and cosmic consciousness, here there is manifested an essential disharmony between humanity and nature, and between humanity and God. That is, although "the cycles of the soul are sure as those / Of sap," in nature seasonal cycles ensure the eternal return of spring, whereas in human beings there is no such guarantee, for they possess the will to seek union with God within.

It is not guaranteed that God,
Coming from the south with light and love,
Will touch the seed, melt our crusts
And bestir Himself in us
When earth moves from cold to warmth.

Rather, a person's spirit must "break free" in a Kierkegaardian leap of faith, before "winter shall give way to spring within."

"They Are Not Missed" describes God, time, and eternity in the context of Old Testament religious faith. This poem opens with a series of metaphors, suggesting that much in the same way that old paths "forget the buried feet," ancestral trees "their fallen leaves," and old houses "the births and death that echo in / Their rooms," God is similarly indifferent to "the souls who shared / His glory once, long ago." That is, God, here described as "the ancient one," teleologically suspends the temporal in favor of the eternal. Like Abraham in Kierkegaard's famous parable of the conflict between the claims of man and the claims of God, the ethical and religious, man must acquiesce to God's providence, His prudent and omniscient management of the universe. Indeed, in this poem there exists no tension between the ethical and the religious; rather, there is complete acceptance of the responsibilities of human beings to seek "or sink . . . / Till past and present meet, and time ends."

A profound rejection of Gurdjieffian idealism, "To Gurdjieff Dying," is a carefully wrought Italian sonnet, with variations in rhyme scheme. The poem employs end rhymes in the opening and closing lines of both the octave and the sestet, with intermediate iterating end rhymes, while retaining the traditional iambic pentameter. The octave disparages Gurdjieff for "Knowing the Buddhic law but to pervert / Its power of peace into dissevering fire." He is also described as a seducer "coiled as a serpent round the phallic Tau / and sacramental loaf," and as a false prophet, "Son of the Elder Liar." The sestet further reproves him for having

> deformed the birth-bringings of light
> Into lust-brats of black imaginings,
> Spilling Pan-passions in the incarnate round
> Of hell and earth. . . .

The concluding lines invoke the "Lords of the Shining Rings / Skilled in white magic," the authority of religion itself, to "Save even Gurdjieff from his hell forthright." Light and dark imagery here effectively contrasts the "black imaginings" of Gurdjieffian idealism and the "white magic" of religious faith.

In the prose poem "Greet the Light" (Box 50, Folder 33, JTC), the poet rehearses the several stages of his spiritual development from the perspective of a religious plane of consciousness. The poem develops around contrasting images of outer light (the sun) and inner light (God's divine presence), but in both instances light functions as a metaphor for the spiritual life.

The first three stanzas invoke the youthful, sun-worshipping poet of "Words for a Hymn to the Sun," in chronicling the first stage of his spiritual development. Here the poet associates sunlight with the universal light of Orientalism and transcendentalism, thereby symbolizing God as the principle of energy manifested in all life-forms:

> I arose at dawn to greet the sun . . .
> I hailed the sun,
> and praised the glory, and prayed to be sustained.

130

He concedes that his "sun worship" was not entirely selfless but that when he worshiped "it was the sun in front, / myself behind." As his devotion to idealism increased, so did his egotism, as he sought "to be a god to men." Thus in his mature years, as the poet describes it,

> I swung around
> So that I was in front, the sun behind
> The time came when I secretly believed
> I was greater than the light.

The middle stanzas describe his transition from sun worship to the rationalism of Gurdjieffian thought. Rejecting his earlier idealism as superstition and nonsense, he develops "a hard cold mind full of small facts and other men's theories":

> So I pushed myself back until I lost myself.
> So I pushed God back until I lost God.
> So I veiled the light
> and was pleased that I lived in darkness.

Here, as in "To Gurdjieff Dying," the poet employs dark imagery to characterize the period of his devotion to Gurdjieffian sublime egotism.

The final two stanzas describe his religious plane of consciousness. As in the opening stanzas, he uses light imagery to symbolize true spiritual consciousness, but here it is the "inner light" of Quaker religious faith, not the outer light of universal consciousness. More important, he reaffirms his pre-Gurdjieffian idealism:

> . . . today, I know the youth, the lover of the sun,
> To have been right; though as youth he was
> Related mainly to the outer light.
> Now I arise at intervals to wait upon and greet the inner light . . .
> I hail the inner light, and seek that glory
> and pray to be perfected
> So that it may shine through me.

During this final period in Toomer's career, there is continuing evidence of idealist reification; however, there is some effort to overcome it. On the one hand, we see struggles against reification in "The Angel Begori," specifically in Ahwell's incisive criticisms of Hitler and Nazism. Similarly, Toomer's attacks on poverty and oppression in India

in "The Colombo-Madras Rail" reveal social and political consciousness. And in both works, as well as in the poems, there is an emerging
skepticism toward Eastern religious idealism. On the other hand, his
fragmented, alienated self remains in his use of the divided protagonist
in "The Angel Begori," torn between historical facts and idealist specula-
tions. And in "The Colombo-Madras Rail" the social and political
commentary is secondary to personal narratives of the family's trip to
Madras. The poems of this period are characterized by the poetics of
alienation and praise. Here we witness not only Toomer's unsuccessful
attempts to reconcile the (social) claims of humankind and the (religious) claims of God but also his frustrated desires for mystical union
with God. That is, his acceptance of Quaker religious idealism actually
further alienated him from the concept of God as he had come to
understand it—that human and divine are one, and that the self is
therefore God. As a consequence, in much of the poetry of this period
we find the poet struggling to renounce the self and accept God's
providence. And even in the poems of orthodox Quakerism, where he
accepts the paradox of religious faith, the poet recognizes his "lowered
status," his alienation from God.

The Lost Dancer: The Failure of Idealism

All social life is essentially *practical*. All mysteries which lead theory to
mysticism find their rational solution in human practice and in the
comprehension of this practice.
—Marx, "Eighth Thesis on Feuerbach"

The philosophers have only *interpreted* the world in various ways;
the point is to *change* it.
—Marx, "Eleventh Thesis on Feuerbach"

In one of his finest poems, "The Lost Dancer," Jean Toomer symbolizes
the failure of idealism as a dancer, unable to find a "source of magic" to
unify himself and his dance in mystical harmony. The dancer figure, reminiscent of Yeats's in "Among School Children," serves as an appropriate
metaphor for Toomer the artist, perpetually searching for new forms of
idealism to harmonize his fragmented personality and restore union
between himself and society. His "split in personality," however, did not
derive from "double-consciousness"; rather, his self-fragmentation pro-
ceeded from his wholesale alienation *as an American,* exiled from all races
and from himself. As a result of America's elaborate system of racial
classification for African-Americans of "mixed blood," what I shall term
"race fetishism" or "race reification," Toomer developed a split in personality between his status as a human being and his "second nature"
classification as a thing (octoroon, quadroon, mulatto, etc.). His social
character then appeared to him as an objective character (he had been
labeled by society), and he began seeing himself as a unique individual. It
was as if half of him, his second nature, had become an objective,
independent thing, regulated by social laws he could neither transform

133

nor control. In time, this second self became an abstraction, and he used it to project an idealized version of himself (the "First American"), a new social order (America as a raceless utopia), and a new order of humanity (the "New American"). In sum, he began regarding an idealized abstraction of himself as if it possessed a material existence. On the one hand, he perceived himself as a thing, a category; on the other, and more important, his subjectivity was reduced to thoughts of his own alienation and to contemplation of a solution to this malady.

On a personal level, Toomer created a reified self, one which would harmonize his divided personality and reunite him with society. Toward this end, he maintained that his several ethnic strains conferred upon him a mystical selfhood and a transcendental vision of America. On a social level, he used this reified notion of himself, that he was one of the first conscious members of a new raceless social order, to project a utopian American society. In this way, he assumed the dual role of mystical seer and objective observer; in both instances he presumed to take a *contemplative* stance *outside* of racial polemics. Toomer indeed conforms to R. W. B. Lewis's definition of the New American Adam: "an individual emancipated from history, happily bereft of ancestry, untouched and undefiled by the usual inheritances of family and race."[1]

Toomer's idealist epistemology represented his attempt to transcend the conflicts and struggles engendered by a dynamic and realistic relationship with society. Within his mind, he escaped this dialectic by absorbing it into mysticism and higher consciousness. Such an escape via consciousness results in a split in personality that effectively restores the original dialectic. That is, the alienated individual who seeks unification with society through transcendent subjectivity experiences a more insidious form of alienation, which is reification. The irony that inheres in transcendental metaphysics, then, is that it invites the intolerable imperfections of the existing world as a precondition for continuing to maintain intact the world of perfection in the intellect or spirit. Clearly, this is no avenue to social change; nor does Toomer's "New American" idealism provide a tenable solution to racism within the culture of capitalism.

Positing the self as the origination of a new social and political order, on the basis of a privileged notion of the self as having special mystical powers, is at best solipsistic, at worst, fascistic. Such ahistorical millennialism does not consider the collective as a catalyst for social change. Moreover, while the idea of a raceless society is in harmony with

134

the principles of democratic idealism—stressing the unity of spirit in a diversity of minds—it is unrealistic if not accompanied by praxis, a political agenda for reformation of America's system of racial classification. Owing to his fair skin and his withdrawal into mysticism and idealistic metaphysics, Toomer did not participate in the struggles of African-Americans for racial equality. In this context, skeptics may legitimately ask whether his New American philosophy represented a clever attempt to dodge being identified as an African-American. Yet Toomer correctly perceived that racial classifications hid the true relations of people among themselves, converting people into objects of a rational and impersonal system that fostered alienation and diminished social interaction. Rather than combining this knowledge with social praxis, however, and aligning himself with rank-and-file antiracists, he exiled himself from all races and adopted a self-conscious and idealist conception of race and society.

But self-consciousness and contemplation do not accomplish social change. Indeed, any system which begins with the individual ego as its defining principle is doomed to fail. "For if man is made the measure of all things, and if with the aid of that assumption all transcendence is to be eliminated without man himself being measured against this criterion . . . the man himself is made into an absolute and he simply puts himself in the place of those transcendental forces he was supposed to explain, dissolve and systematically replace."[2] Moreover, social change can be accomplished only by praxis, not merely by thought or contemplation. Ostensibly, idealism dissolves the subject-object problem into the identical subject-object, reuniting thought and existence; yet, in turn, this leads the theory of thought to transcend the limits of thought itself, and the problem remains. The solution Marx proposes is to transform philosophy into praxis: "The philosophers have only *interpreted* the world in various ways," he argues; "the point is to *change* it."[3] Lukács concurs in his essay on reification:

> As long as man adopts a stance of intuition and contemplation, he can only relate to his own thought and to the objects of the empirical world in an immediate way. . . . As he wishes only to know the world and not to change it he is forced to accept both the empirical, material rigidity of existence and the logical rigidity of concepts as unchangeable. His mythological analy-

ses are not concerned with the concrete origins of this rigidity nor with the real factors inherent in them that could lead to its elimination. They are concerned solely to discover how the *unchanged nature* of these data could be conjoined whilst leaving them unchanged and how to explain them *as such*.[4]

The identical subject-object does not then inhere in the philosophy of thought; rather, it crises from the dialectical interplay of thought *and* praxis. As an alienated African-American and intellectual, Toomer needed above all to feel a sense of belonging. That he was unable to find it is not only a commentary on his materializing of abstractions; it is also a commentary on the failure of American democracy.

Born in 1894, Toomer came of age as a writer and philosopher in the opening decades of the twentieth century, a period many historians regard as the most intensely racist in American history. In the years between 1900 and 1920, American racism reached its apotheosis in the politics of apartheid, realized as Jim Crow laws. According to C. Vann Woodward, there was far less sympathy, tolerance, and understanding between black and white Americans in the first decade of the century than there had been even during Reconstruction.[5] This is corroborated by the noted black author Charles Chesnutt, who, in 1903, proclaimed that "the rights of [African-Americans] are at a lower ebb than at any time during the thirty-five years of their freedom, and the race prejudice more intense and uncompromising."[6] To be sure, hundreds of Jim Crow laws were adopted during this whole period, many of which were enforced at the local level by "whites only" and "colored" signs in theaters and restaurants, on restroom doors and over water fountains, in waiting rooms and over ticket windows. There were even Jim Crow Bibles for African-American witnesses in court proceedings, and Jim Crow elevators for separate transportation within buildings. At the very height of this reign of racism, there was much literature, sociology, and history written to advance disenfranchisement and white supremacy, such as Thomas Dixon's trilogy *The Leopard's Spots: A Romance of the White Man's Burden* (1902), *The Clansman: An Historical Romance of the Ku Klux Klan* (1905), and *The Traitor: A Story of the Fall of the Invisible Empire* (1907); Charles Carroll's *The Negro: A Beast* (1900); William P. Calhoun's *The Caucasian and the Negro in the United States* (1902); and Robert Shufeldt's *The Negro: A Menace to American Civilization* (1907).

136

During the second decade, World War I created new hope for first-class citizenship, as more than 360,000 African-Americans entered military service. America represented itself to the world as a crusader for democracy, and this naturally raised the hopes of black Americans for democracy at home. Yet in the years immediately following the war, there was a resurgence of racism. The Klu Klux Klan boasted a record five million members; there were twenty-five race riots in America's cities during the last six months of 1919; and in the same year, more than seventy African-Americans were lynched, some of them veterans still in uniform. "There was no apparent tendency toward abatement or relaxation of the Jim Crow code of discrimination and segregation in the 1920s," writes Woodward. "In fact the Jim Crow Laws were elaborated and further expanded in those years."[7] For African-Americans of all shades and classifications, the opening decades of the twentieth century laid bare the contradictions of American democracy, and its failure. It is within this climate of racial disharmony that Toomer lived, haunted by ghosts of his racial heritage while trying to transcend the polemics of race. Indeed, he did not take a position in either racial camp, as he sat on the sidelines and assumed the role of moderator and objective observer, proposing transcendental consciousness as the solution to America's race problems.

Despite all evidence to the contrary, Toomer believed that America was evolving into an amalgamated, raceless society; surely, he must be defined as the quintessential democratic idealist. Moreover, he is perhaps the most American of American writers; as a corollary of his democratic idealism, he conceived of himself as participating in the creation of a new and uniquely American literature. In his now-famous letter to James Weldon Johnson, he writes: "My view of this country sees it composed of people who primarily are Americans, who secondarily are of various stocks or mixed stocks. . . . as regards art I particularly hold this view. I see our art and literature as primarily American art and literature."[8] Similarly, in a letter to Waldo Frank, he says, "I cannot think of myself as being separated from you in the dual task of creating an American literature, and of developing a public, however large or small, capable of responding to our creations."[9] Throughout his canon, Toomer presents glorified visions of America's grandeur and diversity, including the urban landscape of Washington, D.C. in "Seventh Street" and "Avey," and of Chicago in "Bona and Paul" and Mr. Limp Krok's Famous 'L'Ride";

the scenic Shenandoah River valley near Harpers Ferry in "Tell Me" and the majestic Catskill Mountains in "Break"; Maine's Atlantic coast in *York Beach* and California's Pacific coast in "Caromb"; the grand panoramic sweeps between North and South in *Cane;* the picturesque imagery of the American Southwest in "Imprint for Rio Grande" and "I Sit in My Room"; the paeans to America's diversity and unity in "The Blue Meridian"; and the shifting, kaleidoscopic images of New England, the eastern seaboard, the South, the Northwest, the Midwest, the Southwest, and the California coast in "It Is Everywhere."

For more than six decades, Jean Toomer criticism has been limited primarily to *Cane,* owing to the large number of unpublished manuscripts that have remained essentially unexamined. As a result, it has been difficult to provide a comprehensive evaluation of Toomer's position in modern American literature. Yet today the several phases of his career as a writer and philosopher can be examined, and the pattern is that of idealism. During the early years of his career, Oriental idealism provided the basis for a transcendental philosophy of mediation between self and world, a philosophy of oneness in duality. Later, as a disciple of Gurdjieffian idealism, he practiced austere self-observation, combined with meditations and exercises, to achieve higher levels of consciousness and, ultimately, a mystical harmony with the Absolute, which Gurdjieff called objective consciousness, a union of self and world. And in the final stage of his career, we witness the ascendancy of Quaker religious idealism, with its mystical quietism, its emphasis on the self's direct union with God, and its principle that God is both imminent and transcendent. When we turn to examine the relationship between consciousness and form, the texts themselves chronicle the range of his reified thinking, specifically in his uses of themes, characters, and technical strategies.

Reification is most clearly revealed by the recurrent themes throughout his canon: idealism, democratic idealism, mysticism, utopian messianism, millennialism, pantheism, and higher consciousness through spiritual self-development. Yet at the very center of Toomer's Romantic-Symbolist aesthetic is his idealist conception of the self, which is evident in his creation of characters. The most widely recurring character type in his writings is the symbolic hero, Jean Toomer in fictional disguise. This symbolic hero is evident in such patently autobiographical works as "Withered Skin of Berries" (David Teyy), *Natalie Mann*

(Nathan), *Cane* ("the spiritual entity behind the work"), "Caromb" (John Andrews), "Eight-Day World" (Hugh Langley), "A Drama of the Southwest" (Lewis Bourne), "The Gallonwerps" (Prince Klondike), and "Pilgrims, Did You Say?" (John). Yet another version of the symbolic hero, informed by Toomer's idealist devotion to mysticism and higher consciousness, is the visionary mystic or seer, as in *Balo*, "Withered Skin of Berries," "The Blue Meridian," "Winter on Earth," "Eight-Day World," and "The Gallonwerps," and the character of the spiritual guide or mentor, as in *Natalie Mann*, "Avey," "Withered Skin of Berries," and *The Sacred Factory*. A third type of symbolic hero is the divided protagonist or the divided self, which often utilizes a Socratic dialogue between two versions of the self, the equivalent of an interior monologue. This technique convincingly illustrates the alienated, private world of the hero's self and is seen in "Delivered at the Knighting of Lord Durgling," "Kabnis," "Fronts," *York Beach,* "A Drama of the Southwest," and "The Angel Begori." Variations of the symbolic hero are further evident in Toomer's narrative perspectives: the alienated narrator as exiled hero, in "Beehive," "Harvest Song," "Bona and Paul," "Fern," "Kabnis," and "Caromb"; and the spectatorial narrator or neutral observer in "Karintha," "Becky," "Carma," "Fern," "Easter," *York Beach,* and "Winter on Earth."

Toomer's symbolic heroes are a corollary of his idealist conception of the self. They are alienated and fragmented; they are visionaries and observers. And they are static, two-dimensional, allegorical types that symbolize idealism and higher consciousness. Toomer's retreat from society into the private realm of idealism and mysticism allowed him to experience life only abstractly, as an observer, a descriptive chronicler. As a corollary, his characters demonstrate a peculiar lack of depth:

> The descriptive method does not present things poetically, but transforms people into inanimate things, into details of still life. The individual traits of people simply coexist and are described one after the other instead of being intertwined and thus revealing the complete living oneness of an individual in his most diverse manifestations. . . . The isolation of a writer from active participation in the struggles of life, in the abundant variety of life, makes all questions of a total outlook *abstract*. It does not matter whether this abstraction finds its

expression in pseudoscientific theories, mysticism or indifference to the great problems of life.[10]

The most obvious influences of Symbolist idealism in Toomer's writings are manifested formally as linguistic and stylistic deformations. Linguistic "defamiliarization" is realized in such poems as "Poem in C," "Sound Poem (I)," and "Face," and in the lyrical ensemble "Earth," "Air," "Fire," and "Water." It is also evident in the Symbolist narratives "Rhobert," "Easter," and "Of a Certain November." Stylistic defamiliarization is seen in Toomer's technique of collapsing poetry and prose to create hybrid forms, like the prose poems "Seventh Street," "Rhobert," "Calling Jesus," "Greet the Light," and "Imprint for Rio Grande"; and the lyrical narratives "Karintha," "Becky," "Carma," and "Fern." According to Karl Uitti, Symbolist writers "tried systematically to discover and impose a highly personal way of seeing things. The process of systematic deformation—linguistic, aesthetic and moral—was the author's answer to all anti-individualism, and was his way of amplifying upon what he thought was a great and new truth: 'the world is my representation.' . . . For Symbolists language is as inalienable a faculty of Self as imagination or the five senses."[11] Style, similarly, is a function of the self: "Through language experience is kept in rhythm with the Self; thus the Self imposes a style upon experience with which, so to speak, it comes in contact."[12] Toomer's linguistic and stylistic deformations are similarly functions of his antirealistic, antinaturalistic predilections, rejecting the truth of external, objective phenomena. And like his Symbolist forebears, he advocated a highly personal way of seeing things in art. His private and often arcane symbology is also a function of his Symbolist idealism, as in "Rhobert," "Easter," "The Gallonwerps," "Of a Certain November," and *The Sacred Factory*. In attempting to use symbols to evoke a reality beyond the senses, he often confused and bewildered readers to the point that they dismissed these works as unintelligible or indecipherable. This is particularly the case in *The Sacred Factory*, where all of the major symbols requisite for interpretation are borrowed from the language of Gurdjieff's system. Toomer's ultimate failure as a Symbolist writer is therefore attributable to his idealist conception of the self, particularly the self's radical defamiliarization of form.

Imagist influences in Toomer's writings inhere in his art of literary portraiture, in his attempts to "essentialize" and "spiritualize" experience as a moment of vision. This technique is manifested not only in his poems but also in his narratives. In *Cane,* for example, his "spiritual design" spatializes the narrator's experiences into a constellation of five stages or moments of racial consciousness, resulting in a portrait of the artist. Similarly, "Winter on Earth" employs spatial form to create multiple, parallel perspectives of life in the modern world, in this way allowing the reader to contemplate diverse yet contemporaneous events spatially. And in "Eight-Day World" he employs a series of epiphanies to spatialize plot into a moment of vision, in this way dramatizing an idea popularized by E. M. Forster—"Only Connect." Toomer's use of spatial form locates him within the modernist tradition of Gertrude Stein, James Joyce, Virginia Woolf, T. S. Eliot, and Ezra Pound—all writers who "engaged in transmuting the time world of history into the timeless world of myth."[13] For a Symbolist writer like himself, time, like character, language, and style, was a function of the self, to be fashioned as a mystical moment of vision. "Time exists only apart from temporal boundaries, as an eternal present, a coefficient of the Self. Past, present, future—all are contained in memory, and memory is no more than a kind of linguistic consciousness."[14] This was consistent with his Imagist aesthetics, for he, like Pound, attempted to represent experience as "an intellectual and emotional complex in an instant of time." Yet Toomer's transmutation of the time world of history into a contemplative stance including static portraits and moments of vision is also consistent with his retreat from active social engagement and historical consciousness. As Lukács defines it, the contemplative stance transforms "the basic categories of man's immediate attitude to the world: it reduces space and time to a common denominator and degrades time to the dimension of space."[15] In reifying millennialism, Toomer dissociated himself from the time world of history and wished for a period of universal idealist consciousness and social justice.

Yet in some works Toomer resists materializing abstractions and challenges the social reality he presumes merely to observe. By far, *Cane* manifests the highest degrees of racial, social, and historical consciousness. "Bona and Paul," for example, chronicles the protagonist's awakening to an awareness of his African-American heritage, as well as the social realities of racism. This awareness continues throughout the Karintha cycle, where life is presented from the perspective of an African-American attempting to participate in the black community and rediscover his lost ancestry. "Lost and Dominant" similarly manifests high degrees of social and historical awareness in its representations of postwar America as a wasteland. Here Toomer criticizes the moral and spiritual bankruptcy of the 1920s in a plea for social change. His efforts against idealist reification are also evident in "The Colombo-Madras Rail," where he attacks poverty and the caste system in India; his efforts are even more definitive in "The Angel Begori," which contains diatribes against Hitler's perverted idealism, German imperialism, and the evils of Nazism.

The interplay between reified and idealist consciousness, on the one hand, and degrees of social and historical consciousness, on the other, discloses that while Toomer's canon is nearly eclipsed by his devotion to mysticism and higher consciousness, the metaphysics of thought, he nevertheless fought against materializing abstractions in some of his works. Reified idealism notwithstanding, there are several minor masterpieces among his published and unpublished works, minor classics which are significant contributions to modern American literature. From the aesthetic period there is the masterwork, *Cane,* an artful amalgamation of literary forms. The best poems are "Song of the Son," "Conversion," and "Harvest Song"; the best prose poems, "Seventh Street" and "Calling Jesus"; the best lyrical narratives, "Karintha" and "Fern"; and the best prose or realistic narratives, "Blood-Burning Moon," "Avey," and "Bona and Paul." And "Kabnis," originally composed as a play, is a powerful drama about identity and entity within the black community. Performed by Howard University's Repertory Theater during its 1923–24 season, *Balo* superbly dramatizes the mystical dimensions of African-American culture; also, *Natalie Mann* has contemporary appeal on the subject of black feminism and the male ego. In this context, it constitutes stimulating and provocative theater. Beyond *Cane* and the plays, Toomer wrote several excellent poems, such as "Tell Me," "Skyline," "Gum," and "Banking Coal," as well as the Imagist lyrics "Five Vignettes," "Storm Ending," "And Pass," "Her Lips Are Copper Wire," and "Face." From the ethical period the finest narratives are *York Beach,* the Gothic short story "The Eye," and the short story collection "Lost and Dominant." Within this collection, "Easter" and "Winter on Earth" rank among the finest short stories in modern American fiction. The best poems of this period are "The Lost Dancer," "The Gods Are Here," "Upward Is This Actuality," "Be with Me," "I Sit in

My Room," "It Is Everywhere," and "The Blue Meridian." The best play of this period, *The Sacred Factory,* constitutes excellent modern drama in the tradition of Brechtian epic theater. From the religious period, there are several excellent lyrics, such as "The Chase," "The Promise," "They Are Not Missed," "To Gurdjieff Dying," and "See the Heart." Also, students of existential or Quaker literature will find rich resources in many other poems of this period.

Toomer's literary canon constitutes a study in the phenomena of the spirit, not only in its spiritualist philosophies—Oriental idealism, African-American mysticism, Gurdjieffian idealism, and Quaker religious idealism—but also in its dramatization of consciousness. What this dramatization consistently reveals is the failure of idealism to transcend alienation via thought and Toomer's reified self struggling pathetically to convert idealist metaphysics into social realities, without the concomitance of praxis. In idealism Toomer sincerely believed he had discovered a way to harmonize his fragmented personality and restore union between himself and society. Yet in the end of his career as a writer and philosopher, as in the beginning, he remained a victim of alienation, a contemplative mystic and visionary exiled within the prison-house of thought.

NOTES

PREFACE

1. Reidar Thomte, *Kierkegaard's Philosophy of Religion* (Princeton: Princeton University Press, 1948), 36.

2. Ibid., 49–50.

3. Ibid., 204.

INTRODUCTION. IDEALISM AND ALIENATION

1. Darwin Turner, *In a Minor Chord: Three Afro-American Writers and Their Search for Identity* (Carbondale: Southern Illinois University Press, 1971), 59.

2. W. E. B. DuBois, *The Souls of Black Folks* (Chicago: A. C. McClurg, 1903), 3.

3. Georg Lukács, *History and Class Consciousness: Studies in Marxist Dialectics,* trans. Rodney Livingston (Cambridge: MIT Press, 1971), 87.

4. Karl Marx, *Selected Writings,* ed. David McClellan (Oxford: Oxford University Press, 1977), 436.

5. Lukács, *History and Class Consciousness,* 88.

6. Ibid., 89.

7. Karl Marx and Frederick Engels, *The German Ideology,* ed. C. J. Arthur (New York: International Publishers, 1981), 121.

8. Lukács, *History and Class Consciousness,* 121.

9. Ibid., 200.

10. For biographical information on Toomer and his grandfather, I am indebted to Cynthia Kerman and Richard Eldridge, *The Lives of Jean Toomer: A Hunger for Wholeness* (Baton Rouge: Louisiana State University Press, 1987).

11. Ibid., 18–19. The spelling, emphasis, sentence structure, and grammar appear as in the original letter, which is in the possession of Margery Toomer Latimer.

12. Ibid., 27.

13. Ibid., 51.

14. Ashley Montagu, *Man's Most Dangerous Myth: The Fallacy of Race* (Cleveland: World Publishing Company, 1964), 23–24. For a summary of the debate over race among physical anthropologists, see Leonard Lieberman, "The

Debate over Race: A Study in the Sociology of Knowledge" *Phylon* 29 (Summer 1968): 127–41.

15. Evelyn Underhill, *Mysticism: A Study in the Nature and Development of Man's Spiritual Consciousness* (London: Metheun, 1911), 15.

16. Quoted in William Ralph Inge, *Christian Mysticism* (London: Metheun, 1899), 339.

17. Andrew Lehman, *The Symbolist Aesthetic in France, 1885–1895* (Oxford: Basil Blackwell, 1950), 54.

18. Underhill, *Mysticism*, 94.

19. Darwin Turner, ed., *The Wayward and the Seeking: A Collection of Writings by Jean Toomer* (Washington, D.C.: Howard University Press, 1980), 119–20.

20. Arthur Symons, *The Symbolist Movement in Literature* (New York: E. P. Dutton, 1919), 5.

21. Charles Feidelson, *Symbolism and American Literature* (Chicago: University of Chicago Press, 1953), 18, 50.

22. Jean Toomer, "Poetry and Spiritual Rebirth," Jean Toomer Collection, Box 25, Folder 20. The Jean Toomer Collection is housed in the Beinecke Rare Book and Manuscript Library, Yale University, New Haven (hereinafter cited as JTC).

23. Turner, *The Wayward and the Seeking*, 54, 438.

24. Toomer, "Poetry and Spiritual Rebirth."

25. Toomer, "The Subject Matter of Art," JTC, Box 42, Folder 37.

26. Turner, *The Wayward and the Seeking*, 120.

27. Toomer, "The Psychology and Craft of Writing," JTC, Box 28, Folder 29.

28. Toomer, letter to Alfred Steiglitz, 7 October 1924, JTC.

29. Michel Waldberg, *Gurdjieff: An Approach to His Ideas,* trans. Steve Cox (London: Routledge and Kegan Paul, 1981), 78–82.

30. Ibid., 85.

31. Richard Gregg, *Self Transcendence* (London: Victor Gollancz, 1956), 31.

32. Richard Maurice Bucke, *Cosmic Consciousness: A Study in the Evolution of the Human Mind* (New York: E. P. Dutton, 1923), 72–75. To illustrate instances of mystical or cosmic consciousness, Bucke cites, among others, Gautama Buddah, Jesus Christ, Mohammed, Dante, William Blake, and Walt Whitman.

33. Kenneth Walker, *A Study of Gurdjieff's Teaching* (London: Jonathan Cape, 1957), 106. I am indebted to Walker for his illuminating discussions of Gurdjieffian philosophy, as well as for the Ray of Creation illustration.

34. Ibid., 116.

35. Quakerism is founded on idealist religious philosophy. Indeed, Underhill reminds us that "religions as a rule are steeped in idealism: Christianity in particular is a trumpet call to an idealistic conception of life, Buddhism little less" (*Mysticism*, 15).

36. Toomer, "Why I Joined the Society of Friends," JTC Box 28, Folder 19.
37. Ibid.
38. Toomer, "The Message of Quakerism," JTC Box 70, Folder 5.

1. ORIENTALISM AND RACIAL CONSCIOUSNESS

1. The poems discussed in this chapter may be located in *The Collected Poems of Jean Toomer,* ed. Robert B. Jones and Margery Toomer Latimer (Chapel Hill: University of North Carolina Press, 1988), 3–20.

2. Gertrude Stein, *Selected Writings,* ed. Carl Van Vechten (New York: Vintage Books, 1962), 461.

3. Robert A. Bone, *The Negro Novel in America* (New Haven: Yale University Press, 1965), 80.

4. Renato Poggioli, *The Theory of the Avant-Garde,* trans. Gerald Fitzgerald (Cambridge: Harvard University Press, 1968), 127.

5. Turner, *The Wayward and the Seeking,* 147.

6. Ibid.

7. Jean Toomer, *Balo,* in *Plays of Negro Life: A Source-Book of Native American Drama,* ed. Alain Locke and Montgomery Gregory (Westport, Conn.: Negro Universities Press, 1970), 284.

8. Turner, *The Wayward and the Seeking,* 299.

2. *CANE*

1. Turner, *The Wayward and the Seeking,* 20.

2. Toomer, "The Psychology and Craft of Writing."

3. Roman Jakobson and Morris Halle, *Fundamentals of Language* (The Hague: Mouton, 1971), 91–92.

4. Roman Jakobson, "Linguistics and Poetics," in *Style in Language,* ed. Thomas Sebeok (Cambridge: MIT Press, 1960), 358.

5. Robert Scholes, *Structuralism in Literature* (New Haven: Yale University Press, 1974), 26.

6. Jakobson, "Linguistics and Poetics," 370.

7. Victor Shklovsky, "Art as Technique," in *Russian Formalist Criticism,* trans. Lee T. Lemon and Marion J. Reis (Lincoln: University of Nebraska Press, 1965), 12.

8. Victor Erlich, *Russian Formalism: History-Doctrine* (The Hague: Mouton, 1965), 177.

9. Jakobson, "Linguistics and Poetics," 370–71.

10. Quoted in Erlich, *Russian Formalism,* 181.

11. Jonathan Culler, *Structuralist Poetics* (Ithaca: Cornell University Press, 1975), 164; Ralph Freedman, *The Lyrical Novel* (Princeton: Princeton University Press, 1963), 10, 35, 36, 38, 179; Karl Uitti, *The Concept of Self in the Symbolist Novel* (The Hague: Mouton, 1961), 42–60.

12. These selections are from Jean Toomer, *Cane* (New York: Liveright

Publishing, 1975). Further references are to this edition and will appear parenthetically with page numbers only.

13. Susan Bernard, *The Prose Poem from Baudelaire to the Present,* trans. Alan F. Rister (Paris: Librairie Nizet, 1959), 14–15. Bernard also quotes Mme. Durry, who maintains that prose poems share in common "the same desire to escape from known and familiar language, a wish to invent a hitherto unknown language in which at last may be expressed perhaps what men will never succeed in explaining by means of words" (12). See also Maurice Chapelan's introduction to *Anthology of the Prose Poem* (Paris: Julliard, 1946), where he notes that it is the very absence of generic conventions which confers upon the prose poem "a dynamism all the other genres of traditional lyricism have lost" (16); and Vista Clayton, *The Prose Poem in French Poetry of the Eighteenth Century* (New York: Columbia University Press, 1936). Part 2 of Clayton's book is devoted to recalling the controversies concerning the relative value of verse and of prose, to presenting the theories on poetic prose and on the rhythm of prose, and to seeking out the principal elements that define poetic prose.

14. Freedman, *Lyrical Novel,* 273.

15. Robert Scholes and Robert Kellogg, *The Nature of Narrative* (London: Oxford University Press, 1966), 237.

16. Gertrude Stein, "Portraits and Repetitions," in *Writings and Lectures: 1911–1945,* ed. Patricia Meyerowitz (London: Peter Owen, 1967), 109.

17. Stein, *Selected Writings,* 333–35.

18. See Blyden Jackson, "Jean Toomer's *Cane:* An Issue of Genre," in *The Twenties,* ed. Warren French (Deland, Fla.: Everett/Edwards, 1975), 317–33.

19. Toomer, letter to Waldo Frank, 12 December 1922, JTC Box 3, Folder 6. Several months earlier, Toomer projected a formal design ostensibly modeled after Whitman's *Leaves of Grass:* "I've had the impulse to collect my sketches and poems under the title perhaps of *Cane.* Such pieces as K. C. A. ["Karintha," "Carma," and "Avey"] and 'Kabnis' (revised) coming under the sub-head of Cane Stalks, Vignettes under Leaf Traceries in Washington" (letter to Waldo Frank, 19 July 1922). By December of 1922, however, Cane had evolved into a Whitmanian "Song of Myself." As for the curves or arcs, two appear *in the text* between "Bona and Paul" and "Kabnis," and one appears between "Blood-Burning Moon" and "Seventh Street." These arcs plot the structure of spiritual design.

20. See Charles Scruggs, "The Mark of Cain and the Redemption of Art: A Study in Theme and Structure of Jean Toomer's *Cane," American Literature* 44 (May 1972): 276–91. Scruggs argues that Toomer uses the biblical account of Cain's descendants to depict the black experience in mythical terms (277); see also Rudolph Byrd, *Jean Toomer's Years with Gurdjieff: Portrait of an Artist, 1923–1936* (Athens: University of Georgia Press, 1990), 16–48. Byrd attempts to show how the theme of "man's lack of and search for wholeness" unifies the works in *Cane* (17).

21. Wayne Booth, *The Rhetoric of Fiction* (Chicago: University of Chicago Press, 1961), 151.

22. Underhill, *Mysticism,* 205–7.

23. *The Secret of the Golden Flower: A Chinese Book of Life,* trans. Richard Wilhelm, with a foreword and commentary by Carl Jung (New York: Harcourt, Brace and World, 1962), 99, 102, 103.

24. Boris Tomashevsky, "Thematics," in *Russian Formalist Criticism,* 68.

25. Underhill, *Mysticism,* 206.

26. Ibid., 262.

27. Ibid., 287.

28. Ibid., 463.

29. Ibid., 480.

30. Jean Toomer, "Autobiographical Note," JTC, Box 64, Folder 15. In a letter to *The Liberator,* dated 19 August 1922, Toomer writes: "From my point of view I am naturally and inevitably an American. I have strived for a spiritual fusion analogous to the fact of racial intermingling. Without denying a single element in me, with no desire to subdue one to another, I have sought to let them function as complements. I have tried to let them live in harmony. . . . Now I cannot conceive of myself as aloof and separated. My point of view has not changed; it has deepened; it has widened."

31. Freedman, *Lyrical Novel,* 28. There are essentially three distinct points of view in *Cane:* the lyrical "I" (as in the poems), the first-person narrator (as in "Avey"), and the third-person narrator (as in "Karintha"). While Toomer's spiritual design seems to imply a first-person point of view, owing to its self-reflexive narrator, all three points of view may be ascribed to the perspective of the "spiritual entity," or implied narrator. As Freedman notes, "Since the formal presentation of a self is a 'self-reflexive' method, most lyrical novels indeed seem to require a single point of view. But actually the tradition of lyrical fiction is considerably more generous; it is capable of including many novels which feature several important characters or suggest a panoramic form" (15).

32. Ibid., 17.

33. Shklovsky, "Art as Technique," 22–23. Shklovsky defines poetic language as highly "defamiliarized" or "roughened" language.

34. Freedman, *Lyrical Novel,* 9.

35. Joseph Frank, *The Widening Gyre* (Bloomington: Indiana University Press, 1963), 16.

36. Freedman, *Lyrical Novel,* 2, 6.

37. Roland Barthes, *Writing Degree Zero and Elements of Semiology,* trans. Annette Lavers and Colin Smith (Boston: Beacon Press, 1970), xvii and 9–18.

38. Culler, *Structuralist Poetics,* 140–60.

39. Ibid., 150–51.

40. Ibid., 151.

41. Fredric Jameson, "Metacommentary," *PMLA* 86 (January 1971): 13.

42. John McClure, letter to Sherwood Anderson, 29 January 1924, JTC, Box 1, Folder 1.

3. ART AND GURDJIEFFIAN IDEALISM

1. In his unpublished review of Richard Aldington's "Art of Poetry," written at least two years before his association with Gurdjieff, Toomer maintains that literature should be moral (i.e., contain a message) as well as aesthetic. Citing a metaphor of the poem as gemstone, he argues that writers should be as concerned about "the spirit behind the gem" as much as "its external form." Thus, by "moral" he implies that the writer had a responsibility to inspire higher, spiritual consciousness. Aldington's essay appeared in *Dial* 69 (July–December 1920): 166–80. Toomer's review may be located in the JTC, Box 55, Folder 6.

2. These works may be located in *Collected Poems*, 39–87. See xxxi–xxxii for a comprehensive listing of Toomer's poems. Toomer also wrote a book of aphorisms and maxims entitled *Essentials* (1931), modeled after "Sayings of Gurdjieff" (See Walker, *Study*, 209–16). Toomer's *Essentials* was recently edited and reintroduced by Rudolph P. Byrd (Athens: University of Georgia Press, 1991). As *Essentials* is not a literary text, it is not discussed in the present study.

3. Turner, *The Wayward and the Seeking*, 120–21.

4. Ibid., 121.

5. Toomer, "A First Ride," JTC, Box 26, Folder 4.

6. Toomer, "The Crock of Problems," JTC, Box 32, Folder 8.

7. Walt Whitman, *Leaves of Grass*, ed. James E. Miller (Boston: Houghton Mifflin, 1959), 128.

8. Bucke, *Cosmic Consciousness*, 3 (my emphasis).

9. R. W. B. Lewis, *The American Adam* (Chicago: University of Chicago Press, 1955), 51.

10. For additional interpretations of this poem, see Nellie McKay, *Jean Toomer, Artist* (Chapel Hill: University of North Carolina Press, 1984), 213–24; Bernard Bell, "Jean Toomer's 'Blue Meridian': The Poet as Prophet of a New Order of Man," *Black American Literature Forum* 14 (1980): 77–80; and Byrd, *Jean Toomer's Years with Gurdjieff*, 152–75.

11. For additional interpretations of "The Gallonwerps," see McKay, *Jean Toomer, Artist*, 211, and Byrd, *Jean Toomer's Years with Gurdjieff*, 90–107.

12. Toomer, "Eight-Day World," chap. 7, "Spinning," 58. Page citations in the text are to this novel.

13. Ibid., chap. 9, "Sunset and Two Men," 89–90.

14. Ibid., chap. 36, "Deep Waters," 307.

15. Ibid., chap. 37, "On and On," 325.

16. D. H. Lawrence, *Women in Love* (New York: Penguin Books, 1976), 137.

17. For additional discussions of "Eight-Day World," see McKay, *Jean Toomer, Artist*, 211 and Byrd, *Jean Toomer's Years with Gurdjieff*, 107–25.

18. Jean Toomer's story "The Eye" may be located in JTC, Box 51, Folder 11. Further citations will be to page numbers only. Precisely when this story was written is unknown. There is no date on the facsimile copy, and there are no intratextual references useful in dating it. I am sure, nonetheless, that it was written in the years between 1923 and 1939, for it does not bear the hallmarks of

either the aesthetic or the religious period. Deciphering the facsimile copy is tedious and laborious. Comprising eighteen pages of typed manuscript, with extensive and numerous corrections on every page, the text contains strikeovers, deleted (and inserted) words and sentences, typographical errors, interpolated pages, and handwritten emendations often bordering on illegibility.

19. These conventions are extrapolated from the following sources: William Patrick Day, *In the Circles of Fear and Desire* (Chicago: University of Chicago Press, 1985), 13–74; David Punter, *The Literature of Terror* (London: Longman Press, 1980), 1–21; Terry Heller, *The Delights of Terror* (Urbana: University of Illinois Press, 1987); 1–42; Elizabeth McAndrews, *The Gothic Tradition in Literature* (New York: Columbia University Press, 1979), 3–107; Cora Ann Howells, *Love, Mystery, and Misery: Feeling in Gothic Fiction* (London: Athlone Press, 1978), 5–27; and Leslie Fiedler, *Love and Death in the American Novel* (New York: Stein and Day, 1960), 126–41. Comprehensive bibliographies on Gothic fiction appear in the works listed here by Punter, Heller, and McAndrews, and in Frederick S. Frank, *Gothic Fiction: A Master List of Twentieth Century Criticism and Research* (Westport, Conn.: Meckler Corporation, 1988).

20. Northrop Frye, *The Secular Scripture: A Study of the Structure of Romance* (Cambridge: Harvard University Press, 1976), 97.

21. For discussions on animals and animal imagery related to the grotesque, see Wolfgang Kayser, *The Grotesque in Art and Literature* (New York: McGraw-Hill, 1966), 57, 115, 152, 182–83, 198, and 209. Kayser's comments on domestic animals, like the dog, and on vermin (182) are especially illuminating in the light of Toomer's uses of these images in "The Eye." In this context, it is significant to note that "The Eye" was originally entitled "The Hound."

22. Day, *Circles of Fear and Desire,* 27.

23. McAndrews, *Gothic Tradition,* 81–82.

24. For additional studies of the evil-eye phenomenon, particularly its feature of empowerment, see Clarence Mahoney, *The Evil Eye* (New York: Columbia University Press, 1976), v–xvi; Tobin Siebers, *The Mirror of Medusa* (Berkeley: University of California Press, 1983), 27–56; Lawrence DiStassi, *Mal Occhio* (San Francisco: North Point Press, 1981), 15–60; and Frederick T. Ellworthy, *The Evil Eye* (London: Collier Press, 1958), 1–25.

25. Joost Meerlo, *Intuition and the Evil Eye* (Wassenaar, Netherlands: Servire Publishers, 1971), 15.

26. Day, *Circles of Fear and Desire,* 20.

27. McAndrews, *Gothic Tradition,* 48–49.

28. Day, *Circles of Fear and Desire,* 97.

29. These poems may be located in *Collected Poems.* "A Drama of the Southwest" may be found in JTC, Box 49, Folder 3. For additional discussion of this play, see Byrd, *Jean Toomer's Years with Gurdjieff,* 140–42.

4. THE POSTWAR DECADE

1. Frederick J. Hoffman, *The Twenties* (New York: Free Press, 1962), 99.

2. Warren French, "Afternote," in *The Twenties,* ed. French, 325–33.

French includes Jean Toomer in an impressive array of American writers influenced by T. S. Eliot. Toomer indeed greatly admired Eliot, describing him as "an artist in the use of words" ("The Psychology and Craft of Writing").

3. See the Bibliography for a listing of Toomer's published and unpublished short stories. While there has been no comprehensive analysis of "Lost and Dominant," Nellie McKay provides cogent and provocative analyses of "Mr. Costyve Duditch," "Easter," and "Winter on Earth," in her *Jean Toomer, Artist*, 205–10; also, Darwin Turner provides cursory glosses of "Drackman," "Mr. Costyve Duditch," "Love on a Train," and "Winter on Earth" in *In a Minor Chord*, 44–49. In their recent biography of Toomer, Kerman and Eldridge allude to "Lost and Dominant" as a collection of stories and poems (*Lives of Jean Toomer*, 182); there are no poems in this volume, however, as the title page and contents clearly indicate.

4. For discussions of the city as a modern wasteland in the literature of the twenties, see Kingsley Widmer, "The Waste Land and the American Breakdown," in *The Twenties*, ed. French, 477–78 and 484–86. Toomer announces the urban setting on the title page of "Lost and Dominant": "A striking view of the skyscraper world, our modern world with its power, speed, and vivid activity is reproduced in the dramatic pages of this book."

5. A similar untimely discussion of death in the midst of a party casts a pall over the gathering at the conclusion of Virginia Woolf's *Mrs. Dalloway*, written three years before "Mr. Costyve Duditch."

6. See "Theater" in *Cane*, 50–53.

7. For a discussion of "The Lost Dancer," as well as the complete text of the poem, see *Collected Poems*, xx–xxi and 39.

8. T. S. Eliot, *The Waste Land* in *The Complete Poems and Plays* (New York: Harcourt, Brace and World, 1962). This passage occurs at the end of "The Burial of the Dead": "Oh keep the Dog far hence, that's friend to men, / Or with his nails he'll dig it up again!"

9. Ibid., "What the Thunder Said," ll. 386–90.

10. "Two Professors" was originally a chapter in "Eight-Day World." Toomer also projects a model utopia based on spiritual values in section four of "Winter on Earth," as well as in "The Blue Meridian," his Whitmanian affirmation of democratic idealism.

11. In accordance with Gurdjieff's teachings, the metaphor of sleep describes a trance state induced by negative self-awareness. To awaken from this state is to claim "objective" consciousness. For additional discussions of sleeping and waking metaphors in Gurdjieffian philosophy, see Walker, *Study of Gurdjieff's Teaching*, 38, 44, and elsewhere.

12. Originally, Toomer wrote this story to be included in "The Gallonwerps"; both were completed in 1927.

13. For a discussion of spatial form in modern literature, see Frank, *Widening Gyre*, 9–14.

14. Throughout "Lost and Dominant," the image of modern woman represents either the triumph or the failure of love, the former as in the third and

fourth frames of "Winter on Earth," the latter as in "Drackman," "Love on a Train," and "The Young Man Tripped On."

15. Eliot, *Waste Land,* "The Burial of the Dead," ll. 31–42.

16. James Joyce, "The Dead," in *Dubliners,* ed. Robert Scholes and A. Walton Litz (New York: Viking Press, 1969), 223–24. Eliot uses rain and thunder imagery as the basis for interpreting the ending of *The Waste Land.*

17. Toomer, "Hugh Lorimer Dreamed," JTC, Box 51, Folder 14.

18. Toomer, "Lump," JTC, Box 51, Folder 21.

19. Toomer, "Elise," JTC, Box 51, Folder 10.

20. Toomer, "Of a Certain November," JTC, Box 51, Folder 23.

21. Toomer, "Man's Home Companion," JTC, Box 49, Folder 8.

22. Turner, *The Wayward and the Seeking,* 386–87.

5. QUIET REBEL

1. For a summary of the Articles of Faith for this group, see "Friends of Being," JTC, Box 70, Folder 1.

2. Franklin Davenport, "Mill House," *BANC!* 2 (June 1972): 6–7.

3. Jessamyn West, ed., *The Quaker Reader* (New York: Viking Press, 1962), 23–25.

4. Thomte, *Kierkegaard's Philosophy of Religion,* 214.

5. Ibid., 61.

6. For contrasting analyses of "human spirituality," which Kierkegaard terms "Religion A," and "Christian spirituality," which he terms "Religion B," see ibid., 85–96, 93–96, 212–13.

7. McKay, *Jean Toomer, Artist,* 9.

8. Toomer, "The Angel Begori," JTC, Box 51, Folder 2. Page numbers in the text refer to this novel.

9. Toomer, "The Colombo-Madras Rail," JTC, Box 49, Folders 2, 10, and 15.

10. Toomer, letter to "Family in America," 3 November 1939, quoted in Kerman and Eldridge, *Lives of Jean Toomer,* 245.

11. Toomer, India Journal, 25–27 October 1939, JTC, Box 17, Folder 4.

12. The poems discussed in this chapter may be located in *Collected Poems,* 91–104.

CONCLUSION. THE LOST DANCER

1. Lewis, *American Adam,* 5.

2. Lukács, *History and Class Consciousness,* 187.

3. Karl Marx, "Eleventh Thesis on Feuerbach," in Marx and Engels, *German Ideology,* 123.

4. Lukács, *History and Class Consciousness,* 202.

5. C. Vann Woodward, *The Strange Career of Jim Crow* (Oxford: Oxford

University Press, 1966), 96. I am indebted to Woodward for the statistics in this discussion.

6. Quoted in ibid.

7. Ibid., 116.

8. Toomer, letter to James Weldon Johnson, 11 July 1930, JTC, Box 1, Folder 4.

9. Toomer, letter to Waldo Frank, 2 August 1922, JTC, Box 3, Folder 6.

10. Georg Lukács, "Idea and Form in Literature," in *Marxism and Human Liberation,* ed. E. San Juan (New York: Dell Publishing, 1973), 123, 126.

11. Uitti, *Concept of Self,* 55–56.

12. Ibid., 62.

13. Frank, *Widening Gyre,* 60.

14. Uitti, *Concept of Self,* 62.

15. Lukács, *History and Class Consciousness,* 89.

BIBLIOGRAPHY

THE LITERARY CANON OF JEAN TOOMER

Unpublished works cited in the various sections below are located in the Jean Toomer Collection, Beinecke Rare Book and Manuscript Library, Yale University, New Haven.

Published Volumes

Cane. Foreword by Waldo Frank. New York: Boni and Liveright, 1923. Reprint, foreword by Arna Bontemps. New York: Harper and Row, 1969. Reprint, introduction by Darwin Turner. New York: Liveright Publishing, 1975.

The Collected Poems of Jean Toomer. Ed. Robert B. Jones and Margery Toomer Latimer. Chapel Hill: University of North Carolina Press, 1988.

Essentials: Definitions and Aphorisms. Chicago: H. Dupee. 1931. Reprint, ed. Rudolph P. Byrd. Athens: University of Georgia Press, 1991.

The Wayward and the Seeking. Ed. Darwin Turner. Washington, D.C.: Howard University Press, 1980.

Unpublished Novels

"The Angel Begori" (also entitled "Exile's Bridge"). 1940.
"Caromb." 1932.
"Eight-Day World" (originally entitled "Transatlantic"). 1929. Revised 1934.
"The Gallonwerps." 1927.

Novella

York Beach (originally entitled "Istil"). In *The New American Caravan: A Yearbook of American Literature,* ed. Alfred Kreymborg, Lewis Mumford, and Paul Rosenfeld. New York: Macaulay, 1929.

Short Stories
(excluding the stories in Cane*)*

PUBLISHED

"Easter." *Little Review* 11 (Spring 1925): 3–7.
"Mr. Costyve Duditch." *Dial* 85 (December 1928): 460–76.
"Of a Certain November" (also entitled "November Tenth"). *Dubuque Dial* 4 (December 1935): 107–12.

BIBLIOGRAPHY

"Winter on Earth." In *The Second American Caravan: A Yearbook of American Literature,* ed. Alfred Kreymborg, Lewis Mumford, and Paul Rosenfeld, 694–715. New York, 1928. Reprinted in *The Wayward and the Seeking.*

"Withered Skin of Berries." In *The Wayward and the Seeking.* Written in 1922.

UNPUBLISHED

In 1929 Toomer assembled an anthology of ten short stories he called "Lost and Dominant" (also entitled "Winter on Earth"). This collection comprises three published stories ("Mr. Costyve Duditch," "Easter," and "Winter on Earth") as well as all of the following that were written before 1930 (except "Elise").

"Break." Ca. 1925.
"Drackman." Ca. 1928.
"Elise." Ca. 1926.
"The Eye" (also entitled "The Hound"). Ca. 1930.
"Fronts." 1928.
"Hugh Lorimer Dreamed." Ca. 1932.
"Love on a Train" (also entitled "Skillful Dr. Coville"). 1928.
"Lump" (also entitled "Clinic"). Ca. 1936.
"Mr. Limp Krok's Famous 'L' Ride." 1927.
"Pure Pleasure." 1927.
"Two Professors." 1929.

Plays

PUBLISHED

Balo: A One-Act Sketch of Negro Life. In *Plays of Negro Life,* ed. Alain Locke and Montgomery Gregory. New York: Harper and Brothers, 1927; Westport, Conn.: Negro University Press, 1970. Written during the winter of 1921–22.

Natalie Mann. In *The Wayward and the Seeking.* Written during the winter of 1921–22. After several revisions, Toomer dated the final page "February 1922."

The Sacred Factory: A Religious Drama of Today (also entitled "Saint Homo" and "The Saints of Men"). In *The Wayward and the Seeking.* Written in 1927.

UNPUBLISHED

"The Colombo-Madras Rail" (also entitled "Pilgrims, Did You Say?" and "Tourists in spite of Themselves"). 1940.
"A Drama of the Southwest" (also entitled "The Elliotts"). 1935.
"The Gallonwerps, or Diked: A Satirical Farce for Marionettes." 1927.
"Man's Home Companion." 1933.

Poems

PUBLISHED

"And Pass." In *The Wayward and the Seeking.*
"Angelic Eve." In *The Wayward and the Seeking.*

BIBLIOGRAPHY

"As the Eagle Soars." *Crisis* 41, no. 4 (1932): 116.
"At Sea." In *Black American Literature: Poetry,* ed. Darwin Turner (Columbus, Ohio: Charles E. Merrill, 1969).
"Banking Coal." *Crisis* 24, no. 2 (1922): 65.
"Beehive." In *Cane.*
"[The] Blue Meridian." In *The American New Caravan,* ed. Alfred Kreymborg, Lewis Mumford, and Paul Rosenfeld. New York: W. W. Norton, 1936.
"Brown River, Smile." *Pagany* 3 (1932): 29–33.
"Conversion." In *Cane.*
"Cotton Song." In *Cane.*
"The Days Ripen." *Friends Intelligencer* 101 (1944): 39.
"Five Vignettes." In *Black American Literature: Poetry.*
"Georgia Dusk." *Liberator* 5, no. 9 (1922): 25.
"Gum." *Chapbook* 36 (1923): 22.
"Harvest Song." *Double Dealer* 4, no. 24 (1922): 258.
"Here." *Friends Intelligencer* 105 (1948): 280.
"Honey of Being." In *The Wayward and the Seeking.*
"Imprint for Rio Grande." *New Mexico Sentinel,* 12 January 1938, p. 6.
"The Lost Dancer." In *Black American Literature: Poetry.*
"Men." In *The Wayward and the Seeking.*
"Mended." In *The Wayward and the Seeking.*
"Nullo." In *Cane.*
"One Within." In *The Wayward and the Seeking.*
"Peers." In *The Wayward and the Seeking.*
"Portrait in Georgia." In *Cane.*
"Prayer." In *Cane.*
"Reapers." In *Cane.*
"See the Heart." *Friends Intelligencer* 104 (1947): 423.
"Sing Yes." In *The Wayward and the Seeking.*
"Song of the Son." *Crisis* 23, no. 6 (1922): 261.
"White Arrow." *Dial* 86 (1929): 596.

UNPUBLISHED

Over his lifetime Toomer assembled three collections of his unpublished poems, all now located in the Jean Toomer Collection at Yale. The first, a loosely bound, untitled collection made in 1931, is divided into three parts: the extended prose poem "Sing Yes," twenty-eight lyric poems, and "The Blue Meridian." During the next three years he added eleven poems to this collection, deleted others, and rearranged the titles, retaining the overall tripartite structure. This second collection he personally copyrighted in 1934, entitling it "The Blue Meridian and Other Poems." Toomer projected two other volumes, which were to be called "Day Will Come" (also entitled "Rise") and "As Hands Unturned."

The third, and by far the most complete and comprehensive of Toomer's volumes of unpublished poetry, is "The Wayward and the Seeking," completed circa 1940. It contains seventy poems, fifty of which (indicated below with an asterisk) do not appear in either of the earlier collections. The volume is divided into seven sections as follows:

I

"I See Her Lovely There"
"White Arrow"*
"Grace"*
"It Used to Be"
"Wedger"*
"Wolf from Lamb"
"Mended"*
"Peers"*
"One Within"*
"Frozen Assets"*
"The Lost Dancer"
"This He Taught Me"
"People"*
"Men"*

II

"Living Earth"*
"Rhymes for Chilren"*
"At Sea"
"T.F.E." (same as "T. K. E." in the 1934 edition)
"Unsuspecting"*
"This Bone"
"Not Those"*
"Discredit"*
"Also Persuaded"*
"Sound Poem" (I)
"Sound Poem" (II)

III

"Vague Opening"
"Why These"
"They Are Not Missed"*
"Cloud"*
"Faint Drift"
"Stretch" (same as "Stretch, Sea" in the 1934 edition)
"Be with Me"*
"Prayer" (I)*
"Thanksgiving"*
"Prayer" (II)*
"Beggar into Son"*

IV

"First Seal"*
"The Gods Are Here"*

"Organs in the Storm"*
"Thine"*
"Two Parts"*
"Our Growing Day"*
"Desire"*
"Here and There"*
"Rest"*
"Conquer This"*
"Presence"*
"Prayer" (III)
"Preparation"*
"The Secret"*

V
"The Promise"*
"I Will"*
"The Days Ripen"*
"The Chase"*
"Foundling"*
"Come What May"*
"Easter"*
"Master"*
"Prayer" (IV)*
"Bend and Lift"*
"Witness"*
"The Second Arc"*

VI
"Imprint for Rio Grande"
"It Is Everywhere"*
"Greet the Light"*
"Let Us Go"*
"How Many Lives"
"It Must Be"
"Sing Yes"

VII
"The Blue Meridian"

Unpublished Autobiographical Writings

"Earth Being." 1929–30.
"Outline of an Autobiography." 1931–32.
"On Being an American." 1934.
"Book X." 1935.
"From Exile in Being" (with revisions as "The Second River"). 1937–46.
"Incredible Journey." 1941–48.

159

"The Second River" (also entitled "Why I Entered the Gurdjieff Work"). 1952–54.

Reviews

PUBLISHED REVIEWS BY TOOMER

"The Critic of Waldo Frank: Criticism, an Art Form." Review of *Waldo Frank: A Study* (1923), by Gorham B. Munson. *S4N,* no. 30 (January 1924): n. pag.
"Oxen Cart and Warfare." Review of *The White Oxen and Other Stories* (1924), by Kenneth Burke. *Little Review* 10 (Autumn–Winter 1924–25): 44–48.
Review of *The Captain's Doll* (1923), by D. H. Lawrence. *Broom* 5, no. 1 (August 1923): 47–54.
Review of *Faint Perfume* (1923), by Zona Gale. *Broom* 5, no. 2 (October 1923): 180–81.
Review of *Holiday* (1923), by Waldo Frank. *Dial* 75 (October 1923): 383–86.

OTHER WORKS REVIEWED BY TOOMER (UNPUBLISHED)

After All (1925), by George F. Hummel.
And Now to Live Again (1944), by Betsy Barten.
"The Art of Poetry" (1920), by Richard Aldington.
Castle Conquer (1923), by Padriac Colum.
The Cloud of Unknowing: A Version in Modern English of a Fourteenth-Century Classic (1948).
The Confessions of Jacob Boehme (1920), comp. and ed. W. Scott Palmer.
Dance of Fire (1935), by Lola Ridge.
Helistropium (1912), by Jeremias Drexelius.
Hizzaner Big Bill Thompson (1930), by John Bright.
Indian Crisis (1943), by John S. Hoyland.
Kilvert's Diary (1947), ed. William Plomer.
The Leaning Tower (1934), by Fred Rothermell.
A Man Can Live (1947), by Bernard Iddings Bell.
A Method of Prayer (1951), by Johannes Kelpius, ed. E. Gordon Alderfer.
The Path of the Saint (1947), anonymous.
Port of New York (1924), by Paul Rosenfeld.
Prayer and the Lord's Prayer (1947), by Charles Goce.
A Preface to Prayer (1944), by Gerald Heard.
The Vegetable (1923), by F. Scott Fitzgerald.

JEAN TOOMER BIBLIOGRAPHY, 1923–1992

1923

Armstrong, John. "The Real Negro." Review of *Cane. New York Tribune,* October 14, 1923, p. 26.
Brickell, Herschell. Review of *Cane. Literary Review of the New York Evening Post,* December 8, 1923, p. 333.

BIBLIOGRAPHY

D. E. D. Review of *Cane*. *Brooklyn Life*, November 10, 1923, 3.

Frank, Waldo. Foreword to *Cane*, vii–xi. New York: Boni and Liveright, 1923.

Gregory, Montgomery. "Our Book Shelf." Review of *Cane*. *Opportunity* 1 (December 1923): 374–75.

Josephson, Matthew. "Great American Novels." Review of *Cane*. *Broom* 5 (October 1923): 178–80.

Kerlin, Robert T. *Negro Poets and Their Poems*, 275–77. Washington, D.C.: Associated Publishers, 1923.

Lasker, Bruno. "Doors Opened Southward." Review of *Cane*. *Survey*, November 1, 1923, pp. 190–91.

"Literary Vaudeville." Review of *Cane*. *Springfield Republican*, December 23, 1923, p. 9a.

Littell, Robert. Review of *Cane*. *New Republic*, December 26, 1923, p. 126.

O'Brien, Edward J. "The Best Short Stories of 1923." *Boston Evening Transcript*, December 1, 1923, p. 3.

Review of *Cane*. *Boston Evening Transcript*, December 15, 1923, p. 8.

1924

Braithwaite, William Stanley. "The Negro in American Literature." *Crisis* 28 (September 1924): 204–10.

DuBois, W. E. B., and Alain Locke. "The Younger Literary Movement." *Crisis* 27 (February 1924): 161–63.

Parsons, Alice Beal. "Toomer and Frank." *The World Tomorrow* 7 (March 1924): 96.

Review of *Cane*. *Dial* 76 (January 1924): 92.

1925

Braithwaite, William Stanley. "The Negro in American Literature." In *The New Negro*, ed. Alain Locke, 19–44. New York: Albert and Charles Boni, 1925.

Locke, Alain. "Negro Youth Speaks." In *The New Negro*, ed. Locke, 47–53. New York: Albert and Charles Boni, 1925.

Munson, Gorham. "The Significance of Jean Toomer." Review of *Cane*. *Opportunity* 3 (September 1925): 262–63.

Rosenfeld, Paul. "Jean Toomer." In *Men Seen: Twenty-Four Modern Authors*, 227–33. New York: Dial, 1925.

1926

Hughes, Langston. "The Negro Artist and the Racial Mountain." *Nation*, June 23, 1926, pp. 692–94.

Kerlin, Robert T. "Singers of New Songs." Review of *Cane*. *Opportunity* 4 (May 1926): 162.

Sergeant, Elizabeth Shepley. "The New Negro." *New Republic* May 12, 1926, pp. 371–72.

161

BIBLIOGRAPHY

1927

Locke, Alain, ed. *Four Negro Poets*, 5–6. "The Pamphlet Poets" Series. New York: Simon and Schuster, 1927.

———, ed., with Montgomery Gregory. *Plays of Negro Life: A Source Book of Native American Drama*, 271–86. New York: Harper, 1927.

1928

Green, Elizabeth Lay. *The Negro in Contemporary Literature: An Outline for Individual and Group Study*, 51–52. College Park, Md.: McGrath, 1928.

Munson, Gorham. "The Significance of Jean Toomer." In *Destinations: A Canvass of American Literature Since 1900*, 178–86. New York: J. H. Sears, 1928.

Oxley, Thomas Lloyd G. "The Negro in the World's Literature." *New York Amsterdam News*, March 28, 1928, p. 8.

1929

Kreymborg, Alfred. *Our Singing Strength: An Outline of American Poetry 1620–1930*, 561, 573, 575. New York: Coward-McCann, 1929.

Review of "Mr. Costyve Duditch." *Salient* 2 (February 1929): 18–19.

1930

Brawley, Benjamin. *The Negro in Literature and Art in the United States*, 123. New York: Duffield, 1930.

Hicks, Granville. "Balm in Gilead." Review of *York Beach*. *Hound & Horn* 3 (January–March 1930): 276–80.

Johnson, James Weldon. *Black Manhattan*, 274. New York: Knopf, 1930.

1931

Munson, Gorham. Review of *Essentials: Definitions and Aphorisms*. *New York World-Telegram*, April 7, 1931, p. 25.

Review of *Essentials: Definitions and Aphorisms*. *Buffalo Courier Express*, June 21, 1931.

Review of *Essentials: Definitions and Aphorisms*. *New Orleans Times-Picayune*, April 12, 1931, p. 30.

1932

Baltimore Afro-American, August 27, 1932.

Holmes, Eugene. "Jean Toomer, Apostle of Beauty." *Opportunity* 10 (August 1932): 252–54, 260.

"Just Americans." *Time*, March 28, 1932, p. 19.

New York Herald Tribune, March 18, 1932, p. 9.

New York World-Telegram, March 17, 1932, p. 1.

St. Louis Argus, March 1932.

Thurman, Wallace. *Infants of Spring*, 221. New York: Macauley, 1932.

BIBLIOGRAPHY

1934

Baltimore Afro-American, November 24, 1934.

Baltimore Afro-American, December 1, 1934.

Barton, Rebecca Chalmers. *Race Consciousness and American Negro Literature,* passim. Greifswald, Prussia: H. Dollmeyer, 1934.

1935

Kerlin, Robert T. *Negro Poets and Their Poems,* 275–77. Washington, D.C.: Associated Publishers, 1923; revised and enlarged, 1935.

1936

Oxley, Thomas Lloyd G. "The Black Man in World Literature." *Philadelphia Tribune,* June 25, 1936.

1937

Brown, Sterling. *The Negro in American Fiction,* 153–54. Washington, D.C.: Associates in Negro Folk Education, 1937.

———. *Negro Poetry and Drama,* 67–68. Washington, D.C.: Associates in Negro Folk Education, 1937.

1938

Johnson, James Weldon. *Along This Way,* 375–76. New York: Viking, 1938.

1939

Redding, J. Saunders. *To Make A Poet Black,* 104–6. Chapel Hill: University of North Carolina Press, 1939.

1940

Hughes, Langston. "Gurdjieff in Harlem." *The Big Sea,* 241–43. New York: Knopf, 1940; New York: Hill and Wang, 1963.

1941

Brown, Sterling, Arthur P. Davis, and Ulysses Lee, eds. *The Negro Caravan,* 15–16. New York: Dryden, 1941.

1947

Bontemps, Arna. "The Harlem Renaissance." *Saturday Review of Literature* (March 22, 1947), pp. 12–13, 44.

Franklin, John Hope. *From Slavery to Freedom: A History of Negro Americans,* 503–4. New York: Knopf, 1947. Third edition, revised 1967.

1948

Gloster, Hugh M. *Negro Voices in American Fiction,* 128–30. Chapel Hill: University of North Carolina Press, 1948.

Weber, Brom. *Hart Crane: A Biographical and Critical Study,* 223. New York: Bodley Press, 1948.

1949

Redding, J. Saunders. "American Negro Literature." *American Scholar* 18 (Spring 1949): 137–48.

1950

Locke, Alain. "Self-Criticism: The Third Dimension in Culture." *Phylon* 11 (Fourth Quarter 1950): 391–94.

1951

Cowley, Malcolm. *Exile's Return: A Literary Odyssey of the 1920s,* 179–80. New York: Viking Press, 1951.

1953

Jones, Howard Mumford, ed., with Walter B. Rideout. *Letters of Sherwood Anderson,* 118–20. Boston: Little, Brown, 1953.

Locke, Alain. "From *Native Son* to *Invisible Man:* A Review of the Literature of the Negro for 1952." *Phylon* 14 (First Quarter 1953): 34–44.

1956

Butcher, Margaret Just. *The Negro in American Culture,* 147. New York: Knopf, 1956; New York: New American Library, 1957.

1958

Bone, Robert. *The Negro Novel in America,* 80–89. New Haven: Yale University Press, 1958. Revised edition, 1965.

1961

Toomer, Jean. *Cane.* Translated into Japanese by Hajime Kajima. Tokyo: Hayakawa Shobô, 1961. (Kokujin bungaku zenshû 4.) Reprinted in Japanese by Hayakawa Shobô, 1967.

1963

Wagner, Jean. *Les poètes nègres des États-Unis, le sentiment racial et religieux dans la poésie de P. L. Dunbar à L. Hughes.* Paris: Librairie Istra, 1963. Translated by Kenneth Douglas as *Black Poets of the United States: From Paul Laurence Dunbar to Langston Hughes,* 259–81. Urbana: University of Illinois Press, 1973.

1965

Jahn, Jahnheinz. *A Bibliography of Neo-African Literature From Africa, America, and the Caribbean,* 309. New York: Praeger, 1965.

Weber, Brom, ed. *The Letters of Hart Crane 1916–1932,* 149, 155, 162, 166–67, 185, 195. Berkeley: University of California Press, 1965.

BIBLIOGRAPHY

1966

Bontemps, Arna. "The Negro Renaissance: Jean Toomer and the Harlem Writers of the 1920's." In *Anger and Beyond: The Negro Writer in the United States,* ed. Herbert Hill, 20–36. New York: Harper, 1966.

Fullinwider, S. P. "Jean Toomer, Lost Generation or Negro Renaissance?" *Phylon* 27 (Fourth Quarter 1966): 396–403.

Jahn, Jahnheinz. *Geschichte der neoafrikanischen Literatur.* Düsseldorf-Köhn: Eugen Diederichs, 1966. Translated by Oliver Coburn and Ursual Lehrburger as *Neo-African Literature,* 196. New York: Grove Press, 1968.

Jones, Leroi. "The Myth of a 'Negro Literature.'" In *Home: Social Essays,* 105–16. New York: Morrow, 1966.

Littlejohn, David. *Black on White: A Critical Survey of Writing by American Negroes,* 58–61. New York: Grossman, 1966.

1967

Dillard, Mabel Mayle. "Jean Toomer: Herald of the Negro Renaissance." *Dissertation Abstracts* 28 (1967): 3178A–79A. Ohio University.

Frank, Waldo. Foreword to Reprint of *Cane,* vii–xi. New York: University Place Press, 1967.

Goede, William. "Tradition in the American Negro Novel." *Dissertation Abstracts* 28 (1967): 260A. University of California, Riverside.

Hayden, Robert. *Kaleidoscope: Poems by American Negro Poets,* 50. New York: Harcourt, Brace & World, 1967.

Turner, Darwin T. "And Another Passing." *Negro American Literature Forum* 1 (Fall 1967): 3–4.

―――. "The Failure of a Playwright." *CLA Journal* 10 (June 1967): 308–18.

Turpin, W. E. "Four Short Fiction Writers of the Harlem Renaissance." *CLA Journal* 11 (September 1967): 59–72.

1968

Chapman, Abraham, ed. *Black Voices: An Anthology of Afro-American Literature,* 63. New York: New American Library, 1968.

Emanuel, James A., and Theodore L. Gross, eds. *Dark Symphony, Negro Literature in America,* 95–98. New York: Free Press, 1968.

Margolies, Edward. *Native Sons: A Critical Study of Twentieth Century Negro American Authors,* 38–40. Philadelphia: Lippincott, 1968.

Review of *Cane. Choice* 5 (December 1968): 1312.

1969

Bone, Robert. "The Black Classic that Discovered 'Soul' is Rediscovered after 45 Years." Review of *Cane. New York Times Book Review,* January 19, 1969, pp. 3, 34.

Bontemps, Arna. Foreword to Reprint of *Cane,* vii–xvi. New York: Harper and Row, 1969.

BIBLIOGRAPHY

Fullinwider, S. P. *The Mind and Mood of Black America*, 133–44. Homewood, Ill.: Dorsey, 1969.

Goede, William J. "Jean Toomer's Ralph Kabnis: Portrait of the Negro Artist as a Young Man." *Phylon* 30 (First Quarter 1969): 73–85.

Goode, Stephen H. *Index to American Little Magazines 1920–1939*, 307. Troy, N.Y.: Whitston, 1969.

Jellinek, Roger. Review of *Cane*. *New York Times*, January 21, 1969, p. 45.

Lieber, Todd. "Design and Movement in *Cane*." *CLA Journal* 13 (September 1969): 35–50.

Moore, Gerald. "Poetry in the Harlem Renaissance." In *The Black American Writer*, vol. 2. Ed. C. W. E. Bigsby, 67–76. Deland, Fla.: Everett/Edwards, 1969. Baltimore: Penguin, 1971.

Munson, Gorham. "Letter to the Editor." *New York Times Book Review* (February 16, 1969), 7, 54.

Nower, Joyce. "Foolin' Master." *Satire Newsletter* 7 (Fall 1969): 5–10.

Turner, Darwin T. "Jean Toomer's *Cane*: A Critical Analysis." *Negro Digest* 18 (January 1969): 54–61.

————. "Jean Toomer (1894–1967)." *A Bibliographical Guide to the Study of Southern Literature*, ed. Louis D. Rubin, Jr., 311–12. Baton Rouge: Louisiana State University Press, 1969.

————, ed. *Black American Literature: Fiction*, 53–54. Columbus, Ohio: Charles E. Merrill, 1969.

————, ed. *Black American Literature: Poetry*, 53–59. Columbus, Ohio: Charles E. Merrill, 1969.

Unterecker, John. *Voyager: A Life of Hart Crane*, 325–29. New York: Farrar, Straus and Giroux, 1969.

1970

Ackley, Donald G. "Theme and Vision in Jean Toomer's *Cane*." *Studies in Black Literature* 1 (Winter 1970): 45–65.

Bell, Bernard W. "The Afro-American Novel and Its Tradition." *Dissertation Abstracts International* 31 (1970): 2373-A. University of Massachusetts.

Christian, Barbara. "Spirit Bloom in Harlem: The Search for a Black Aesthetic During the Harlem Renaissance, The Poetry of Claude McKay, Countee Cullen, and Jean Toomer." *Dissertation Abstracts International* 34 (1970): 308-A. Columbia University.

Ellison, Curtis William. "Black Adam: The Adamic Assertion and the Afro-American Novelist." *Dissertation Abstracts International* 32 (1970): 1508-A. University of Minnesota.

James, Charles L., ed. *From the Roots, Short Stories by Black Americans*, 71. New York: Dodd, Mead, 1970.

Kearns, Francis E., ed. *The Black Experience: An Anthology of American Literature for the 1970's*, 405–6. New York: Viking, 1970.

Kraft, James. "Jean Toomer's *Cane*." *Markham Review* 2 (October 1970): 61–63.

Lomax, Alan, and Raoul Abdul, eds. *3000 Years of Black Poetry,* 193. New York: Dodd, Mead, 1970.

Mason, Clifford. "Jean Toomer's Black Authenticity." *Black World* 20 (November 1970): 70–76.

McKeever, Benjamin F. "*Cane* as Blues." *Negro American Literature Forum* 4 (July 1970): 61–63.

Reilly, John M. "The Search for Black Redemption: Jean Toomer's *Cane.*" *Studies in the Novel* 2 (Fall 1970): 312–24.

Stein, Marian. "The Poet-Observer and Fern in Jean Toomers *Cane.*" *Markham Review* 2 (October 1970): 64–65.

Turner, Darwin T. *Afro-American Writers,* 73–74. New York: Appleton-Century, Crofts, 1970.

Williams, Kenny J. *They Also Spoke: An Essay on Negro Literature in America, 1787–1930,* 265. Nashville: Townsend, 1970.

1971

Bell, Bernard. "A Key to the Poems in *Cane.*" *CLA Journal* 14 (March 1971): 251–58.

Bigsby, C. W. E. *The Black American Writer.* Vol. 1, *Fiction,* 23, 55, 60. Baltimore: Penguin Books, Inc., 1971.

———. *The Black American Writer.* Vol. 2, *Poetry and Drama,* 60, 72. Baltimore: Penguin Books, Inc., 1971.

Brown, Robert Michael. "Five Afro-American Poets: A History of the Major Poets and their Poetry in the Harlem Renaissance." *Dissertation Abstracts International* 32 (1971): 3990-A. University of Michigan.

Cancel, Rafael A. "Male and Female Interrelationships in Toomer's *Cane.*" *Negro American Literature Forum* 5 (Spring 1971): 25–31.

Chase, Patricia. "The Women in *Cane.*" *CLA Journal* 14 (March 1971): 259–73.

Davis, Arthur P., and Saunders Redding, eds. *Cavalcade: Negro American Writing from 1760 to the Present,* 285. Boston: Houghton Mifflin, 1971.

Durham, Frank. "The Poetry Society of South Carolina's Turbulent Year: Self-Interest, Atheism, and Jean Toomer." *Southern Humanities Review* 5 (Winter 1971): 76–80.

———, ed. *The Merrill Studies in* Cane. Columbus, Ohio: Charles E. Merrill, 1971.

Fischer, William C. "The Aggregate Man in Jean Toomer's *Cane.*" *Studies in the Novel* 3 (Summer 1971): 190–215.

Ford, Nick Aaron, ed. *Black Insights: Significant Literature by Black Americans 1760 to the Present,* 150. Waltham, Mass.: Ginn, 1971.

Grant, Sister Mary Kathryn. "Images of Celebration in *Cane.*" *Negro American Literature Forum* 5 (Spring 1971): 32–34, 36.

Gross, Theodore L. *The Heroic Ideal in American Literature,* 142–46. New York: Free Press, 1971.

Hayashi, Susanna Campbell. "Dark Odyssey: Descent into the Underworld in Black American Fiction." *Dissertation Abstracts International* 32 (1971): 5790-A. Indiana University.

Huggins, Nathan I. *The Harlem Renaissance,* 179–87. New York: Oxford University Press, 1971.

McPherson, James M., Laurence B. Holland, James M. Banner, Jr., Nancy J. Weiss, and Michael D. Bell. *Blacks in America: Bibliographical Essays,* 251–53. New York: Doubleday, 1971.

Miller, Ruth, ed. *Blackamerican Literature, 1760 to Present,* 373–74. Beverly Hills, Calif.: Glencoe-Macmillan, 1971.

O'Brien. John. "'Becoming' Heroes in Black Fiction: Sex, Iconoclasm, and the Immanence of Salvation." *Studies in Black Literature* 2 (Autumn 1971): 1–5.

Rubin, Lawrence. "The Castaways: A Study of Three Poets of the Harlem Renaissance." *Dissertation Abstracts International* 34 (1971): 6658A. Columbia University.

Singh, Raman K. "The Black Novel and Its Tradition." *Colorado Quarterly* 20 (Summer 1971): 23–29.

Starke, Catherine Juanita. *Black Portraiture in American Fiction: Stock Characters, Archetypes, and Individuals,* 101–2. New York: Basic Books, 1971.

Turner, Darwin T. "Jean Toomer: Exile." In *In a Minor Chord: Three Afro-American Writers and Their Search for Identity,* 1–60. Carbondale: Southern Illinois University Press, 1971.

Waldron, Edward E. "The Search for Identity in Jean Toomer's 'Esther.'" *CLA Journal* 14 (March 1971): 277–80.

Westerfield, Hargis. "Jean Toomer's 'Fern': A Mythical Dimension." *CLA Journal* 14 (March 1971): 274–76.

1972

BANC! 2 (May–June 1972). Special Number on Jean Toomer [Published by Fisk University Library, Special Collections].

Barksdale, Richard, and Kenneth Kinnamon, eds. *Black Writers of America,* 500–502. New York: Macmillan, 1972.

Bontemps, Arna, ed. *The Harlem Renaissance Remembered,* 51–61. New York: Dodd, 1972.

———. "Remembering *Cane.*" *BANC!* 2 (May–June 1972): 9–10.

Chandler, Sue P. "Books by Jean Toomer in the Fisk University Library Special Collections." *BANC!* 2 (May–June 1972): 17.

———. "Fisk University Library Archives: Jean Toomer Collection, List of Published Works." *BANC!* 2 (May–June 1972): 15–16.

———. "Material on or Writings by Jean Toomer to be found in Selected Titles in Special Collections." *BANC!* 2 (May–June 1972): 17–18.

Davenport, Franklin. "Mill House." *BANC!* 2 (May–June 1972): 6–7.

Duncan, Bowie. "Jean Toomer's *Cane:* A Modern Black Oracle." *CLA Journal* 15 (March 1972): 323–33.

Durham, Frank. "Jean Toomer's Vision of the Southern Negro." *Southern Humanities Review* 6 (Winter 1972): 13–22.

BIBLIOGRAPHY

Farrison, W. Edward. "Jean Toomer's *Cane* Again." *CLA Journal* 15 (March 1972): 295–302.

Gilpin, Patrick J. "Charles S. Johnson: Entrepreneur of the Harlem Renaissance." In *The Harlem Renaissance Remembered,* ed. Arna Bontemps, 215–46. New York: Dodd, Mead, 1972.

Harrison, Paul Carter. *The Drama of Nommo,* 112–18. New York: Grove Press, 1972.

Helbling, Mark Irving. "Primitivism and the Harlem Renaissance." *Dissertation Abstracts International* 33 (1972): 5724A. University of Minnesota.

Innes, Catherine L. "The Unity of Jean Toomer's *Cane.*" *CLA Journal* 15 (March 1972): 306–22.

Kent, George E. *Blackness and the Adventure of Western Culture.* Chicago: Third World Press, 1972. *Passim.*

Krasny, Michael Jay. "Jean Toomer and the Quest for Consciousness." *Dissertation Abstracts International* 32 (1972): 6982A. University of Wisconsin, Madison.

Long, Richard A., and Eugenia W. Collier, eds. *Afro-American Writing: An Anthology of Prose and Poetry,* vol. 2, 308, 393–94. New York: New York University Press, 1972.

Ludington, C. J., Jr. "Four Authors View the South." *Southern Humanities Review* 6 (Winter 1972): 1–4.

Mintz, Steven. "Jean Toomer: A Biographical Sketch." *BANC!* 2 (May–June 1972): 1–3.

Otto, George Edward. "Religious Society of Friends." *BANC!* 2 (May–June 1972): 8.

Royster, Philip. Review. *BANC!* 2 (May–June 1972): 11–14.

Scruggs, Charles W. "The Mark of Cain and the Redemption of Art: A Study in Theme and Structure of Jean Toomer's *Cane.*" *American Literature* 44 (May 1972): 276–91.

Schockley, Ann Ellen. "Dedicated to Jean Toomer." *BANC!* 2 (May–June 1972): i–ii.

Smith, James Frederick, Jr. "From Symbol to Character: The Negro in American Fiction of the Twenties." *Dissertation Abstracts International* 33 (1972): 3672A. Pennsylvania State University.

Spofford, William K. "The Unity of Part One of Jean Toomer's *Cane.*" *Markham Review* 3 (May 1972): 58–60.

Thompson, Larry E. "Jean Toomer: As Modern Man." In *The Harlem Renaissance Remembered,* ed. Arna Bontemps, 51–62. New York: Dodd, Mead, 1972.

Watkins, Patricia. "Is There a Unifying Theme in *Cane?*" *CLA Journal* 15 (March 1972): 303–5.

Welch, William. "The Gurdjieff Period." *BANC!* 2 (May–June 1972): 4–5.

1973

Barnet, Sylvan, Morton Berman, and William Burto, eds. *Nine Modern Classics: An Anthology of Short Novels,* 351, 445–49. Boston: Little, Brown, 1973.

BIBLIOGRAPHY

Dickerson, Mary Jane. "Sherwood Anderson and Jean Toomer: A Literary Relationship." *Studies in American Fiction* 1 (Spring 1973): 163–75.

Harris, Trudier. "The Tie That Binds: The Function of Folklore in the Fiction of Charles Chesnutt, Jean Toomer and Ralph Ellison." *Dissertation Abstracts International* 34 (1973): 2489A. Ohio University.

Hart, Robert C. "Black-White Literary Relations in the Harlem Renaissance." *American Literature* 44 (January 1973): 612–28.

Henderson, Stephen. *Understanding the New Black Poetry,* 47. New York: Morrow, 1973.

Kousaleos, Peter G. "A Study of the Language, Structure and Symbolism in Jean Toomer's *Cane* and N. Scott Momaday's *House Made of Dawn.*" *Dissertation Abstracts International* 34 (1973): 2631A. Ohio University.

Krasny, Michael J. "Design in Jean Toomer's *Balo.*" *Negro American Literature Forum* 7 (Fall 1973): 103–4.

Mellard, John M. "Solipsism, Symbolism, and Demonism: The Lyrical Mode in Fiction." *Southern Humanities Review* 7 (Winter 1973): 37–51.

Schraufnagel, Noel. *From Apology to Protest: The Black American Novel.* Deland, Florida: Everett/Edwards, Inc., 1973.

Trachtenberg, Alan, ed. *Memoirs of Waldo Frank,* 102–8. Amherst: University of Massachusetts Press, 1973.

Wagner, Jean. *Les poètes nègres des États-Unis, le sentiment racial et religieux dans la poésie de P. L. Dunbar à L. Hughes.* Paris: Librairie Istra, 1963. Translated by Kenneth Douglas as *Black Poets of the United States: From Paul Laurence Dunbar to Langston Hughes,* 259–81. Urbana: University of Illinois Press, 1973.

Whitlow, Roger. *Black American Literature: A Critical History,* 80–83. Chicago: Nelson Hall, 1973.

1974

Bell, Bernard. "Portrait of the Artist as High Priest of Soul: Jean Toomer's *Cane.* *Black World* 23 (September 1974): 4–19, 92–97.

Blackwell, Louise. "Jean Toomer's *Cane* and Biblical Myth." *CLA Journal* 17 (June 1974): 535–42.

Blake, Susan. "The Spectatorial Artist and the Structure of *Cane.*" *CLA Journal* 17 (June 1974): 516–34.

College Language Association Journal [*CLA Journal*]. 17 (June 1974). Special Number on Jean Toomer.

Crewdson, Arlene J. "Invisibility: A Study of the Works of Toomer, Wright, and Ellison." *Dissertation Abstracts International* 35 (1974): 1092A–93A. Loyola University, Chicago.

Davis, Arthur P. *From the Dark Tower: Afro-American Writers 1900 to 1960,* 44–51, 57–58. Washington, D.C.: Howard University Press, 1974.

Davis, Charles T. "Jean Toomer and the South: Region and Race as Elements Within a Literary Imagination." *Studies in the Literary Imagination* 7 (Fall 1974): 23–37. Reprinted in *Black is the Color of the Cosmos,* ed. Henry Louis

Gates, 235–51. New York: Garland Press, 1982. Also reprinted in *The Harlem Renaissance Re-Examined,* ed. Victor A. Kramer, 185–99. New York: AMS, 1987.

Dillard, Mabel. "Jean Toomer: The Veil Replaced." *CLA Journal* 17 (June 1974): 468–73.

Fisher, Alice P. "The Influence of Ouspensky's *Tertium Organum* Upon Jean Toomer's *Cane.*" *CLA Journal* 17 (June 1974): 504–15.

Griffin, John C. "A Chat with Marjorie Content Toomer." *Pembroke Magazine* 5 (1974): 15–27.

———. "Jean Toomer: A Bibliography." *South Carolina Review* 7 (Spring 1974): 61–64.

Jackson, Blyden, and Louis D. Rubin. *Black Poetry in America: Two Essays in Historical Interpretation,* 33–35. Baton Rouge: Louisiana State University Press, 1974.

Jones, Norma Ramsay. "Africa, as Imaged by Cullen and Co." *Negro American Literature Forum* 8 (Spring 1974): 263–67.

Kopf, George. "The Tensions in Jean Toomer's 'Theater.'" *CLA Journal* 17 (June 1974): 498–503.

Kramer, Victor A. "The 'Mid-Kingdom' of Crane's 'Black Tambourine' and Toomer's *Cane.*" *CLA Journal* 17 (June 1974): 486–97.

McCarthy, Daniel P. "'Just Americans': A Note on Jean Toomer's Marriage to Margery Latimer." *CLA Journal* 17 (June 1974): 474–79.

McNeely, Darrell Wayne. "Jean Toomer's *Cane* and Sherwood Anderson's *Winesburg, Ohio:* A Black Reaction to the Literary Conventions of the Twenties." *Dissertation Abstracts International* 36 (1974): 890A–91A. University of Nebraska.

Matthews, George C. "Toomer's *Cane:* The Artist and His World." *CLA Journal* 17 (June 1974): 543–59.

Reilly, John. "Jean Toomer: An Annotated Checklist of Criticism." *Resources for American Literary Study* 4 (Spring 1974): 27–56.

Richmond, Merle. "Jean Toomer and Margery Latimer." *CLA Journal* 18 (December 1974): 300.

Riley, Roberta. "Search for Identity and Artistry." *CLA Journal* 17 (June 1974): 480–85.

Rosenblatt, Roger. *Black Fiction,* 54–64. Cambridge: Harvard University Press, 1974.

Smith, Cynthia Janis. "Escape and Quest in the Literature of Black Americans." *Dissertation Abstracts International* 36 (1974): 287A. Yale University.

Turner, Darwin. "An Intersection of Paths: Correspondence between Jean Toomer and Sherwood Anderson." *CLA Journal* 17 (June 1974): 455–67.

1975

Antonides, Chris. "Jean Toomer: The Burden of Impotent Pain." *Dissertation Abstracts International* 36 (1975): 8054A. Michigan State University.

Bone, Robert. "Jean Toomer." In *Down Home: A History of Afro-American Short*

Fiction from Its Beginnings to the End of the Harlem Renaissance, 204–38 passim. New York: G. P. Putnam's, 1975.

Christ, Jack. "Jean Toomer's 'Bona and Paul': The Innocence and Artifice of Words." *Negro American Literature Forum* 9 (Summer 1975): 44–46.

French, Warren. "Afternote." *The Twenties: Fiction, Poetry, Drama.* Ed. Warren French, 325–33. Deland, Florida: Everett/Edwards, 1975.

Gayle, Addison. "The Confusion of Identity." *The Way of the New World: The Black Novel in America,* 98–104. Garden City: Anchor Press, 1975.

Griffin, John C. "Two Poems by Jean Toomer." *Pembroke Magazine* 6 (1975): 67–68.

Gysin, Fritz. *The Grotesque in American Negro Fiction: Jean Toomer, Richard Wright, and Ralph Ellison.* Cooper Monograph 22, 36–90, 276–79. Bern: Francke, 1975.

Helbling, Mark. "Sherwood Anderson and Jean Toomer." *Negro American Literature Forum* 9 (Summer 1975): 35–39.

Jackson, Blyden. "Jean Toomer's *Cane:* An Issue of Genre." In *The Twenties: Fiction, Poetry, Drama,* ed. Warren French, 317–33. Deland, Florida: Everett/Edwards, 1975.

Jung, Udo. "'Spirit-Torsos of Exquisite Strength': The Theme of Individual Weakness vs. Collective Strength in Two of Toomer's Poems." *CLA Journal* 19 (December 1975): 261–67.

Kerman, Cynthia. "Jean Toomer? Enigma." *Indian Journal of American Studies* 7 (Fall 1975): 67–78.

Krasny, Michael. "The Aesthetic Structure of Jean Toomer's *Cane.*" *Negro American Literature Forum* 9 (Summer 1975): 42–43.

———. "Jean Toomer's Life Prior to *Cane:* A Brief Sketch of the Emergence of a Black Writer." *Negro American Literature Forum* 9 (Summer 1975): 40–41.

MacKethan, Lucinda H. "Jean Toomer's *Cane:* A Pastoral Problem." *Mississippi Quarterly* 28 (Fall 1975): 423–34.

Scruggs, Charles W. "Jean Toomer: Fugitive." *American Literature* 47 (March 1975): 84–96.

Shaw, Brenda Joyce Robinson. "Jean Toomer's Life Search for Identity as Realized in *Cane.*" *Dissertation Abstracts International* 36 (1975): 7427A. Middle Tennessee State University.

Taylor, Clyde. "The Second Coming of Jean Toomer." *Obsidian* 1 (Winter 1975): 37–57.

Turner, Darwin. Introduction to *Cane,* ix–xxv. New York: Liveright Publishing Corporation, 1975.

1976

Baker, Houston. "Journey Toward Black Art: Jean Toomer's *Cane.*" *Singers of Daybreak: Studies in Black American Literature.* Washington: Howard University Press, 1976. 53–80.

Faulkner, Howard. "The Buried Life: Jean Toomer's *Cane.*" *Studies in Black Literature* 7 (Winter 1976): 1–5.

Griffin, John C. "Jean Toomer: American Writer (A Biography)." *Dissertation Abstracts International* 37 (1976): 2180A. University of South Carolina.

Jackson, Blyden. *The Waiting Years: Essays on American Negro Literature,* 189–97. Baton Rouge: Louisiana State University Press, 1976.

Larson, Charles. "Reconsideration." A Review of *Cane. New Republic,* June 19, 1976, pp. 30–32.

Martin, Odette C. "*Cane:* Method and Myth." *Obsidian* 2 (Spring 1976): 5–20.

Perry, Margaret. "Two Outcasts." In *Silence to the Drums: A Survey of the Literature of the Harlem Renaissance,* 32–44. Westport, Conn.: Greenwood Press, 1976.

Quirk, Tom, and Robert E. Fleming. "Jean Toomer's Contributions to *The New Mexico Sentinel.*" *CLA Journal* 19 (June 1976): 524–32.

Redmond, Eugene B. *Drumvoices: The Mission of Afro-American Poetry,* 174–79. Garden City: Anchor Press, 1976.

Rankin, William. "Ineffability in the Fiction of Jean Toomer and Katherine Mansfield." In *Renaissance and Modern: Essays in Honor of Edwin M. Moseley,* ed. Murray J. Levith, 160–71. Saratoga Springs, N.Y.: Skidmore College, 1976.

Rusch, Frederik L. "Every Atom Belonging to Me as Good Belongs to You: Jean Toomer and His Bringing Together of the Scattered Parts." *Dissertation Abstracts International,* 37 (1976): 6488A–89A. SUNY, Albany.

Singh, Amritjit. *The Novels of the Harlem Renaissance: Twelve Black Writers, 1923–1933,* 64–69. University Park: Pennsylvania State University Press, 1976.

Solard, Alain. "The Impossible Unity: Jean Toomer's 'Kabnis.' " In *Myth and Ideology in American Culture,* ed. Regis Durand, 175–94. Villeneuve d'Ascq: U de Lille III, 1976.

Twombly, Robert C. "A Disciple's Odyssey: Jean Toomer's Gurdjieffian Career." *Prospects: An Annual Journal of American Cultural Studies* 2 (Fall 1976): 437–62.

Van Mol, Kay R. "Primitivism and Intellect in Toomer's *Cane* and McKay's *Banana Bottom:* The Need for an Integrated Black Consciousness." *Negro American Literature Forum* 10 (Summer 1976): 48–52.

1977

Brannan, Tim. "Up From the Dusk: Interpretations of Jean Toomer's 'Blood-Burning Moon.' " *Pembroke Magazine* 8 (1977): 167–72.

Eldridge, Richard L. "Jean Toomer's *Cane:* The Search for American Roots." *Dissertation Abstracts International* 38 (1977): 6723A–24A. University of Maryland.

Howell, Elmo. "Jean Toomer's Hamlet: A Note on *Cane.*" *Interpretations* 9 (1977): 70–73.

Jung, Udo. "Jean Toomer's 'Fern.' " In *The Black American Short Story in the Twentieth Century: A Collection of Critical Essays,* ed. Peter Bruck, 53–69. Amsterdam: Grüner, 1977.

———. "'Nora' is 'Calling Jesus': A Nineteenth-Century European Dilemma in an Afro-American Garb." *CLA Journal* 21 (December 1977): 251–55.

Page, James A., ed. "Jean Toomer." *Selected Black American Authors: An Illustrated Bio-Bibliography,* 266–67. Boston: G. K. Hall, 1977.

Taylor, Carolyn G. "'Blend Us With Thy Being': Jean Toomer's Mill House Poems." *Dissertation Abstracts International* 38 (1977): 1397A. Boston College.

Withrow, Dolly. "Cutting Through Shade." *CLA Journal* 21 (September 1977): 98–99.

1978

Miller, Ruth, and Peter J. Katopes. "The Harlem Renaissance: Arna Bontemps, Countee Cullen, James Weldon Johnson, Claude McKay, and Jean Toomer." *Black American Writers: Bibliographical Essays.* vol. 1. Ed. M. Thomas Inge et al, 165–66, 182–86. New York: St. Martins Press, 1978.

Rusch, Frederik L. "Meetings of Allen Tate and Jean Toomer." *American Notes and Queries* 17 (December 1978): 60.

1979

Clark, Michael. "Frustrated Redemption: Jean Toomer's Women In *Cane,* Part One." *CLA Journal* 22 (June 1979): 319–34.

Collins, Paschal Jay. "Jean Toomer's *Cane:* A Symbolistic Study." *Dissertation Abstracts International* 39 (1979): 4255A. University of Florida.

Dorris, Ronald. "The Bacchae of Jean Toomer." *Dissertation Abstracts International* 40 (1979): 324A. Emory University.

Eldridge, Richard. "The Unifying Images in Part One of Jean Toomer's *Cane.*" *CLA Journal* 22 (March 1979): 187–214.

Johnson, Abby Arthur, and Ronald Mayberry Johnson. *Propaganda and Aesthetics: The Literary Politics of Afro-American Magazines in the Twentieth Century.* passim. Amherst: University of Massachusetts Press, 1979.

Jung, Udo. "Die Dichtung Jean Toomers und die Negerrenaissance." In *Black Literature: Zur afrikanischen und afroamerikanischen Literatur,* ed. Eckhard Breitinger, 295–316. Kritische Information 73. München: Wilhelm Fink Verlag, 1979.

Ogunyemi, Chikwenye Okonjo. "From a Goat Path in Africa: Roger Mais and Jean Toomer." *Obsidian* 5 (Winter 1979): 7–21.

Schultz, Elizabeth. "Jean Toomer's 'Box Seat': The Possibility for 'Constructive Crises.'" *Black American Literature Forum* 13 (Spring 1979): 7–12.

1980

Bell, Bernard. "Jean Toomer's *Blue Meridian:* The Poet as Prophet of a New Order of Man." *Black American Literature Forum* 14 (Summer 1980): 77–80.

Benson, Brian Joseph, and Mabel Mayle Dillard. *Jean Toomer.* Twayne Monograph 389. Boston: G. K. Hall, 1980.

Bigsby, C. W. E. *The Second Black Renaissance: Essays in Black Literature,* passim. Westport, Conn.: Greenwood Press, 1980.

BIBLIOGRAPHY

Greene, J. Lee. "The Pain and the Beauty: The South, the Black Writer, and Conventions of the Picaresque." In *The American South: Portrait of a Culture. Southern Literary Studies,* 264–88. Baton Rouge: Louisiana State University Press, 1980.

Helbling, Mark. "Jean Toomer and Waldo Frank: A Creative Friendship." *Phylon* 41 (June 1980): 167–78.

Rusch, Frederik L. "The Blue Man: Jean Toomer's Solution to His Problems of Identity." *Obsidian* 6 (Spring–Summer 1980): 38–54.

———. "A Tale of the Country Round: Jean Toomer's Legend, 'Monrovia.'" *MELUS* 7 (Summer 1980): 37–46.

Turner, Darwin, ed. *The Wayward and the Seeking: A Collection of Writings by Jean Toomer.* Washington: Howard University Press, 1980.

Walker, Alice. "The Divided Life of Jean Toomer": Review of *The Wayward and the Seeking. New York Times Book Review,* July 13, 1980, pp. 11, 16.

1981

Barthold, Bonnie. *Black Time: Fiction of Africa, the Carribean and the United States,* 158–63. New Haven: Yale University Press, 1981.

Brinkmeyer, Jr., Robert H. "Wasted Talent, Wasted Art: The Literary Career of Jean Toomer." *Southern Quarterly* 20 (Winter 1981): 75–84.

Gibson, Donald B. "Jean Toomer: The Politics of Denial." In *The Politics of Literary Expression: A Study of Major Black Writers,* 155–81. Westport, Conn.: Greenwood Press, 1981.

Ikonné, Chidi. *From DuBois to Van Vechten: The Early New Negro Literature, 1903–1926,* 125–44 passim. Westport, Conn.: Greenwood Press, 1981.

Lewis, David L. *When Harlem Was in Vogue,* 58–74 passim. New York: Knopf, 1981.

McKay, Nellie Y. "Forerunners in the Tradition of Black Letters." *Harvard Educational Review* 51 (February 1981): 158–62.

Payne, Ladell. *Black Novelists and the Southern Literary Tradition,* 38–53 passim. Athens: University of Georgia Press, 1981.

Pickney, Darryl. "Phantom." Review of *The Wayward and the Seeking. New York Review of Books,* March 5, 1981, pp. 34–36.

Rusch, Frederik L. Review of *The Wayward and the Seeking. MELUS* 8 (Spring 1981): 83–85.

Wallace, Carolyn Reid. "Jean Toomer: Death on the Modern Desert." *Dissertation Abstracts International* 42 (1981): 2135A. George Washington University.

1982

Bowen, Barbara E. "Untroubled Voice: Call-and-Response in *Cane.*" *Black American Literature Forum* 16 (Spring 1982): 12–18.

Candela, Gregory Louis. "Melodramatic Form and Vision in Chestnutt's *The House Behind the Cedars,* Dunbar's *The Sport of the Gods,* and Toomer's *Cane.*" *Dissertation Abstracts International* 42 (1982): 4826A. University of New Mexico.

Jones, Robert B. "Symbolist Aesthetics in Modern American Fiction: Studies in Gertrude Stein and Jean Toomer." *Dissertation Abstracts International* 42 (1982): 3595A–96A. University of Wisconsin, Madison.

Perry, Margaret. *The Harlem Renaissance: An Annotated Bibliography and Commentary,* 138–58. New York: Garland Press, 1982.

1983

Bush, Ann Marie, and Louis D. Mitchell. "Jean Toomer: A Cubist Poet." *Black American Literature Forum* 17 (Fall 1983): 106–8.

Ford, Nick Aaron. "Jean Toomer and His *Cane.*" *Langston Hughes Review* 2 (Spring 1983): 16–27.

Golding, Alan. "Jean Toomer's *Cane:* The Search for Identity through Form." *Arizona Quarterly* 39 (Spring 1983): 197–214.

Nwankwo, Nkem. "Cultural Primitivism and Related Ideas in Jean Toomer's *Cane.*" *Dissertation Abstracts International* 43 (1983): 2669A. Indiana University.

Rice, Herbert. "Repeated Images in Part One of *Cane.*" *Black American Literature Forum* 17 (Fall 1983): 100–105.

1984

Bus, Heiner. "Jean Toomer and the Black Heritage." In *History and Tradition in Afro-American Culture,* ed. Gunter Lenz, 56–83. Frankfurt: University of Frankfurt-Main Press, 1984.

Cooke, Michael G. "Tragic and Ironic Denials of Intimacy: Jean Toomer, James Baldwin, and Ishmael Reed." In *Afro-American Literature in the Twentieth Century: Achievement of Intimacy,* 177–99 passim. New Haven: Yale University Press, 1984.

Dieke, Ikenna. "Archetypal Patterns in African, Afro-American, and Caribbean Literature." *Dissertation Abstracts International* 44 (1984): 2140A. Southern Illinois University.

Harris, Trudier. *Exorcising Blackness: Historical and Literary Lynching and Burning Rituals,* 80–81. Bloomington: Indiana University Press, 1984.

Kellner, Bruce. "Jean Toomer." In *The Harlem Renaissance: A Historical Dictionary for the Era,* 358–59. Westport, Conn.: Greenwood Press, 1984.

McKay, Nellie Y. *Jean Toomer, Artist: A Study of His Literary Life and Work, 1894–1936.* Chapel Hill: University of North Carolina Press, 1984.

Rohrberger, Mary. "The Question of Regionalism: Limitation and Transcendence." In *The American Short Story: 1900–1945: A Critical History,* ed. Philip Stevick, 147–82. Boston: Twayne, 1984.

1985

Bradley, David. "Looking Behind *Cane.*" *Southern Review* 21 (Summer 1985): 682–94.

Byerman, Keith E. *Fingering the Jagged Grain: Tradition and Form in Recent Black Fiction,* passim. Athens: University of Georgia Press, 1985.

BIBLIOGRAPHY

Byrd, Rudolph P. "Jean Toomer and the Afro-American Literary Tradition." *Callaloo* 8 (Spring–Summer 1985): 310–19.

Caldeira, Maria Isabel. "Jean Toomer's *Cane:* The Anxiety of the Modern Artist." *Callaloo* 8 (Fall 1985): 544–50.

Hall, Fred. "*Cane* by Jean Toomer: Theatre Review." *Atlanta Voice,* 27 April–3 May 1985, p. 6.

Johnson, Issac Johnny. "The Autobiography of Jean Toomer: An Edition." *Dissertation Abstracts International* 46 (1985): 702A. Purdue University.

Julien, Claude. "The Eye That Cannot/Will Not See: Location and Intertextuality in Jean Toomer's 'Becky.'" *Journal of the Short Story in English* 5 (Autumn 1985): 23–29.

Shourie, Usha. *Black American Literature,* passim. New Dehli: Cosmo Publications, 1985.

Solard, Alain. "Myth and Narrative Fiction in *Cane:* 'Blood-Burning Moon.'" *Callaloo* 8 (Fall 1985): 551–62.

Thompson, Chezia Brenda. "Hush, Hush—Somebody's Callin' Ma Name: Analyzing and Teaching Jean Toomer's *Cane.*" *Dissertation Abstracts International* 46 (1985): 1282A. Carnegie-Mellon University.

1986

Byrd, Rudolph P. "Jean Toomer: Portrait of an Artist, The Years with Gurdjieff, 1923–1936." *Dissertation Abstracts International* 46 (1986): 3350A. Yale University.

Hogue, Lawrence W. *Discourse and the Other: The Production of the Afro-American Text,* passim. Durham: Duke University Press, 1986.

Moore, Lewis D. "Kabnis and the Reality of Hope: Jean Toomer's *Cane.*" *North Dakota Quarterly* 54 (Winter 1986): 30–39.

Noyes, Sylvia G. "A Particular Patriotism in 'York Beach.'" *CLA Journal* 29 (March 1986): 288–94.

Rice, Herbert W. "An Incomplete Circle: Repeated Images in Part Two of *Cane.*" *CLA Journal* 29 (June 1986): 442–61.

Rusch, Frederik L. "Jean Toomer's Early Identification: The Two Black Plays." *MELUS* 13 (Spring–Summer 1986): 115–24.

1987

Baker, Houston A. *Modernism and the Harlem Renaissance,* passim. Chicago: University of Chicago Press, 1987.

Bell, Bernard. *The Afro-American Novel and Its Tradition,* 96–99. Amherst: University of Massachusetts Press, 1987.

Dixon, Melvin. In "To Wake the Nations Underground: Jean Toomer and Claude McKay." In *Ride Out the Wilderness: Geography and Identity in Afro-American Literature,* 33–42. Urbana University of Illinois Press, 1987.

Hubbard, Dolan. "Preaching the Lord's Word in a Strange Land: The Influence of the Black Preacher's Style on Black American Prose Fiction." *Dissertation*

Abstracts International 47 (1987): 2585A. University of Illinois, Champaign-Urbana.

Jones, Robert B. "Jean Toomer as Poet: A Phenomenology of the Spirit." *Black American Literature Forum* 21 (Fall 1987): 253–73. Reprinted in *Black Literature Criticism,* vol. 3. Ed. James P. Draper, 1761–67. Detroit: Gale Research Inc., 1992.

Kulii, Elon A. "Literature, Biology and Folk Legal Belief: Jean Toomer's 'Kabnis.'" *University of South Florida Language Quarterly* (Spring–Summer 1987): 5–7, 49, 54.

Mackey, Nathaniel. "Sound and Sentiment, Sound and Symbol." *Callaloo* 10 (Winter 1987): 33–37.

Munro, C. Lynn. "Jean Toomer: A Bibliography of Secondary Sources." *Black American Literature Forum* 21 (Fall 1987): 276–87.

Rampersad Arnold. "His Own Best Disciple." Review of *The Lives of Jean Toomer: A Hunger for Wholeness. New York Times Book Review,* (August 30, 1987), 7, 9.

1988

Bone, Robert. "Jean Toomer." In *Down Home: Origins of the Afro-American Short Story,* 204–38. New York: Columbia University Press, 1988.

Callahan, John F. "'By de Singin' uh de Song': The Search for Reciprocal Voice in *Cane.*" In *In the African-American Grain: The Pursuit of Voice in Twentieth-Century Black Fiction,* 62–114. Urbana: University of Illinois Press, 1988.

Christensen, Peter. "Sexuality and Liberation in Jean Toomer's 'Withered Skin of Berries.'" *Callaloo* 11 (Summer 1988): 616–26.

Dawson, Emma J. Waters. "Images of the Afro-American Female Character in Jean Toomer's *Cane,* Zora Neale Hurston's *Their Eyes Were Watching God,* and Alice Walker's *The Color Purple.*" *Dissertation Abstracts International* 48 (1988): 2627A. University of South Florida.

Estes-Hicks, Onita. Review of *The Lives of Jean Toomer: A Hunger for Wholeness. CLA Journal* 31 (June 1988): 490–97.

Flowers, Sandra Hollin. "Solving the Critical Conundrum of Jean Toomer's 'Box Seat.'" *Studies in Short Fiction* 25 (Summer 1988): 301–5.

Gates, Henry Louis. *The Signifying Monkey: A Theory of Afro-American Literary Criticism.* 178–79. New York: Oxford University Press, 1988.

Hajek, Friederike. "The Change of Literary Authority in the Harlem Renaissance: Jean Toomer's *Cane.*" *Literarische Diskurse und historischer Prozess: Beiträge zur englischen und amerikanischen Literatur und Geschichte,* ed. Brunhild de la Motte, 106–14. Potsdam, GDR: Pädagogische Hochschule Karl Liebknecht, 1988.

Hudzik, Robert. Review of *The Collected Poems of Jean Toomer. Library Journal,* March 1, 1988, p. 68.

Johnson, Charles. *Being and Race: Black Writing Since 1970,* passim. Bloomington: Indiana University Press, 1988.

Jones, Robert B., and Margery Toomer Latimer, eds., *The Collected Poems of Jean Toomer*. Chapel Hill: University of North Carolina Press, 1988.

Kerman, Cynthia, and Richard Eldridge. *The Lives of Jean Toomer: A Hunger for Wholeness*. Baton Rouge: Louisiana State University Press, 1988.

Lubiano, Waheema H. "Meeting with the Machine: Four Afro-American Novels and the Nexus of Vernacular, Historical Constraint, and Narrative Strategy." *Dissertation Abstracts International* 48 (1988): 2874A–75A. Stanford University.

Mitchell, Carolyn A. "Henry Dumas and Jean Toomer: One Voice." *BALF* 22 (Summer 1988): 297–309.

O'Daniel, Therman B., ed. *Jean Toomer: A Critical Evaluation*. Washington, D.C.: Howard University Press, 1988.

Raynor, Jerry. "Jean Toomer—'To Curl Forever in a Barnyard Flower.'" Review of *The Collected Poems of Jean Toomer*. *Daily Reflector* [Greenville, N.C.], June 5, 1988, D-5.

Reckley, Ralph, Sr. "The Vinculum Factor: 'Seventh Street' and 'Rhobert' in Jean Toomer's *Cane*." *CLA Journal* 31 (June 1988): 484–89.

Review of *The Collected Poems of Jean Toomer*. *American Literature* 60 (October 1966): 515.

Review of *The Collected Poems of Jean Toomer*. Fayetteville [N.C.] *Observer-Times*, May 5, 1988, p. 5.

St. Andrews, B. A. "Gurdjieff and the Literary Cult." *University of Windsor Review* 21 (1988): 46–51.

Scruggs, Charles. "Textuality and Vision in Jean Toomer's *Cane*." *Journal of the Short Story in English* 10 (Spring 1988): 93–114.

Selman, Robyn. "Passing Fancies: Jean Toomer's Identity Crisis." Review of *The Collected Poems of Jean Toomer*. *Voice Literary Supplement*, July 1988, p. 19.

S. L. Z. Review of *The Collected Poems of Jean Toomer*. *Kliatt* [Newsletter Issue], June 1988, pp. 15–16.

Thornton, Jerome E. "'Goin on de Muck': The Paradoxical Journey of the Black American Hero." *CLA Journal* 31 (March 1988): 261–80.

Turner, Darwin, ed. Cane: *An Authoritative Text, Backgrounds, Criticism*. New York: W. W. Norton & Company, 1988.

1989

Aubert, Alvin. "Archetypal Victim." Review of *The Collected Poems of Jean Toomer*. *American Book Review* 59 (January–February 1989): 12, 21.

Byrd, Rudolph P. "Jean Toomer and the Writers of the Harlem Renaissance: Was He There with Them?" In *The Harlem Renaissance: Revaluations,* ed. Amritjit Singh, William S. Shiver, and Stanley Brodwin, 209–18. New York: Garland Press, 1989.

Margolies, Edward. "American Biography: Anderson, Dreiser, Toomer." *English Studies: A Journal of English Languages and Literature* 4 (August 1989): 372–76.

179

BIBLIOGRAPHY

Rosenberg, Liz. "Simply American and Mostly Free." Review of *The Collected Poems of Jean Toomer. New York Times Book Review* (February 19, 1989), p. 24.

1990

Byrd, Rudolph P. *Jean Toomer's Years with Gurdjieff: Portrait of an Artist, 1923–1936.* Athens: University of Georgia Press, 1990.

Estes-Hicks, Onita Marie. "Jean Toomer: A Biographical and Critical Study." *Dissertation Abstracts International* 51 (1990): 850A. Columbia University.

Jones, Robert B. "Jean Toomer's *Lost and Dominant:* Landscape of the Modern Waste Land." *Studies in American Fiction* 18 (Spring 1990): 77–86.

Kerblat-Houghton, Jeanne. "Mythes ruraux et urbains dans *Cane* de Jean Toomer (1894–1967)." In *Mythes ruraux et urbains dans la culture américaine,* 67–77. Aix-en-Provence: Univ. de Provence, 1990.

Melhem, D. H. *Heroism in the New Black Poetry: Introductions and Interviews,* 19. Lexington: University of Kentucky Press, 1990.

1991

Byrd, Rudolph P., ed. *Essentials: Definitions and Aphorisms by Jean Toomer.* Athens: University of Georgia Press, 1991.

Fabre, Michel. *From Harlem to Paris: Black American Writers in France, 1840–1980,* 129–32. Urbana: University of Illinois Press, 1991.

Hedgepeth, Chester M., Jr. "Jean Toomer." *Twentieth Century African-American Writers and Artists,* 287–88. Chicago: American Library Association, 1991.

Jones, Gayle. "Blues Ballad: Jean Toomer's 'Karintha.'" In *Liberating Voices: Oral Tradition in African-American Literature,* 70–79. Cambridge: Harvard University Press, 1991.

1992

Jones, Robert B. "Gothic Conventions in Jean Toomer's 'The Eye': A Study in Terror and Insanity." *Studies in American Fiction* 20 (Autumn 1992): 209–17.

SECONDARY SOURCES

Barthes, Roland. *Writing Degree Zero and Elements of Semiology.* Trans. Annette Lavers and Colin Smith. Boston: Beacon Press, 1970.

Bernard, Susan. *The Prose Poem from Baudelaire to the Present.* Trans. Alan F. Rister. Paris: Librairie Nizet, 1959.

Bone, Robert A. *The Negro Novel in America.* New Haven: Yale University Press, 1965.

Booth, Wayne. *The Rhetoric of Fiction.* Chicago: University of Chicago Press, 1961.

Bucke, Richard Maurice. *Cosmic Consciousness: A Study in the Evolution of the Human Mind.* New York: E. P. Dutton, 1923.

Chapelan, Maurice, ed. *Anthology of the Prose Poem.* Paris: Julliard, 1946.

Clayton, Vista. *The Prose Poem in French Poetry of the Eighteenth Century.* New York: Columbia University Press, 1936.

Culler, Jonathan. *Structuralist Poetics.* Ithaca: Cornell University Press, 1936.

Day, William Patrick. *In the Circles of Fear and Desire.* Chicago: University of Chicago Press, 1985.

DiStassi, Lawrence. *Mal Occhio.* San Francisco: North Point Press, 1981.

DuBois, W. E. B. *The Souls of Black Folks.* Chicago: A. C. McClurg, 1903.

Eliot, T. S. *The Waste Land.* In *The Complete Poems and Plays.* New York: Harcourt, Brace and World, 1962.

Ellworthy, Frederick T. *The Evil Eye.* London: Collier Press, 1958.

Erlich, Victor. *Russian Formalism: History-Doctrine.* The Hague: Mouton, 1965.

Feidelson, Charles. *Symbolism and American Literature.* Chicago: University of Chicago Press, 1953.

Fiedler, Leslie. *Love and Death in the American Novel.* New York: Stein and Day, 1960.

Frank, Frederick S. *Gothic Fiction: A Master List of Twentieth Century Criticism and Research.* Westport, Conn.: Meckler Corporation, 1988.

Frank, Joseph. *The Widening Gyre.* Bloomington: Indiana University Press, 1963.

Freedman, Ralph. *The Lyrical Novel.* Princeton: Princeton University Press, 1963.

French, Warren, ed. *The Twenties.* Deland, Fla.: Everett/Edwards. 1975.

Frye, Northrop. *The Secular Scripture: A Study of the Structure of Romance.* Cambridge: Harvard University Press, 1976.

Gregg, Richard. *Self-Transcendence.* London: Victor Gollancz, 1956.

Heller, Terry. *The Delights of Terror.* Urbana: University of Illinois Press, 1987.

Hoffman, Frederick J. *The Twenties.* New York: Free Press, 1962.

Howells, Cora Ann. *Love, Mystery, and Misery: Feeling in Gothic Fiction.* London: Athlone Press, 1978.

Inge, William Ralph. *Christian Mysticism.* London: Metheun, 1899.

Jakobson, Roman, and Morris Halle. *Fundamentals of Language.* The Hague: Mouton, 1971.

Jameson, Fredric R. "Metacommentary." *PMLA* 86 (January 1971): 13.

Joyce, James. *Dubliners.* Ed. Robert Scholes and A. Walton Litz. New York: Viking Press, 1969.

Kayser, Wolfgang. *The Grotesque in Art and Literature.* New York: McGraw-Hill, 1966.

Kerman, Cynthia, and Richard Eldridge. *The Lives of Jean Toomer: A Hunger for Wholeness.* Baton Rouge: Louisiana State University Press, 1987.

Lawrence, D. H. *Women in Love.* New York: Penguin Books, 1976.

Lehman, Andrew. *The Symbolist Aesthetic in France, 1885–1895.* Oxford: Basil Blackwell, 1950.

Lewis, R. W. B. *The American Adam.* Chicago: University of Chicago Press, 1955.

BIBLIOGRAPHY

Locke, Alain, and Montgomery Gregory. *Plays of Negro Life: A Source-Book of Native American Drama.* Westport, Conn.: Negro Universities Press, 1970.

Lukács, Georg. *History and Class Consciousness: Studies in Marxist Dialectics.* Trans. Rodney Livingston. Cambridge: MIT Press, 1971.

McAndrews, Elizabeth. *The Gothic Tradition in Literature.* New York: Columbia University Press, 1979.

Mahoney, Clarence. *The Evil Eye.* New York: Columbia University Press, 1976.

Marx, Karl. *Selected Writings.* Ed. David McClellan. Oxford: Oxford University Press, 1977.

Marx, Karl, and Frederick Engels. *The German Ideology.* Ed. C. J. Arthur. New York: International Publishers, 1981.

Meerlo, Joost. *Intuition and the Evil Eye.* Wassenaar, Netherlands: Servire Publishers, 1971.

Montagu, Ashley. *Man's Most Dangerous Myth: The Fallacy of Race.* Cleveland: World Publishing, 1964.

Poggioli, Renato. *The Theory of the Avant-Garde.* Trans. Gerald Fitzgerald. Cambridge: Harvard University Press, 1968.

Punter, David. *The Literature of Terror.* London: Longman Press, 1980.

Russian Formalist Criticism. Trans. Lee T. Lemon and Marion J. Reis. Lincoln: University of Nebraska Press, 1965.

San Juan, E., ed. *Marxism and Human Liberation: Essays on History, Culture, and Revolutions by Georg Lukacs.* New York: Dell Publishing, 1973.

Scholes, Robert. *Structuralism in Literature.* New Haven: Yale University Press, 1974.

Scholes, Robert, and Robert Kellogg. *The Nature of Narrative.* London: Oxford University Press, 1966.

Sebeok, Thomas, ed. *Style in Language.* Cambridge: MIT Press, 1960.

The Secret of the Golden Flower: A Chinese Book of Life. Trans. Richard Wilhelm, with a foreword and commentary by Carl Jung. New York: Harcourt, Brace and World, 1962.

Siebers, Tobin. *The Mirror of Medusa.* Berkeley: University of California Press, 1983.

Stein, Gertrude. *Selected Writings.* Ed. Carl Van Vechten. New York: Vintage Books, 1962.

———. *Writings and Lectures: 1911–1945.* Ed. Patricia Meyerowitz. London: Peter Owen, 1967.

Symons, Arthur. *The Symbolist Movement in Literature.* New York: E. P. Dutton, 1919.

Thomte, Reidar. *Kierkegaard's Philosophy of Religion.* Princeton: Princeton University Press, 1948.

Turner, Darwin. *In a Minor Chord: Three Afro-American Writers and Their Search for Identity.* Carbondale: Southern Illinois University Press, 1971.

Underhill, Evelyn. *Mysticism: A Study in the Nature and Development of Man's Spiritual Consciousness.* London: Metheun, 1911.

Uitti, Karl. *The Concept of Self in the Symbolist Novel.* The Hague: Mouton, 1961.

BIBLIOGRAPHY

Waldberg, Michel. *Gurdjieff: An Approach to His Ideas*. Trans. Steve Cox. London: Routledge and Kegan Paul, 1981.

Walker, Kenneth. *A Study of Gurdjieff's Teaching*. London: Jonathan Cape, 1957.

West, Jessamyn, ed. *The Quaker Reader*. New York: Viking Press, 1962.

Whitman, Walt. *Leaves of Grass*. In *Complete Poetry and Selected Prose*, ed. James E. Miller. Boston: Houghton Mifflin, 1959.

Woodward, C. Vann. *The Strange Career of Jim Crow*. Oxford: Oxford University Press, 1966.

INDEX

185